# ROT in HELL

## Peter Dupas – the mutilating monster

T0342862

# Jim Main

Publishing

Published by:

Bas Publishing
ABN 30 106 181 542
PO Box 2052
Seaford Vic 3198
Tel/Fax: (03) 5988 3597
Web: www.baspublishing.com.au
Email: mail@baspublishing.com.au

National Library of Australia Cataloguing-in-Publication entry

| | |
|---|---|
| Author: | Main, Jim, 1943- |
| Title: | Rot in hell : Peter Dupas the mutilating monster / Jim Main. |
| ISBN: | 9781920910969 (pbk.) |
| Subjects: | Dupas, Peter Norris, 1953- |
| | Rapists--Victoria--Melbourne. |
| | Serial murderers--Victoria--Melbourne. |
| | Serial murder investigation--Victoria--Melbourne. |
| | Serial rape investigation--Victoria--Melbourne. |
| Dewey Number: | 364.1523099451 |

Layout & Design: Ben Graham

*This book is dedicated to all Peter Dupas'*
*victims, including all those left to grieve.*

*"He is a very dangerous young person who will continue to offend where females are concerned and will possibly cause the death of one of his victims if he is not straightened out."*
– A police report on Peter Dupas in 1974.

*"We never forget that murdered people have families who need to know what happened."*
– Detective Senior Sergeant Jeff Maher, of the Victoria Police Homicide Squad.

*"Every victim matters."*
– Justice Phillip Cummins, in August, 2007, sentencing Peter Dupas to a third term of life imprisonment, even though the multiple murderer already was serving two life sentences.

*"There was an absolute determination to bring Mersina Halvagis' killer to justice."*
– Detective Senior Constable Paul Scarlett.

# Acknowledgements

This book could not have been written without the magnificent contribution of several Victoria Police officers. In particular, I thank Detective Senior Sergeant Jeff Maher and Detective Senior Constable Paul Scarlett, not only for the time and patience they afforded me, but also for playing major roles in bringing Peter Dupas to justice. The dedication they showed was remarkable and reflected the highest standards of police investigation and procedure. I also thank the Victoria Police Media and Corporate Communication Department's Ms Vicki Vassilopoulos and Acting Senior Sergeant Peter Sambell for their splendid co-operation.

# Contents

# Introduction

In a less civilised era than this, Peter Norris Dupas would have been sentenced to death. Depending on the Victorian government of the time (Labor always was vehemently opposed to the death penalty), he might have been taken to a place of execution, had his arms and legs tied together, a hood placed over his head and had a trap door open under him to send him to his death. There even would be some now who would argue that Dupas deserves nothing less, but this is an antiquated eye for an eye argument and the mutilating monster knows he will "rot in hell" for the rest of his life. No pardons, no parole.

Dupas, the overweight killer with what are described as "man-boobs", could pass for a mild-mannered office worker — a man nobody would guess could kill with such cold-blooded ruthlessness and determination for his sick satisfaction. In fact, not even the woman he lived with knew of his deadly dark past or his perverted present. His life was a secret and probably always will be.

What drove this otherwise seemingly normal man to act with such depravity in killing three women — Nicole Patterson, Margaret Maher and Mersina Halvagis? In writing this book I set out to answer this question but came up almost empty-handed. No one really knows what drove Dupas to kill these women with such ferocious brutality. Over more than 30 years of sexual depravity he was questioned and examined by psychologists and psychiatrists. None was able to discover the monster behind the mask of normality. And, despite years of treatment and analysis, Dupas returned to his old degenerate behaviour like a dog returning to its own vomit. He raped and raped, and killed, killed and killed again.

His killings were so vicious and so evil that I almost stopped writing this book in sympathy with Dupas' victims and their families and friends. My task was chilling in the extreme and made me wonder of man's inhumanity to man. How could any human being do this to another? Again and again?

Understandably, many of those I wanted to interview for this book only wanted to forget, not remember. Dupas not only killed, but traumatised many, many others and, in particular, the families of those he murdered. I therefore apologise to all those affected by this book for rekindling the agony they have suffered. Despite what might be suggested in crime fiction, the conviction of a killer does not bring closure. Nothing can. There is always a void, impossible to fill or forget. The pain is forever.

Yet it is important that society does not breed, let alone encourage through inactivity or misguided good intentions, those like Dupas. When Justice Frank Vincent sentenced the evil and apparently remorseless Dupas to life imprisonment for the murder of 28-year-old Northcote psychotherapist Nicole Patterson in 1999, he rhetorically asked him: "How did you come to be as you are?" It is a question no one has been able to answer as police could find no evidence of Dupas being molested as a boy or, indeed, suffering from any early psychological damage. Justice Vincent also pointed to Dupas' litany of sexual perversions and wondered how the pudgy-faced monster could have been released time and time again, only to re-offend time and time again. Parole for Dupas was a licence to continue his dissolute activities.

The manner in which Dupas was released on parole time and time again to continue his depraved activities has been echoed in the United Kingdom, much to the British public's disgust. Serial rapist Christopher Braithwaite also was released on parole and even worse, released without charge pending further enquiries, only to kill young mother Stacey Westbury on August 9, 2007, while her 10-month-old son slept in a cot just metres away.

Women's right campaigner Katherine Rake said as Braithwaite started a life sentence: "The fact Braithwaite was released on bail shows that criminal justice agencies have utterly failed to implement adequate safeguards."

Braithwaite pleaded guilty to stabbing a woman in February, 2005, and, instead of being jailed, was given a two-year community order. The following month he allegedly raped a woman five times and was charged only after Stacey Westbury's death. In March, 2007, he allegedly raped and falsely imprisoned another woman and was released without charge pending further enquiries. Little wonder the British were outraged.

The *Herald Sun*, in an editorial following Dupas' conviction for the murder of Nicole Patterson, described Dupas' numerous paroles as "classic revolving door justice". This is why Justice Vincent told the killer he would be "permanently removed from society". He did us all a favour and let us pray that Dupas never again will hear a murmuring brook, feel sand and sea under his feet or enjoy the sound of children laughing. His victims never will. In more basic terms, we pray he never again walks and stalks our streets.

# Prologue

Death, in its most malevolent mood, stalked pretty, brown-haired Mersina Halvagis late on the afternoon of November 1, 1997. Mersina, a 25-year-old who worked in the accounts department at the ANZ Bank's head office in Melbourne, was in love with life. And why not? She was engaged to be married and with fiancé Angelo Gorgievski had bought a block of land in the outer north-eastern suburb of Mill Park. They planned lives of quiet domesticity. Long lives. Happy lives. But all those dreams were shattered that damp and dull spring afternoon.

Mersina worked late on Friday, October 31 — the hobgoblin night of Halloween — and spent that evening at the Mill Park home of her fiance's parents. She stayed there until just after 3pm the following day when she borrowed Gorgievski's car, a red Ford Telstar, with the intention of attending the grave of her maternal grandmother at the sprawling Fawkner Cemetery. Born into a close-knit Greek family, Mersina regularly placed flowers in vases at her grandmother's grave and while she faced the grey-black headstone, would pray silently for her grandmother's soul.

Soon after arriving at the cemetery, Mersina stopped at tea rooms within the grounds and bought a bunch of long-stemmed statis flowers and two bottles of Sprite lemonade from catering manager Elva Hayden, who was the last person to see her alive. This was about 3.47 pm and, from there, Mersina drove to the Seventh Avenue car park for the Greek Orthodox section of the cemetery and then walked to her grandmother's grave in Row M — a distance of just 50 metres.

Within minutes, other cemetery visitors heard screams, initially piercing and then more subdued, like groaning. Then, silence. Mersina had unwrapped the flowers and cut the stems, and was bending over her grandmother's grave when she was attacked from behind. She probably did not see the monster who repeatedly stabbed her but, had she survived, she would have told police he was a podgy, dough-faced middle-aged man with lank fair hair. Witnesses later gave police this description of a man who had been seen stalking women at the Fawkner Cemetery in the previous fortnight. The monster had a name — PETER NORRIS DUPAS.

# CHAPTER ONE

# The Young Monster

Peter Norris Dupas was born in Sydney on July 6, 1953, the son of taxi truck operator George and wife Merle Dupas, who ran Tupperware parties. He was born healthy as the youngest of three children, and moved to Melbourne with his family as a small boy. He was much younger than his brother and sister and therefore treated like an only child. His parents showered affection on him, but as soon as he left home to go to school each day, there was an overwhelming feeling of inadequacy. Dupas later told psychiatrists that his mother was extremely protective and that his father was a perfectionist who made him feel inferior.

Short and built like a dumpling, he was a source of fun for bullies who nicknamed him Pugsley after the fat character in the TV comedy *The Addams Family.* The Melbourne boy known as Pugsley also was the butt of jokes for his slow learning and, despite his apparently warm and loving family, Dupas' life at Waverley High School must have been a misery. He had few, if any, friends and classmates said he appeared to be aloof and dominated by his parents, especially his mother.

Dupas was driven to and from school "in a big white car" and did not mix with other students before, during or after school, except for the times he was involved in schoolyard scuffles after being taunted because of his weight and learning difficulties. He became a fat, obviously unhappy teenager with limited social skills. He was, in the words of schoolmates, "ordinary". However, Dupas in later life proved that he was anything but ordinary and, in fact, became one of Australia's most notorious killers.

The roly-poly Dupas first came to police attention when he was still at school and just 14. While living with his family at Mt Waverley in February, 1968, he ingratiated himself with a neighbour, a 27-year-old mother, and asked if he could help her peel potatoes. Wearing school clothes, he then repeatedly stabbed the unsuspecting woman inflicting several wounds. The attack was unprovoked. Dupas had said goodbye to the neighbour before returning through a back door. As the woman entered the laundry, Dupas rushed at her while holding the vegetable knife and the woman told police: "He had the handle in his hand and the blade was pointing at me. He then lunged forward at me and made a stabbing movement at my stomach with the knife. He did not say anything, and I was saying 'Peter, what's wrong?'

"I managed to grab hold of his hand holding the knife. We struggled violently then for a long time. Almost straight away he knocked me down on to the floor and he fell on top of me ... I kept trying to talk to him, trying to find out what was wrong ... when he couldn't get a good lunge at me with the knife he grabbed my hair and I started to become exhausted and I started to panic. I then started to scream as loud as I could.

"As I was screaming he placed his hand into my mouth and tried to force his hand down my throat. When he did this I could not make any sound. He kept on covering my nose and mouth with the palm of his hand. We were still struggling violently on the floor and I was trying to crawl and wriggle along on the floor.

"All of a sudden he stopped struggling with me, looked at the knife, turned it towards himself and then slowly let me get up. This took a long time and it all happened so very slowly. I finally got to my feet and, after a lot of coaxing, he let me take the knife from him. I don't remember what I did with the knife, but I hid it somewhere. After I did this he became very hysterical and nearly fell on the floor; he was sobbing and crying."

Amazingly, this courageous woman tried to comfort Dupas and took him into the loungeroom. He told her to call the police but, instead, she rang his mother and then his brother at work. They arrived at the woman's house about 10 or 15 minutes later and the woman told them what happened.

The woman later told police she pleaded with Dupas to release her, but he told her: "I can't stop now; they'll lock me up."

When apprehended, Dupas told police he did not know why he had attacked the woman and claimed he couldn't even remember having the knife in his hand. Despite the terrible circumstances, Dupas was treated leniently in being placed on probation for 15 months, ordered to have psychiatric treatment and admitted to the Larundel Psychiatric Hospital. The future killer had been rapped over the knuckles with a feather, even allowing that the woman he attacked suffered relatively minor injuries of five stitches to her fingers and face, scratches to the face and neck and bruising to her back.

During Dupas' first admission, the bodies of two elderly women who had died of natural causes were horribly mutilated in a nearby hospital morgue. There was nothing then or after Dupas' later convictions to suggest he was involved, but the mutilations were unique in light of future events and left police deeply concerned. The attacks on the bodies of these two silver-haired grandmothers were horrific in the extreme. A depraved monster had desecrated their dignity in death. Both had their breasts and vaginas removed and long, deep cuts were slashed into their thighs. Whoever had mutilated these women obviously had a serious psychological problem.

The young mother Dupas attacked in her home told the Melbourne *Herald Sun* many years later, on his life sentence for murdering Nicole Patterson: "I feel free. I feel very relieved, as though a weight has been lifted from my shoulders. I felt as if I've been hiding all these years. What if I saw him in the street? It was always a possibility."

Dupas, whose absence from school during his time at Larundel was never explained to classmates, left school on completion of Year 11 and he started working as an apprentice fitter and turner with General Electrics in the outer eastern suburb of Notting Hill. Again, he appeared to be an ordinary young man, with no obvious friends and no apparent interests.

Dupas' second brush with the law followed in March, 1972, when he was convicted for being unlawfully on premises after being found in the rear yard of a house in Oakleigh at the witching hour of midnight. The man who lived in the house had spotted Dupas peeping through a bathroom window and chased after the 18-year-old. Only Dupas knew what he had in his mind, but it now could be assumed he was not intending to pick fruit from a tree or smell the roses. Dupas, when confronted by police, told them he had been taking a short cut to his car after "taking a stroll". He was fined $50.

A hint of what Dupas might have been intending came 20 months later when he was convicted of rape, housebreaking and stealing. Dupas had parked his car near a home in the eastern suburb of Mitcham on November 5, 1973, and lifted the bonnet in pretence of having motor trouble. He then knocked on his victim's front door, pointed to his car and asked the woman if he could borrow a screwdriver. As the woman rummaged in search of a screwdriver, Dupas — armed with a knife — let himself into the house, threatened the woman and grabbed hold of her 18-month-old baby's arm to reinforce his threat of violence. He then bound the woman's hands and feet and took her to a bedroom where he fondled her breasts and bit a nipple before raping her. Dupas also slapped the woman during the horrifying rape.

Amazingly, Dupas repeated his ruse of a car breakdown to enter the homes of two other women in the same area. He stole money at one house, but did not commit any crime in the second incident. He was identified by all three women and when police went to interview him at his parents' then Mt Waverley home about 7am two weeks after he had raped the young woman in Mitcham, he was completely taken by surprise.

After police knocked on the front door, it was opened by Dupas' father, who invited them inside after they said they wanted to speak with Peter. They then told Peter: "Would you get properly dressed and come with us. We want to have a talk to you at the Nunawading CIB office." Dupas asked them if it would take long as he had an examination to take that day, and that was when they told him they wanted to talk to him about a rape.

George Dupas briefly left the loungeroom, but returned as Peter asked the police: "Why can't you talk to me here? I've got an exam this morning, and you've got me all upset." Even though the police officers told Dupas "if you are not involved, well, you have got nothing to worry about", Dupas started crying and told his father: "I don't want to go with them."

George Dupas intervened and told the police officers they would not be taking his son anywhere until contact had been made with the family solicitor and asked them: "How does Peter come to be a suspect?" Detective Sergeant Walter Quinn told George Dupas that the rapist's description matched that of Peter and that the offender also had been seen driving a "red shiny car". And Peter Dupas had a "red shiny car".

Despite saying they wanted to take Peter to the Nunawading CIB office, police continued to ask general questions before telling George Dupas that his son would be subject to an identification parade. The parents' protection of their son was, according to police reports, typical. They would not hear of their son committing such foul crimes and, in many ways, Peter relied on their protection. He did not seem to care about raping a young woman, but cried in front of his father when told he would have to be taken to a police station to be interviewed.

After being found guilty on one count of rape, one of housebreaking and stealing and one of housebreaking with intent to commit a felony, Justice John Leckie told him:

"Leaving aside the so-called pack rapes, this was one of the worst rapes that could be imagined. You raped a young married woman who was previously unknown to you in her own home and on her own bed. You invaded the sanctity of her home by a false story about your car having broken down, relying upon her willingness to help in order to gain admission.

"You threatened her with a knife, you tied her up with a cord, you struck her when she tried to resist and, worst of all, you threatened to harm her baby when she tried to resist. This was no sudden impulse, because you must have left home that morning armed with a knife and provided with the cord to bind your victim."

Justice Leckie then referred to a psychiatric report on Dupas compiled after he was admitted to Larundel in 1968 for his knife attack on his neighbour. Justice Leckie continued: "She (the psychiatrist) considered that on that occasion you lost normal control when pent-up feelings of sexual needs and aggression overwhelmed you.

"This is in contrast to some extent to the crime for which you now are sentenced because, as I have pointed out, you set out from home prepared for what you eventually did. In view of this history I have obtained pre-sentence and psychiatric reports.

"Dr (Allen) Bartholomew conducted a very thorough investigation, but found it difficult to make any definite diagnostic statement in the absence of any admission by you. He is reasonably certain that you have a psycho-sexual problem and you are to be seen as potentially dangerous. The problem of potential danger to the community is also adverted to in the report of a psychologist who tested you.

"A fortnight after the rape you entered the homes of two women in a different suburb, using the same false pretence as you used at Mitcham. In one house you stole some money, in the other you did not commit a further crime, but the jury has found you entered with intent to commit a felony. In that case the woman told you she was expecting her husband home shortly, which may explain why you went no further.

"These further matters are additional reasons why I am unable to accept that the rape was committed in sudden impulse. All these offences would seem to have been premeditated. Moreover, whilst accepting that you are psychologically disturbed, I believe you were fully responsible for your actions …

"In view of the potential danger to the community which you present, there is obviously no alternative but to sentence you to a term of imprisonment. In determining what the length of that sentence should be, I have regard not only to the seriousness of the offences, but also to your youth, your background, the reports I have received … On the count of rape you are sentenced to be imprisoned for nine years, and on each of the breaking counts to six months' imprisonment, cumulative upon each other, but each concurrent with the sentence on the first. That makes a total of nine years, and I fix five years as the term to be served before you become eligible for parole."

There were several interesting aspects to Justice Leckie's sentencing comments, particularly that the rape committed by Dupas "was no sudden impulse". He planned his attack and obviously left home with rape in mind. He had a knife and this, of course, was to be a pattern repeated time and time again, culminating in his convictions for three separate murders. Justice Leckie also referred specifically to whether Dupas was "a potential danger to society". Later events proved he was an enormous and lethal danger, just as Dr Bartholomew predicted. Dr Bartholomew was no clairvoyant, but he obviously knew a potential murderer when he came across one.

Senior Detective Ian Armstrong, of the Nunawading CIB, wrote to the Crown Solicitor on June 6, 1974, with this message: "He (Dupas) is a very dangerous young person who will continue to offend where females are concerned and will possibly cause the death of one of his victims if he is not straightened out."

It was a chilling and prophetic warning and if the residents of Melbourne's eastern suburbs felt safer with the rapist apprehended, found guilty and sentenced, they were wrong. Dupas was sent to the Mont Park Psychiatric Hospital where he was allowed to come and go as he pleased. Even worse, no records were kept of the convicted rapist's departure and return times.

Dupas was sentenced on September 30, 1974, and re-offended less than four months later, on January 6, 1975. He was arrested for loitering with intent and offensive behaviour after he was found in the female showers at the McCrae Foreshore Caravan Park. He even had the nerve to go inside the women's shower block and stand at the open door while he stared at girls taking a shower. The girls screamed and although Dupas quickly fled the scene, he was apprehended after a police operation was put into place. He denied he had been "peeping", but was identified and fined $100 (plus $44 costs) and it now should have been obvious his behaviour was something far more sinister than that of a Peeping Tom.

The convicted rapist was released on September 4, 1979, following recommendations for his parole, even though there was the precautionary rider that it was felt "this man will need a great deal of supervision while on parole".

The report concluded: "Dupas and his family very much desire his parole, and they have strong hopes that he will be released as early as possible. The Parole Officer recommends that Dupas receive parole, but it is felt he will require very close supervision and indefinite psychiatric treatment. It is felt that in some ways Dupas does pose a threat to the community at the moment, although he feels he will not reoffend, his pattern of offending in the past has taken the form of impulsive actions over which he apparently has little control. It is this factor which most concerns the Parole Officer in recommending Dupas for parole. Psychiatric treatment is often ineffective in dealing with this type of personality disorder."

Dupas might have been on parole but re-offended little more than two months later — with four separate attacks on women. Dupas even raped one of his victims in a public toilet in Frankston and another, an elderly woman, was stabbed in the chest before foiling his attempt at raping her. He wore a balaclava and was armed with a knife in each attack and must have left his victims with permanent mental scarring.

The first attack occurred about 11.30pm on November 9, 1979. Soon after a woman was about to leave a cubicle in a toilet block on the Nepean Highway, Frankston, the masked Dupas confronted her and pushed her backwards, turned her around and made her face a wall. After making her remove her pants, he then digitally raped her. Chillingly, he told her that if she didn't do as she was told he would stab and kill her. He even placed a knife over her throat when he heard other people in the toilet block. When he later read the victim's statement, he wrote on the bottom: "I've read this statement and I'm sorry it happened. It's all true."

Just two nights later, a woman was walking along Kars Street, Frankston, when she noticed a man following her. Sensing danger, she started to run but, because he was gaining on her, she stopped to confront her pursuer. Dupas, wearing a balaclava, then rushed towards her and brandished a knife. The woman, now terrified, ran into the centre of the road and started screaming. Dupas immediately stopped running and gestured with his hands for her to keep quiet. When she continued to scream, Dupas fled on foot. The woman later identified the blue balaclava Dupas had been wearing that night and, in a signed statement, Dupas admitted driving to the area armed with a knife, a mask and overalls with the intent to rape.

The third incident took place a week later, about 9.15pm on November 18, 1979. An elderly woman was walking along the Nepean Highway, Frankston, when Dupas grabbed her from behind and dragged her to a vacant block of land and forced her onto the ground. Dupas, wearing a balaclava, told the terrified woman: "Don't scream or I'll kill you." He then tried to remove the woman's cardigan but, despite Dupas' threats, she resisted and started to scream. Dupas moved from on top of his victim and walked away. Although the elderly woman had a lucky escape, Dupas this time inflicted a wound. The woman had to have 14 stitches in a chest wound caused by the assault with a knife. Dupas later admitted laying in wait for the female victim and was armed with a knife, balaclava and rope with the intention of raping her.

Finally in this sequence of attacks, on the next night, a woman was walking along Dandenong Road East, Frankston, when the masked Dupas leapt from a vacant block of land. The fact that he was wearing a balaclava would have indicated that this was no chance encounter and the woman started screaming. Apart from Dupas' frightening appearance, he also was growling. Dupas again fled, but this time was apprehended by police. He told them when interviewed: "I waited in the bushes and the lady came along. I saw her coming and I put on me (sic) mask and jumped out at her. I wanted to rape her."

Dupas was questioned about the other three attacks in the Frankston area and told police he deliberately wore a balaclava when he entered the toilet block in the first of the four attacks "because I was going to find a woman to rape". He added that he used the knife "to scare her with".

He also said in a recorded interview: "I have had a problem for about six years. I'm glad I got caught. It all started again about two weeks ago. I don't know if it was because me (sic) girlfriend left me or what it is. I just find it hard to mix with people and I haven't many friends. I just don't know what to say."

Dupas was convicted of rape, malicious wounding, assault with intent to rob and indecent assault. Despite the escalation of the viciousness of his attacks, there was no increase in penalty. The prosecution was shocked when Dupas was sentenced to just six and a half years' jail, with a minimum term of five years.

# CHAPTER TWO

# The Repeat Rapist

Dupas served little more than that five-year minimum for his series of attacks in and around Frankston and was released in February, 1985. Yet, true to form, he no sooner was a free man than he indulged again in his gross sexual deviations. On March 3, 1985, he went to a beach at Blairgowrie, ostensibly to sunbake. A 21-year-old woman also decided to go to the beach that day and drove to the Portsea back beach and then onto Blairgowrie after telling friends she would return about 4pm.

It was a glorious Melbourne day, with the sun throwing shards of brilliance on the pale, clear water of the eastern side of Port Phillip Bay. Close to shore, waves twinkled before breaking as a frothy cream. Children played with brightly coloured beachballs, built sandcastles or waded with their mothers. Overhead, gulls crawed and aarked in celebration of the radiance of the day. All was quiet and peaceful, or so it seemed and, for one woman, the darkest of eclipses blotted the sun.

The woman parked her car and walked with her dog along an access track to the beach and noted that there were few people in the vicinity. The woman saw half a dozen surfers in the water and saw a man throwing a stick for a dog to chase. The man with the dog was Dupas.

The woman, who already was wearing the bottom part of her two-piece swim outfit under her trousers, put on her bikini top without removing her T-shirt and left her clothing in a pile as she went for a walk along the beach. And, all the time, Dupas was watching and waiting. Finally, he moved to within a couple of metres of her and, as the woman walked across jagged rocks, she said to him: "The rocks are sharp." Dupas merely smiled at her before the woman walked back to her pile of clothes. And Dupas was there again, bare-chested and wearing jeans.

Dupas approached the woman and made a couple of comments she could not hear. Then, when she moved closer to hear what he was saying, Dupas said something about a purple star fish and that "the surf isn't very good".

Now sensing danger, the woman brushed past Dupas when, as quick as a snake and just as dangerous, he grabbed her and put an arm around her throat. He then held a knife to her throat and told her: "If you struggle I will hurt you." The woman told police she could "vaguely remember seeing the knife at that time". It was brown-handled with a silver blade and was similar to a paper knife. Dupas held the knife to her throat and snarled: "Don't struggle; I won't hurt you. If you struggle I will hurt you." He then ordered the woman on to the sand and forced her on to her stomach.

The terrified woman screamed, so Dupas put a hand over her mouth. At this stage the knife was on the beach and when the woman reached out to get hold of it, he snapped: "Don't be foolish".

His intention was obvious as he rolled her on to her back, pulled down her bikini top and started fondling her breasts and kissing her.

The woman later told police: "I was so petrified at the time, it is hard for me to remember exactly how things happened."

Dupas then told the poor victim: "I will take off your panties." He then performed oral sex on her before he removed his jeans and knelt between her legs. He snarled: "Look what I've got for you." The woman in desperation tried to make herself sick by placing her fingers down her throat and even told Dupas: "I think I am going to be sick." She asked him: "Why are you doing this? Why are you hurting me?"

Dupas did not answer and, despite the woman's tears, raped her. He then dressed himself as the woman begged: "Please don't hurt me." Dupas pushed her on to the rocks and fled the scene but, remarkably, not before asking her if she wanted a lift.

The woman was left shaking and sobbing on the beach before walking to the water's edge and waving to surfers. She then turned and saw two men walking towards her from a beach track. The woman told them: "I have been raped. Can you take me to my car?" The men at first found it difficult to believe what they had been told, but she was crying so hysterically that one of them took off to catch up with Dupas.

The other man took the woman to her car and, soon after they drove off, she spotted Dupas. The man, who was driving, stopped the car, got out and grabbed Dupas, who later was handed over to police and questioned at the Rosebud Police Station. He at first denied the attack, but later admitted raping the woman and that she had not encouraged him.

Asked if he knew what he had done was wrong, Dupas replied: "Yes, of course I know it's wrong." Yet, in the same interview, he said he did not want to hurt the woman and even said: "I'm sorry for what happened. Everyone was telling me I'm OK now. I never thought it was going to happen. All I want to do is live a normal life."

Dupas later tried to hang himself while in the Frankston Police Station cells, but it is difficult to know whether he really was attempting to end his life or making a plea for help. Regardless, it might have been better had he succeeded as his failure to kill himself resulted in the deaths of three innocent women. This time he was sentenced to 12 years' imprisonment, with a minimum of 10 years.

Dupas pleaded guilty to one count of indecent assault with aggravating circumstances and one count of rape and Justice Leckie told him in sentencing on June 28, 1985: "The evidence in relation to these offences is that you went in your car to the beach in the vicinity of Blairgowrie, got out of the car, taking with you a knife, with the intention of using that knife — should the opportunity present itself — to frighten a female so that you could have intercourse with her.

"You went down on the beach and this girl was there and you followed her round for some time and then, coming behind her, you forced your arm across her throat and forced her down to the ground, threatened her with the knife, and took her bathing costume off and raped her against her will and without her consent. It must have been a horrifying experience for her."

Justice Leckie explained the reasons why he detailed the background in his sentencing and said prophetically:

**"On the evidence which I have read before me this morning there seems to be a very good chance — if you were at large again — that some other girl might suffer in the same way."**

Or, as it turned out, even worse.

Judge Leckie continued, after referring to Dupas' prior convictions and absence of rehabilitation: "Now, the question is what can I do? I have got that dreadful example of what did happen in front of me … there is a strong probability of your re-offending, that the recidivism rate in cases of your type is between 80 per cent and 90 per cent or even higher."

The judge told Dupas that the rapist was carrying "a loaded gun in his pocket" before adding: "The question of releasing you at this stage is not to be considered. The community, I am sure, would be both outraged and apprehensive if that were to be done. But what is suggested is that a further attempt upon your subsequent release should be made to give you the appropriate treatment, including the medication Depo Provera if no other drug is then considered effective, with of course no guarantee that even that would be effective.

"The situation is that I am not empowered to prescribe conditions of parole when you are eventually released. So I have no guarantee — even in any order that I could make — that you would receive the treatment.

"I accept readily that you feel remorse and that you endeavour to overcome this enormous urge which you must have. But quite simply, I am not prepared to run the risk of some other girl being attacked by you in the same fashion.

"I think the only course open to me, because I am of the opinion that a custodial sentence is the only course open having considered all the other alternatives, I think I can only impose what I regard as an appropriate sentence for the offence, and apply that in contemplation of the earlier offences because not only are these offences accompanied by aggravating circumstances — that you carried a knife with you as an offensive weapon — but because of the prior convictions, there are six other grounds upon which each of these offences is accompanied by aggravated circumstances, in accordance with the provisions of the Crimes Act. One must have sympathy for you, but the community must also be protected.

"On the first count of indecent assault with aggravating circumstances you are sentenced to be imprisoned for six years. On the second count of rape with aggravating circumstances you are sentenced to be imprisoned for 12 years. The two offences were really one, a rolled up matter, and consequently I make those two sentences concurrent, making a total of 12 years. I fix 10 years as the minimum term to be served before you are eligible for parole."

Interestingly, the body of a woman who had been battered to death was found on a nearby beach 18 days earlier. The woman, Helen McMahon, had been sunbathing on February 13, 1985, when viciously attacked. Police still refuse to give full details of this murder as only they and the killer know the precise circumstances of how McMahon was murdered. However, police at the time disclosed that the dead woman was found on her side, naked except for a blood-stained towel placed across her breasts. There is nothing to link Dupas directly with the murder, except that he was living with his family in nearby Frankston on day release when McMahon was murdered. The files on this case are still open.

Dupas, who earlier had been engaged to be married, obviously was a young man with massive sexual and psychological problems and, despite lengthy terms of incarceration, was close to full metamorphosis as monster and killer. He knew he had a serious psychological problem and shortly after his incarceration at Pentridge tried to commit suicide. Although no details are available, he wrote a note to his family, starting with "Dear Mum and Dad".

Dupas, in this letter, apologised for his criminally sexual behaviour and told them: "Where can one start? There are probably hundreds of things we should have said to one another over the years. I guess it's too late now. The most important thing I've got to say is that I love you both."

Dupas then went on to suggest that they (his parents) did not know how much breaking up with his fiancée meant to him and added: "The way I feel at the moment and have for ages is that I'm far better off out of it all. I tried, I really tried to work on myself and my problems (but) I never felt I was getting anywhere." He ended his letter with: "We'll meet again some day."

But did Dupas really work hard at rehabilitating himself? A parole report in 1981 suggested: "He seeks a single magical stroke which will totally explain and totally cure at one fell swoop." This report also indicated that Dupas was "selective" in his acceptance of group learning, even if there was acknowledgement that he had been making some headway.

Nine years later, while serving his sentence for the rape at Blairgowrie, psychiatrist Dr Bartholomew spent one and a half hours with Dupas after having dealings with him over earlier convictions. Dr Bartholomew suggested that Dupas would not admit the truth of his earlier convictions and later was resistant to treatment. Dupas was prescribed drugs to restrict his sexual drive, "but without much success".

In a report to the Adult Parole Board, Dr Bartholomew said: "My main concern is that this man has three separate rapes against his name and some aggressive sexual behaviour before the rapes. This period of freedom between rapes one and two, and two and three was very short and he has really had little or nothing to be termed treatment … he has some capacity to threaten or attempt suicide when depressed and miserable."

Dr Bartholomew suggested it might take "some considerable time" to resolve Dupas' problems and that suicide must be considered as the convicted rapist had "a very brittle personality".

Another report, from a doctor at Mont Park, stated that Dupas did "not present the appearance of a psychiatrically ill person". The report added that Dupas did not acknowledge the need for ongoing medical treatment, but said he would "quite readily" keep appointments if directed to do so. In other words, he appeared to lack motivation.

Significantly, the report said: "Since past behaviour is the single best predictor of future behaviour, it would be naïve to conclude that Mr Dupas is not potentially dangerous. He has violently assaulted three women already, armed with a knife, either overtly threatening their life or implying a threat to it. He admits freely that until three years ago he denied any problems in this area. He now again essentially does the same (and) explains that he no longer has problems because he has sorted them out over the past three years … to his credit, he has organised a rather carefully planned re-entry into the free world."

The report did not make any recommendations "in the way of specific constraints or restrictions" if Dupas was granted parole, but added: "Clearly, given his past history, he will require the maximum possible supervision."

During this latest term of imprisonment he again was treated at the Larundel Psychiatric Hospital and it was during this period he met his future wife, Grace, a much older woman. She was 52 when Dupas met her while she was working as a mental health nurse at Pentridge in 1986. Grace, a divorcee with four adult children, later befriended Dupas and felt some moral responsibility for him, perhaps through pity.

Grace believed Dupas was a "model prisoner" who never caused any problem and was used as a handyman in his part of the prison ("G" Division). His main duties were in the laundry but, because there was inevitable contact with mental health staff, he and Grace often came into contact. Dupas told her "I regard you as a mother image", but Grace maintained an entirely appropriate and professional manner in their contact with each other.

Grace told police in 2001, while Dupas was the main suspect in the Mersina Halvagis murder, she was concerned about Dupas while he was in Pentridge because his "emotions smouldered". She also believed he was capable of suicide, but although he never directly answered her questions about whether he was suicidal, he "gave a negative reaction".

She also told of Dupas' fastidiousness, always wanting to be clean and neat yet, strangely, abandoned his smart appearance for a visit by his parents. She queried him about this but, in return, Dupas merely stared at her. It seemed no one, not even the psychiatric and other medical staff, had the slightest notion of what was occurring in Dupas' mind. It was a locked vault.

Arrangements eventually were made for Dupas to be transferred to Mont Park and this might have been the end of any contact between this odd couple, yet Dupas telephoned Grace from the mental institution. He asked her: "Why haven't any of you been to see me?" Dupas' charge nurse also told Grace that the convicted sex offender "felt let down by the fact that she had not been interested enough" to visit him and see how he was.

Grace decided to visit Dupas at Mont Park, where he told her he not only was infatuated with her, but "was in love" with her. He told her that with her help he could become "a normal person". The relationship then turned personal and Grace met Dupas twice a week at the institution coffee shop. She resigned her nursing position and later told police she felt "some sort of moral obligation to helping this man".

Dupas was transferred back to Pentridge and placed in "B" Division, for sex offenders. Grace visited him once while he was there before he applied to be transferred to Castlemaine. She said she believed Dupas made this request so that she would have to move away from her friends and family and that he could have her to himself, even though he would still be in prison.

When Dupas eventually was transferred to Castlemaine, in 1988, Grace moved to Kyneton so that she could visit him twice a week. She later told police: "During this time at Castlemaine Dupas became very much a man of the world and monopolised me. His unwritten rule was that I write every day."

Amazingly, Dupas even complained that Grace's daily letters had been written on plain white paper. He had seen letters women had sent to other prisoners and these had been written on "pretty paper". Dupas demanded the same as he believed that plain white paper was an act of "putting him down". Grace told police Dupas believed he was better than the other prisoners. "He felt superior," she said.

The extraordinarily possessive Dupas even took exception to Grace taking a friend's three-year-old son for one visit. He got angry when the child sat on her knee, simply because he could not have her undivided attention. He came first, second and last. As Grace said in her 2001 statement to police: "Dupas was a possessive, quietly domineering man. He was immensely jealous of all my friends and anything that I did that did not include him as the focus."

To Grace's amazement, Dupas asked her to marry him. She knew he had been jailed for a sex offence, but knew little of the litany of horrors he already had committed. However, marriage was never going to be a formality and when persmission was refused, the matter went before the Ombudsman and the Health Department. The matter eventually was sorted out and the couple was married in August, 1989. It was a strange marriage, with Dupas in prison and the new Mrs Dupas visiting her husband from a base she had found herself at Carlsruhe.

The good wife continued to visit Dupas, but she felt there was no real love. She later complained to police: "If Dupas was capable of love then he would have loved me. But I do not know if he had this capability. I now regard that I was one of his possessions, no different to any piece of furniture, vehicle or clothing."

Dupas' emotional claims on her increased and, finally, she wondered what she had let herself in for in marrying the man who later would be infamous as a murderous beast. When Dupas was nearing possible release on parole, psychiatric reports filed in December, 1990, indicated he was still a risk to society. One report indicated that the Dupas case would take some considerable time to resolve and another indicated that if Dupas was released he would "require the maximum possible supervision".

Dupas felt late in his sentence that he was ready to return to society and told parole officers he had "continued seeking and attending different programs that are provided in the system that will benefit me and prepare me for my eventual release". He also claimed that being married had given him responsibilies he previously had never experienced.

To back his claim that he could be trusted on the outside he referred to work he had done in and around Castlemaine on the "Community Gang". This involved jobs at the Castlemaine Library, Chewton Cemetery and the Castlemaine Recycling Depot. Dupas also pointed out that he even had attended a "refresher" fitting and machining course at Bendigo TAFE.

When Dupas was released in 1992 after serving just seven years, he went to live with his wife at Carlsruhe. Sadly and despite all his wife had done for him, Dupas felt hard done by and complained that the house was not grand enough and that her car was not good enough for him.

The couple applied through the Common Equity Rental Co-operative (CERC) for a rented house in Woodend and finally moved there in 1993. At last, Dupas seemed happy, even ecstatic — for a while. He was unable to find employment at that time and was on Job-Search, but became the honorary maintenance manager for the CERC and, according to his wife, "walked around the houses with a clipboard, or quoting rules and regulations at the CERC meetings".

While Dupas was looking for work, his wife was the bread-winner. They had few friends but Dupas spoke little of his childhood. However, he disclosed that he once had been engaged to a young woman named Heather and that when she broke off the engagement she handed the ring back to Dupas' parents. Dupas thought poorly of this, but did not elaborate.

He did tell his wife that he had a very unhappy childhood, not only because he was overweight, but also because he lived in a "spotless, almost sterile" house in which he wasn't even allowed to put his fingers on the windows and walls or walk in shoes on the carpet. Dupas also told his wife that his parents bickered and argued but whenever the question arose about why he had a psychological problem in his teens, Dupas clammed up.

The Dupas marriage was not consummated while the sex offender was in prison because he felt the sexual act was a private matter and should be experimented with in his own home and not in a prison room set aside for conjugal visits. However, it appears the marriage was consummated after Dupas was released.

Mrs Dupas, in her 2001 statement, described her and her husband's sex life as very basic and that she would go through with it as a "sense of responsibility" and "sometimes out of revulsion". She eventually reached the stage where she "could not bear him touching me". However, Mrs Dupas said her husband never showed any sign of sexual fantasies or desires and never saw him with any pornographic magazines or films.

Mr and Mrs Dupas lived quietly and modestly, their monthly highlight being a shopping visit together to Sunbury, usually on pension day. It was a humdrum existence, with Mrs Dupas working as a casual at a special accommodation residence and Dupas playing Mr Bigshot with his clipboard, but not earning any money.

If the poor woman expected any form of excitement in marriage to Dupas she would have been sorely disappointed. He had few interests, hated politics, did not read books and spent most of his time watching television or videos. Dupas' only hobby or interest was attending local auctions where he bought boxes of junk to repair items for resale at other auctions. Mrs Dupas said having a conversation with him was "like talking to a parrot".

Dupas not only looked like a nerd, but behaved like one. However, he appeared to have one or two saving graces, according to his wife. She said he rarely got upset and never swore. Yes, he might have been a rapist and (later) a killer, but the worst words from his lips at home were "bugger" and "damn".

Mrs Dupas told police: "I never heard him yell. If he did get upset he became very morbid. He would stare at the floor and just sit there.

He had great trouble looking people in the eye. His eyes would dart around rather than make contact with the other person's eyes. He did have another noticeable trait. Without warning he would have bouts of body shaking and severe perspiration. This would happen frequently, on a weekly basis. He gave no explanation for it, other than saying he was shaky. I got the impression he had been like this for many years."

Mrs Dupas might not have painted a flattering picture of the man she briefly shared her life with, but she made one point in Dupas' favour when she admitted he "never had a pre-occupation with knives". Yet, he had terrorised women with a knife before he met Grace and, of course, he later stabbed women to death.

On release from prison in March, 1992, Dupas lived with her until he again re-offended, but not before being involved in another incident which drew the attention of police.

A teenage girl was riding her horse down a Kyneton lane on September 23, 1993, when she noticed a car stop in front of her. The man in the car wound down a window and told her: "Your horse is bleeding." The girl jumped off her horse to see what was wrong and, while she was looking for any sign of blood on the horse, the man approached her from the rear of his car.

The girl told police in a statement: "As he approached me he said 'here, let me hold the reins, the blood's around the back', or something like that. I didn't let go of the reins but he took hold of them." While the girl was examining the horse, the man put his left arm around her shoulders. He said to her: "Now you are off your horse and I am out of the car we can have a good time."

The girl said "no" and snatched the reins from him and swung the horse's rear around to put the animal between herself and the man. When she remounted and galloped away, she looked behind her and could see the man in the car moving towards her. But as she tried to gallop the horse along the road, it panicked and the girl had trouble controlling it.

She slowed down, but only to turn to the man and snarl: "You fucking dirty bastard." He replied: "Get on the fucking side of the road" before driving off. Her description fitted Dupas almost perfectly. In her statement, the girl said: "The man was in his late 30s to early 40s, he was about 5ft 2in to 5ft 4in. tall. He was shorter than I am. He was wearing gold-framed glasses, had a round face, short hair blondy brown; he spoke like an Australian and he smelt strongly of cigarette smoke." Apart from the physical description, Dupas was a smoker.

The girl had had a narrow escape and said in her statement: "Apart from being very upset and scared, I was not hurt in any way."

This, however, was not the end of the matter as the girl on January 7, 1994, went to the Kyneton Police Station and identified a blue station wagon as the one driven by the bespectacled man who had frightened her so badly. Police then took her to the Kyneton Magistrates' Court building and asked her if there was anyone there who looked like the man who had approached her the previous September.

There were about 40 people in the room, including several police officers, but as soon as she walked in, the girl recognised a man sitting on a bench near the doorway and identified him immediately. She said in a statement: "When I saw this man I became frightened. I walked around the court looking at other people but I already knew it was him. When I walked past him I did not indicate him to the policeman with me. I walked out of the court and then, when a detective asked me if I had seen anyone I know I pointed to the man I now know as Peter Norris Dupas. I am certain he is the one who attacked me."

Dupas, who was not charged over this incident in the Kyneton lane, was in the courtroom the day the girl was asked to attend following a far more sinister attack. Wearing his trademark balaclava, he had attacked a woman in frightening circumstances as she was sitting on a toilet in a restroom block at Lake Eppalock on January 3, 1994.

Obviously unable to control his deviate urges, Dupas parked his car near a group of people which included a young woman who had just been water-skiing. He exchanged greetings with the group before driving 200 metres to a car park near a public toilet block. An hour later, the woman who had been water-skiing, left the group and went to the toilet. She had her shorts and bikini bottom around her ankles as the door was pushed open.

What she saw would have terrified any woman. A man in a balaclava moved towards her with a long-handled knife in one hand. She tried to slam the toilet door shut, but Dupas was too quick and, as the woman tried to defend herself, her left hand was slashed. The masked Dupas tried to turn the woman towards him, but she resisted and screamed. Dupas reacted by trying to drag her out of the cubicle, but eventually realised he had to flee. His victim rushed from the block, told her friends what had happened and they took off after Dupas, who had driven away.

This is what the terrified woman told police: "As I was sitting on the toilet the door pushed open and I tried to push the door shut and said 'no'. I didn't see anyone at this stage.

"The next thing that happened was that I saw a hand and knife come around the door, then a body and I immediately stood up and tried to push the knife away from me ... with my left hand and received cuts to my middle and ring fingers and the palm of my left hand.

"At this stage the male person was standing inside the door of the cubicle. When I tried to push the knife away from me I felt my hand become wet (with her own blood). He then tried to turn me around and was repeatedly saying 'just turn around'.

"My bathers and shorts at this stage were still around my ankles. As he was trying to turn me around I said to him: 'Please don't hurt me. I'll do whatever you want. I'm very frightened. Just tell me what's going on.' While he was repeatedly saying 'just turn around', I kept saying to him: "I'm very frightened. Just tell me what's going on.'

"During this time he was trying to push me around so I would face the back of the toilet wall and at the same time he was waving the knife close to my face and neck. During this I feared for my life and I thought that he wanted to rape me.

"I kept resisting him so he couldn't turn me around and I kept talking to him, repeating what I said earlier to him: 'I'm very frightened. Just tell me what's going on.' I would have repeated this about half a dozen times to him and he would have asked me to turn around about the same number of times.

"After that he turned his back and made to leave the cubicle and he still had hold of my right arm and as he left the cubicle I felt I was being led out of the cubicle. Once we were outside the cubicle he let go of me. He put both of his hands up nine inches in the air; he still had hold of the knife. He then said 'go', and gestured with his hands as if to dismiss me. He then left the toilet block and I remained standing in the doorway of the cubicle."

When the woman "cautiously" left the toilet block, she saw her attacker halfway to his car. She then ran screaming as fast as she could to her friends, who ran after the man later identified as Dupas.

It was a truly terrifying attack and the woman genuinely was in fear of her life. After all, her attacker had a knife, was wearing a creamy-coloured balaclava and seemed intent on causing her considerable harm. She described the knife as being "black-handled and kitchen type" and added in her statement:

"During this incident I feared the worst and was very frightened for my safety and also that I might be raped. I didn't scream because I didn't want to enrage him and I didn't think I would be heard outside the brick wall of the toilet block."

Two of the woman's male friends and her fiancé (an off-duty Australian Federal Police officer) took chase after seeing a blue Ford station wagon reverse and tear up the road. The men tried to chase it on foot but gave up without being able to read the rear number plate. One of them then jumped into his Ford utility, collected his friends, and took chase. They accelerated as fast as they dared and, after about 14 kilometres, spotted the station wagon approaching a roundabout.

The driver of the station wagon accelerated up a hill and even drove through a 75kph zone at about 100kph in an effort to get away. He then braked and turned left into a dirt road in a 60kph zone. However, he underestimated his speed, spun 180 degrees and came to a stop.

The pursuers pulled their car directly in front of the station wagon so there could be no escape and jumped out, but wary that the man they were chasing was in possession of a knife. One of the pursuers told police: "We all approached him. I watched his hands, but he was not carrying any knives. We all grabbed him and forced his hands behind his back and I remember we all demanded he lean over the bonnet of the car. He was struggling and saying: 'What are you doing to me? I haven't done anything.'"

The men asked him about the knife, and were told it was "in the back". One of them then went to a nearby house to telephone the police. They held the attacker face down on the bonnet until the police arrived and although there was little conversation, the man asked them: "What am I supposed to have done?"

Dupas knew full well what he had done and he was fortunate that the men who had chased and grabbed him did not take the law into their own hands. Imagine how the woman's fiancé would have felt! This monster, knife in hand, had barged into a toilet cubicle. The attack might have been a scene from the movie *Psycho*, with the woman seeing only a knife and hand around the cubicle door. She had been frightened out of her wits and many other men who chased and caught up with Dupas might have taken retribution and belted him half to death. To their credit, and probably to the enormous relief of the man who attacked only women, they did nothing unlawful.

Police quickly arrived and put the man described in statements as "the offender" in a police vehicle. Meanwhile, other police searched his car and removed three knives, two balaclavas, electrical tape and condoms. Police later showed the woman one of the balaclavas, made from a shirt-sleeve and she recognised it as the one the attacker was wearing. Importantly, the attacker was wearing a bloodied T-shirt and police later took a blood sample (through a court order) from the woman in the hope it would make a match. A blood sample also was taken from the man captured following the chase — Peter Norris Dupas.

One of the police officers who attended the scene was Detective Senior Constable Calvin Bone, of the Kyneton CIB, who, after telling Dupas of his rights, asked him several questions. The officer started by asking Dupas if the three men who had apprehended him were the ones who had followed him. Dupas replied "yeah" and then was asked if he knew the men. He said: "No, I don't. They assaulted me." Dupas then refused to answer questions until he had spoken with his solicitor.

Fortunately, the woman's physical injuries were not serious, even though the mental wounds would take a long time — if ever — to heal, especially in light of future murders. The woman in the toilet block might have suffered an agonising ordeal, but she was very fortunate.

Dupas was taken to the Kyneton CIB office and, on their way from where he was captured, Detective Senior Constable Bone asked him several questions, including where he lived and whether the blue Ford station wagon was his. Dupas then said the men had assaulted him and would not make any further comment until after he had spoken with a solicitor. Also, the articles taken from Dupas' car were itemised and included a blood-stained black-handled kitchen knife.

Detective Senior Constable Robert Leeder officially interviewed Dupas from 2.02pm the day of the arrest. Dupas, during the usual formalities, interrupted by asking why he could not contact his solicitor. Leeder continued with the formalities, but noticed that Dupas was shaking and offered him a blanket or some warm clothing.

Dupas again asked if he could contact his solicitor and was told this could be done once a warrant on Dupas' property had been executed, but not beforehand. Leeder told him: "I have legal requirements on me for not letting you contact a solicitor or another person at this time". He asked Dupas if he understood this and Dupas merely mumbled "yeah".

The interview was suspended after just nine minutes and resumed at 7pm, with Detective Senior Constable Calvin Bone asking the questions with Leeder present. Dupas indicated that he had, by now, spoken with a solicitor and was advised not to answer any questions. To all questions, Dupas either replied "on legal recommendation" or "no comment" to all questions. He started replying parrot-like with the comment "on legal recommendation I shouldn't answer any of your questions". However, Bone told Dupas that he need say only "no comment" and although Dupas adopted this suggestion, his answers remained parrot-like.

In what was to become a familiar aspect of the questioning of Dupas, his voice was barely audible and he was asked to speak up. The interview concluded with the police officers telling Dupas he would be required to take part in an identification parade and when asked whether he wished to give a blood sample, he replied "no".

Questions asked included:

- "It is alleged that around 11am today you went to Bally Ball at Eppalock. What do you say to that?"
- "It's alleged that whilst you were there you went to the female toilets. What do you say to that?"

- "It's alleged that you followed a female into those toilets. What do you say to that?"
- It's alleged that at the time you went into those toilets you were armed with a knife and other items. What do you say to that?"
- "It's alleged that whilst in those toilets you forced your way into the cubicle where the girl was seated. What do you say to that?"
- It's then alleged that you attacked that girl. What do you say to that?"
- "It's alleged that as a result of your attack the girl suffered injuries to her hand. What do you say to that?"
- It's alleged those injuries were inflicted with a knife. What do you say to that?"
- "It's alleged that your attack caused the girl to become hysterical. What do you say to that?"

Dupas' situation worsened the following day when police visited his wife at the Woodend home. Mrs Dupas told police that when she arrived home from her part-time job she found that the bed clothing had been disturbed and found a pornography video and a book on love positions lying on the bed. She had never seen them before and it can only be assumed that Dupas had intended hiding them when he returned from the "fishing trip" he had told his wife he was making that day.

Police, when they visited Mrs Dupas on January 4, showed her the following items, taken from the car Dupas had been driving the previous day:

- A kitchen knife.
- A wooden block with black tape around it with two knives pushed into the wood.
- A black balaclava with eye-holes.
- A T-shirt sleeve with eye-holes cut into it.
- A jar of Vaseline.
- A red plastic box containing condoms.

- A roll of blue plastic sticking tape.

Mrs Dupas was at a loss to explain the relevance of many of these items, but recognised the kitchen knife as one from her kitchen. She had asked her husband two days earlier to sharpen it. However, she had never previously seen the wooden block with the other two knives.

The black balaclava was part of an item Dupas used to keep in a shed, but she had never seen it with eye-holes cut into it. The T-shirt sleeve appeared to come from an item Dupas had owned. She had told him to throw it out because it was damaged around the neck.

Mrs Dupas was in the habit of keeping a jar of Vaseline in the bathroom but, when she looked for it in the presence of the two police officers, could not find it, a situation she described as "unusual".

She had never previously seen the box containing the condoms and was at a loss to explain "why Peter would have them". Also, Mrs Dupas had never previously seen the blue sticking tape. She thought this was strange as, if there had been any in the house, it would have been old, yet this roll was new.

Finally, Mrs Dupas told police: "I have no idea what Peter was doing at Eppalock on January 3, 1994, as I believed he was fishing just outside of Kyneton where we had gone previously." The evidence, circumstantial and forensic, was overwhelming and it was obvious Dupas was going to serve more years in jail. It also was obvious his marriage was over.

Dupas, according to his wife, was "very possessive" and disliked sharing her company — even when she had to go to work — and was increasingly moody. He had few pleasures and often was lost in his own introspective moods. Finally, he cracked. He returned to his old ways, of terrorising women. The marriage had never been a happy one and Mrs Dupas, to her credit, suggested she had done little more than take pity on Dupas and tried to look after him. She deserved much better and Dupas repaid her trust and loyalty in the most vicious manner imaginable, with worse to come.

Despite what police had found in Dupas' car and his atrocious record of sex attacks, he was handed a sentence of just three years and nine months, with a minimum term of two years. Dupas had pleaded guilty to false imprisonment, but avoided a charge of attempted rape because of lack of evidence.

The police were devastated, but were in a Catch 22 situation. New Victorian legislation meant that serial sexual offenders could be jailed indefinitely, but because there was little chance of proving a sexual offence against Dupas, it was a case of either letting him off with no conviction or having him put away for false imprisonment. Unfortunately for the woman he attacked, this must have been heartbreaking news as she later told of how she was too scared to walk down the passage of her home to go to the toilet at night.

With Dupas pleading guilty, the woman he attacked was not required to give evidence and his counsel, Mr David Cordy, told Judge Leo Hart at a Bendigo hearing of the County Court of Victoria, Criminal Jurisdiction:

"Your Honour will no doubt be very concerned about his prior convictions and what his motives may have been on this occasion, but of course it's a situation where despite what he did, he stopped the behaviour, he released the girl. It's not a case where someone has come along and disturbed him. It's not a case for which he was prevented from exercising his will on the girl by some external means whatsoever.

"He's apparently just snapped out of it, and as I understand her account of it, raised his hands up and said 'go' and just let her go. And, in my submission, Your Honour, that's a matter that ought to stand him in great stead when Your Honour comes to sentence him."

Judge Hart told Dupas in sentencing him on November 21, 1994: "Mr Dupas, your prior convictions and criminal history are breathtaking." The judge noted Dupas' prior convictions and told him: "This offence is not a sexual offence nor a violent offence as those terms are defined and you are not subject, in this case, to the penalties introduced by the Sentencing (Amendment) Act 1993, although you will clearly be found to be a serious sexual offender, as defined, should you ever be convicted of a sexual offence or a violent offence in the future.

"Whilst your motivation for this offence is a proper matter for me to consider in assessing your moral culpability and I infer that your motive was to commit an offence of a sexual nature, I remind myself that no matter what the victim might have thought your purpose was, nor what I might think your purpose was, the offence cannot be elevated or altered thereby to an offence other than what it is and I must sentence you for the offence of false imprisonment and for nothing else.

"That offence, especially in the following circumstances, is nonetheless a serious and significant offence, high on the scale of gravity of such offences. It was not spontaneous; it was planned and you must have been watching and waiting nearby. Steps were taken to conceal your identity, a weapon was used and other equipment was at hand, if required. It was an offence carried out on a single, by that I mean a lone, defenceless woman in degrading circumstances in the seclusion of an isolated toilet block when she was separated from her friends and at your mercy.

"It was calculated to and did engender terror in her mind. It involved a physical assault and the likely consequence of using a knife eventuated. It was a significant affront to her and a serious violation of her rights and self-esteem. What is more, it was carried out by a person with the prior convictions and criminal history that you have …

"Deterrence, both special and general, looms large as a sentencing consideration in this matter, but again I remind myself that you are not subject to the provisions of the Sentencing

(Amendment) Act 1993, and that I must punish you only for the offence charged and not for what I think you were going to do, but did not.

"The only matters that I can think of which tend, to some extent, to mitigate the gravity of the offence and your criminality are that it was mercifully short. That is, the detention was over in minutes, although I am sure it seemed a much longer period for the girl and that you released her voluntarily and not because you were disturbed or prevented from continuing. I do not know why you did this, but it is an important matter in your favour, indeed, a very important matter.

"By ceasing when you did, although you had already offended as I have outlined, you spared the girl the terrible fate you originally intended and which she expected, and you acted in such a manner to give rise to at least the hope and perhaps the prospect that realisation of the significance of what you were about to do activated your conscience in such a way as had not happened on the occasions of your previous offences. I cannot, therefore, preclude the possibility of rehabilitation notwithstanding that your history suggests otherwise …

"Any time you spend in prison will no doubt be 'done hard', as they say, because of the nature of the offences and because of the prison culture. You pleaded guilty to this offence at an earlyish time and thereby spared the victim the trauma of trial and I take into account that plea in reduction of what might otherwise have been the appropriate sentence and the plea, is again, consistent with the hints of conscience that I have referred to …

"Mr Dupas, I sentence you to be imprisoned for a period of three years and nine months. I fix a non-parole period of two years and nine months."

Although Judge Hart did not "preclude the possibility of rehabilitation", he nevertheless would have been bitterly disappointed that Dupas would develop in a cold-blooded multiple killer.

Dupas now was big news in Melbourne. Before being sentenced for his Lake Eppalock attack, the *Sunday Herald Sun* ran the news of his latest sexual offence under the headline RAPE FIEND IN COURT AGAIN.

The *Sunday Herald Sun* reported: "A man described by police as 'Victoria's most vicious serial rapist' has appeared in court again, this time pleading guilty to the assault and unlawful imprisonment of a young woman."

The newspaper described Dupas in terms he would have detested when it reported: "This week Dupas, a small man with glasses, an untidy moustache and thin, straight brown hair, sat quietly in the dock when the Crown outlined the frightening attack."

A *Sunday Herald Sun* reporter asked Dupas' wife if she had anything to say, but she refused to discuss her husband, although she said that the marriage was over.

The newspaper contacted the president of the Victims of Crime Assistance League, Ms Tricia Rhodes, who said: "This case is a perfect example of somebody who, if he is mentally ill, should be kept in a psychiatric hospital at the Governor's pleasure — and if he is not mentally disabled should be kept in for the term of his natural life."

The secretary of the Victoria Police Association, Senior Sergeant Danny Walsh, told the newspaper: "We would expect that the community would be totally outraged and disgusted by the repetitive and persistent sexual offences committed by Dupas. Perhaps it is time the Government looked at special cases and gave the necessary power to ensure that repeat offenders of this nature are removed from society."

Psychiatrists were unable to describe Dupas as mentally ill, even though he obviously had a disturbed and warped mind, while there were no moves to have this "rape fiend" locked away indefinitely. If

Ms Rhodes' suggestion had been adopted, three women would not have died at the monster's hand.

Dupas, in attacking the unfortunate woman at Lake Eppalock, had been well-prepared; he wore a balaclava and carried a knife. His future attacks also were well-planned, but his victims were not so fortunate. He did not let them "go". He killed them.

The monster eventually was paroled after serving just under two years, leaving prison in September, 1996, and moved into a flat in Rose Street, Brunswick, an inner northern Melbourne suburb. His wife had left him soon after the Lake Eppalock incident and after meeting another woman, computer programmer Iolanda Cruz, moved in with her in May, 1997. They had met while they were tenants in separate flats in Rose Street and, after she returned from a holiday in South Africa, Dupas convinced her they should live together.

The de facto couple moved just a little further north, to Coane Street, Pascoe Vale, and it seemed the monster had been tamed. Dupas, who had spent much of his adult life in prison, found employment at a Thomastown furniture factory — Blue Diamond Furniture — as a general hand. It was a humble and mundane occupation, but Dupas had another occupation in mind, one that would bring him notoriety as a multiple murderer and seemingly a man without a heart or conscience.

Dupas spent 12 months with Blue Diamond and, after complaining of wrist injuries, left to start making furniture from his garage at home. He complained of Repetitive Strain Injury (RSI) and had surgery in an effort to overcome this problem. During Dupas' time with Blue Diamond, two women were killed in appalling circumstances, with another to meet her death seven months after he resigned. The third killing, of Nicole Patterson, led to his arrest and conviction for the earlier murder of 40-year-old prostitute Margaret Maher and then of Mersina Halvagis.

# CHAPTER THREE

# An Appointment with Death

In March, 1999, Dupas read an advertisement in a local newspaper which eventually led to the horrific death of the woman who had placed it in the *Northcote Leader*. In reality, it was an invitation to a killer and might as well have been printed with a funereal black border. Attractive and keen to establish a psychotherapy practice, Nicole Patterson advertised her services, unaware she would take calls from a convicted rapist looking for an easy target.

Nicole Amanda Patterson had been born at the Sandringham Hospital, in Melbourne's bayside, on May 28, 1970, the daughter of Pam and William ("Bill") Patterson, who had married in 1967, but separated in 1998. The Pattersons had three children, with Kylie the eldest and then Andrew, with Nicole — who always preferred to be called Nicky — the youngest.

As Pam Patterson cradled and suckled her baby for the first time and showered her with kisses and maternal affection, she could not possibly have imagined the horror that lay ahead for her precious daughter at the hands of a monster.

More than 38 years later, the now Mrs Pam O'Donnell recalled that Nicole was "a brilliant baby — the best any other mother could have". The infant slept through the night from just a few months and "always woke smiling or laughing". Nicole walked at 11 months and was strong-willed from a tender age. "She always knew what she wanted," according to her mother.

As father Bill was a chain store executive, the family moved around the country, not only within Victoria but also to Adelaide and Perth. Nicole was just two years of age when the Pattersons moved to Warracknabeal, where Bill got to know another young family man, a Greek migrant who ran the local fish and chip shop. Bill and his new mate often had a beer together after work and it now is an almost overwhelmingly sad coincidence that the happy, hard-working George Halvagis' daughter Mersina also was murdered by Dupas.

Nicole attended several primary schools and always shone, particularly when at Mentone Park. She sat for a scholarship while there in Grade Three and her proud parents were overjoyed when their little blonde daughter won a half-scholarship to Cato, a campus of MLC (Methodist Ladies' College). Then, in her first year at Cato, she won a full scholarship.

Nicole Patterson was more than just bright; she was extremely talented and also could turn her hand to anything from sport to music. A good swimmer, she also excelled at music and dance and at one stage her parents believed Nicole's education would follow a musical stream as she was highly proficient as a flautist.

The Cato years were interrupted by Bill's transfer to Adelaide and then Perth, but Nicole returned to Cato for years seven and eight and passed the entrance examination for highly prestigious government school, Mac.Robertson's Girls High (named after benefactor, chocolate magnate Sir MacPherson Robertson), on the southern edge of the city of Melbourne. Although extremely bright, Nicole was, on her mother's admission, "not very studious". Mrs O'Donnell explained: "Nicole seemed to get through on natural talent and seemed to breeze through school year after year."

Nicole, according to her mother, also was "a bit of a scallywag". Lively and mischievous, Nicole loved playing pranks, with one of her best remembered by all those at "Mac.Rob" when Nicole was in Year 11. She "borrowed" a triple adaptor and hooked up a tape she played over the school PA system for every student and teacher to hear. It was one of her favourite songs, of the Monty Python gang singing "sit on my face, and tell me that you love me". It earned Nicole a visit to the head's office.

On completing her secondary studies, Nicole attended Swinburne for one year of an Arts course, but would have preferred Media Studies. Unfortunately, her VCE marks fell just short of those necessary for this course and, in hindsight, if Nicole had pursued a career in the media instead of psychotherapy she probably would still be alive today.

Nicole ended her secondary education at Rusden College, completing Bachelor of Education and psychotherapy courses. Although she lived with her mother for a while after the break-up of her parents' marriage, she eventually moved out and lived with friends at various addresses, including one in St Kilda.

Choosing a career in psychotherapy was typical of Nicole, whose mother described her as "always wanting to help others". Mrs O'Donnell, after her daughter's murder, told police that Nicole was "a very intelligent girl". She told them: "Everything she did she did well, whether it was academic or sport, She was emotionally stable and never exhibited any anger. She was quite the opposite actually. She could see goodness in everybody and wanted to help everyone in need and solve the problems of the world. Nicole could see someone with two heads walking towards her and she would not even look at the heads and, instead, just see that person's heart."

Mrs O'Donnell, years after her daughter's murder, cited the example of Nicole helping a young woman who turned up "high" at a clinic. "The girl was what you would describe as spaced out," Mrs O'Donnell said. "Others at the clinic called out 'get rid of her', but Nicky took the girl aside and asked how she could help her. This was typical of her, always thinking of others and always seeing the best, not the worst, in people."

Nicole, while at secondary school, adopted the following motto for life from the works of great Irish playwright George Bernard Shaw: "I rejoice in life for its own sake; life is no brief candle to me." Tragically, that life was snuffed all too soon.

Full of vitality, Nicole sometimes burned her candles at both end. She drank and smoked and loved a good party, until a medical examination revealed an irregular smear. Her doctor recommended a medical option, but Nicole insisted she could solve the problem herself. She gave up smoking and turned to organic food. Her doctor was amazed when a follow-up smear was "all clear".

Nicole, happier than ever in her healthy new lifestyle, moved to a rented house in Harper Street, Northcote, in 1996 and shared the accommodation with a friend until Andrew briefly moved in to be with his younger sister. The fledgling psychotherapist grew vegetables, often supplying her mother with beetroot — "it will do you good" — and revelled in the joys of everyday life.

A young woman who trusted people and loved family life, she adored her sister Kylie's two daughters, Amy and Alisha, and it was obvious to everyone that Nicole one day would love to have children of her own.

Her mother recalled: "We were having a family barbeque one day when little Alisha, just two years of age, tugged at me and asked me to come and see her 'baby'. She led me into a room where Nicole was wrapped in a blanket and pretending to cry and wail like a baby. Little Alisha walked over to her, patted her head and Nicole pretended that she had been soothed to sleep."

Amy and Alisha also use to hide when Nicole would visit and then jump from behind a chair to surprise their aunt, who cherished their company as much as the little girls gave her their unconditional love. It was a tight, loving family, torn in all directions in the most horrible of circumstances.

Nicole, once settled into her Northcote home, converted the front bedroom for her psychotherapy practice, but clients were few and far between. The caring young woman with a social conscience spent much of her time with the private drug counselling group "Breaking the Cycle" and it was in this youth assistance culture that she met boyfriend Richard Smith, a drug and alcohol counsellor.

Nicole's business was slow to take off and her only early clients were those Smith referred to her. Advertising in the local newspaper was the obvious solution, only for the advertisement to be read by Dupas. He subsequently made 15 telephone calls in reply between March 3 and April 12 and eventually made an appointment for 9am on Monday, April 19. Police later were convinced Dupas used the false Christian name of "Malcolm" and provided Nicole with a mobile telephone number. Fortunately for police, she noted the name and number in her personal diary and circled the appointed time of 9am.

Nicole was pleased that her advertisement had paid off and excitedly told friends that she was expecting to see a "new" client. She believed she would be admitting a man known as "Malcolm" to her home but she was visited by a monster with mayhem in mind.

It would not be difficult to guess Nicole's state of excitement that morning. She would have showered, dressed and had breakfast with a song in her heart. Her fledgling psychotherapy business was about to take off with the visit by "Malcolm", a man who wanted to discuss his addiction to gambling — or so she believed. It was enormously significant that Nicole had written that name "Malcolm" in her contact book and had circled that time of 9am.

Nicole, wearing a pale blue top, a darker blue light cardigan, a red skirt and black suede slip-on, wedge-heeled shoes sized seven and a half, had her Northcote home in pristine condition for her visitor. The beige carpet in the "consultancy room" had been cleaned and everything pointed to an air of professionalism, with books on cement-brick and timber shelves, academic qualifications on the wall and knick-knacks and photos on a maroon velvet-covered sideboard. Nicole also had two light brown chairs arranged to face each other, presumably for therapist and client to sit face to face. Perversely in hindsight, a white cuddly toy bear sat atop the bookshelf. It was a perfectly normal scene, not a setting for murder.

The rest of the house in Harper Street was more "lived in". There was a bike in the hallway and Nicole's bedroom was furnished with basic and inexpensive items. Sadly, a doll was propped up in a corner next to her green timber bed. The lounge room was comfortable and cosy, with a gas fire sitting inside an antique timber mantelpiece. A lavender coloured bookcase stood on one side of the brick chimney, with a dining suite on the other side. It was all homely and revealed Nicole was house proud. Neat as a pin.

Significantly, there was a small black suitcase on the floor and, on top of this, there was an answering machine, several ball-point pens and scraps of note papers. These had several notes scribbled on them, including the one with the name "Malcolm" at the top of one off-white page. Underneath was the word "depression". To complete the scene of normal domesticity there was the name and number of a pizza shop and some of its offerings — super supreme (with anchovies and BBQ sauce, but no salami), ham, pineapple and prawns, ham and cheese and margherita with pineapple. Nicole Patterson was never given the chance to order another pizza.

The kitchen was small and neat, with a white laminex top and dark wooden cupboards. In the sink there was a bowl and spoon, and it seemed obvious Nicole's last meal had been cereal, possibly with toast or bread, as there was a small bread and butter knife on the right of the sink, just in front of the microwave.

Nicole was all prepared for her first client and the man who gave his name as Malcolm, the murderous Dupas, could have entered the property in Harper Street from one of two directions. From the left of the property he could have walked a short distance up a cobbled bluestone driveway and then right on to the front porch. Alternatively, he could have entered through a small green cast-iron gate about a metre high and along a concrete path and then left to the porch before coming across a bronze flywire door in front of the main door. It is not difficult to imagine a smiling Nicole greeting her patient/client at the door.

The house itself was typical of those built in Northcote and, indeed, many inner Melbourne suburbs in the Victorian era. It was an off-white weatherboard cottage with a small green bullnose verandah and green roof, verandah posts and downpipes. It was ultra-Victorian except for the low cream-brick fence, which probably would have been built in the 1950s. There were shrubs and rose bushes in the tiny front garden and the driveway ended just a metre or so beyond the narrow porch. It was an unpretentious house in an unpretentious area, even if Northcote in 1999 was booming through renovations and redevelopment.

The house has changed little since Nicole's murder. The green paint has been replaced by white or cream and much of the shrubbery has been removed. The alterations have been merely cosmetic, but nothing could disguise the horror it hosted when Nicole greeted her client.

Nicole would have opened the front door around the appointed time of 9am and this would have been the last time anyone but Dupas would have had the chance to see her alive. However, no one saw Nicole open the door and then close it with her killer about to attack. Nicole even had made herself and Dupas a plunger of coffee. One blue mug was half-full with cold white coffee when police later arrived. The plunger was on its side with coffee spilt into a tray and on to the floor and one empty brown, beige and turquoise pottery mug was found on the carpet. Nicole had been attacked while she was having coffee.

No one saw Nicole on that fateful day of April 19 and about 6.30pm close friend Regina (known as Rena) Hoffman arrived at her home for a pre-arranged dinner. She opened the front door and walked into a scene of utter horror. Nicole's body, in pools of blood, was face up in the front consultation room, her legs crossed at the ankles with her navy blue knickers around and underneath the left ankle.

Worse, Nicole's body had been horrifically mutilated. Her killer had slashed off the top of her light blue top and left it lying in a pool of blood alongside Nicole's left shoulder. The cardigan had been pushed down and Nicole's breasts had been removed. The murdered woman was naked from the waist down and there was a terrible deep and long slash to Nicole's inner right thigh.

Other obvious injuries included a gash to her abdomen, just under her pierced belly-button, and blood around her mouth and neck. Nicole's head was lying slightly to her left and pointing to the doorway leading to the passage, just next to a display of peacock feathers. Her arms were outspread as if she were asleep. It was a truly loathsome scene and although Hoffman immediately telephoned for an ambulance, Nicole was long dead and police launched a murder investigation.

Hoffman, in her statement to police, told of how she had become friendly with Nicole while studying psychotherapy in 1994. They celebrated birthdays together and met at least once a week at drawing classes in North Melbourne.

She added: "Since she graduated Nicky had been building up her work to include counselling sex workers. Nicky graduated 12 months after me because she was required to have an extra 12 months supervised therapy. She did these extra 12 months to improve her skills at counselling.

"This year Nicky had been working at Ardoch Youth in St Kilda. She began late October last year. Nicky's previous job was at 'Breaking the Cycle' and was very good at it. 'Breaking the Cycle' is working with long-term unemployed youth (under 25 years old). She would have a record of all the participants in a particular program and after they had completed their program she would do follow up calls and find them jobs.

"Nicky was an extremely integral friend, very supportive, and trustworthy. She was sensitive and a very intelligent and creative person.

"After we graduated Nicky started a dream analysis group which included four women. This occurred every fortnight and had been regularly occurring since probably January, 1997. The women were ex-students of the psychotherapy course … and one woman would present a dream and generally speaking it was your own dream, wherein we would discuss associations and possible meanings and, at times, it could become emotional. Other times it was laughing and talking about a dream."

Hoffman last saw Nicole alive on the night of April 12 at one of these dream group's meetings. Nicole rang her friend early on the afternoon of Saturday, April 17, and explained that she had a difficult week ahead of her and was having problems in the relationship with boyfriend Richard, who had a seven-year-old daughter and a four-year-old son. After speaking openly about her problems over about an hour, Nicole agreed to have dinner with Hoffman on the Monday night.

Hoffman added in her statement to police: "It was my day off on Monday, April 19, 1999. I went shopping and had a coffee that morning (with a female friend), went home and then went to see my therapist at 3pm. Had a coffee and, after that, went to the bank and came home at about 5pm. I rang Nicky on her mobile, but got a message. I know this was at 5.06pm because I thought I was meant to pick her up at 5.30pm and I would be late, hence my urgency at contacting her.

"The message I left was checking what time we had arranged for me to pick her up, but I said I would try to ring her at work. I rang her at (my) work and was told it was her day off. I then remembered that I was going straight to her house at 6.30. So I rang her on her home number and got the machine and left a message saying ignore my previous silly message on the mobile and I would be there shortly. This was before 5.30pm. At 6.04pm I left home. I looked at the car clock because I knew that I was still running late and wanting to buy some flowers as well, knowing it generally takes half an hour to get to Nicky's house, not including peak hour traffic. The last time I looked at the clock was when I was turning into the High Street area and it was 6.49pm."

Hoffman parked her car outside Nicole's house in Harper Street, just near the driveway. She at first was surprised not to see Nicole's car in the driveway, but quickly remembered that it had been stolen and written off in an accident. Hoffman walked up the driveway, paused to look at the roses and noticed the verandah light was on. She rang the bell and Nicole's dog Bella immediately started barking. Hoffman rang the bell a few more times and when there was no answer, used force to open the door. Hoffman heard music and noticed that the light was on in Nicole's work room and in other rooms. It was then that Hoffman came across a sight she will never forget.

She said in her statement: "I saw her (Nicole) lying naked on the floor in her work room, with her head towards the door. She was lying diagonal and she was lying flat on her back, her head leaning on her left side and there was a rag or material like a silky thing on her left side not touching her. It was soaked in what looked like blood and the carpet looked bloodied. There was something metallic, maybe jewellery, with this silky thing.

"I noticed her wrists; there were some slashes and blood on them and on her chest there was blood. Her bras (sic) were pulled up and loose; the cup was loose and I thought that her breasts were covered with something unrecognisable. It was an orangy yellow colour. Her breasts looked punctured and there was this yellowish thing; I thought she had a top on. There was a bluish tinge to her face. Her eyes were closed. Her right arm was beside her and her left arm was resting. I saw a slash mark on both her wrists. I saw the bottom half of her body; her legs were straight together. I could see her pubic hair, which seemed unmarked. I could not see any blood around her pubic area or legs.

"It was very quiet. I had yelled out 'hi' or 'hello' and she did not respond. That was when I first came in. I thought she was acting; it was like an act but when she continued not to respond and I sort of looked more and realised that there was something terribly wrong. This was not normal. And I knew that she would not put me under that stress anyway.

"I dropped my bag and my flowers and I went in and said 'Nick', to see if she was breathing. I bent down on her right side and ran to the phone in the living room. I tried to dial 000 emergency. I tried a few times, got through and was asked if I wanted police, fire or ambulance. I said 'ambulance' as I believed Nicky had attempted to commit suicide and I wasn't sure if she was dead yet. The operator said: 'We are sending over police and ambulance. Go and put your ear to her nose and mouth to hear her breath and look to see if her chest is rising or falling. I'll wait here.'

"So I ran back at this stage. I went into the (work) room and I remember going really close to her and her eyes were now open and I went through the actions of listening and I touched her chest. I looked at her and her chest and realised that they were her breasts and that there was nothing on them. I saw she was not breathing. I looked for her pulse on her neck (but) could see it wasn't moving. She was cold (when) I touched her chest.

"I ran back to the phone and told him (the operator) that she wasn't breathing. I was crying and he said: 'Do you want me to stay on the phone?' I told him I was going to ring somebody (a friend named Kaalli — full name Holly Kaalli Cargill). I got the answering machine first and then Kaalli picked up and I was crying and I told her that I was at Nicky's and I think Nicky has committed suicide. We were both crying and I told her I had rung the police and the ambulance. She asked me if I wanted her to come over and I didn't know what to do. Then the door was knocked on; the police had arrived."

Constables Sheree McDuff and Anne Howey rushed to Harper Street from the Northcote Police Station and it was then that Hoffman realised her friend had not committed suicide, but had been murdered. Discovering her friend's mutilated body had been a terrible shock and Hoffman was grateful that the two female police officers had been so kind, supportive and sympathetic. In fact, she referred to Constable Howey as "Anne" at the police officer's request and, after seeing Nicole's body placed in an ambulance, Hoffman was driven to the Homicide Squad's headquarters in St Kilda Road to make her statement.

Constable McDuff said in her statement: "Upon arrival at the scene at approximately 6.56pm Howey and I alighted from the divisional van and approached the address entering the front yard through the front gate located on the right hand side of the premises. Howey and myself walked on to the front verandah and proceeded to look through the front window located on the left hand side of the premises. Here I observed a female lying on the lounge room floor who appeared to be deceased and mutilated ...

"As a result of this discovery Howey and I entered the premises via the unlocked security screen and wooden front doors located on the right hand side of the house. Both doors did not display any visible signs of forced entry. Once inside the doorway I observed an evidently distressed female on the telephone at the end of the hallway and a bouquet of flowers beside a black coloured bag lying on the floor directly in the doorway of the front entrance. This female is now known to me as the witness in this matter, Regina Hoffman.

"Howey immediately approached the female on the telephone. Whilst Howey spoke with Hoffman I positioned myself in the doorway of the lounge room where the deceased female lay on the floor. The lounge room is located on the immediate left of the hallway as you walk through the front door.

"Upon looking at the deceased female I observed both of her breasts to have been cut off, multiple stab wounds to her chest area and dried blood on her upper thigh area near her vagina. The female lay on her back on the floor in the crucifix position. Her legs were crossed right over left, resting on a piece of dark coloured cloth. The cloth was folded neatly and placed underneath her heels raising them slightly off the floor. Her arms were laid out to her sides with the palms facing upwards.

"There was a pool of blood on the carpet to the left of Patterson's body. A piece of light blue coloured cloth was scrunched up on the floor near the pool of blood. The deceased's body was naked, with the exception of a bra on her person which had been raised up over her breasts and left sitting high on her chest.

"I also observed a silver coloured necklace on the floor on the left side of Patterson's body. The clasp of the necklace was broken. To the right of Patterson's body was a pair of black coloured ladies clog-type shoes and a red-coloured fleece or similar type material zip-up jacket."

Knowing she was dealing with a murder, Constable Howey immediately called for back-up from the Northcote and Heidelberg stations and the Homicide Squad. Then, at 7.01pm, ambulance officers Tony Cuthbert, Ross Barkla and Rebecca Rose arrived at the house of horror in Harper Street. They agreed immediately it would be a waste of time trying to revive Patterson and returned to their ambulance at the front of the house.

Just three minutes later, Sergeant Brian McCallum arrived and he was followed at 7.20pm by Detective Senior Constables Mal Stevenson and Ross Mitchell and, finally, the Homicide Squad, led by Detective Senior Sergeant Jeff Maher, a lookalike for Hollywood movie star Kevin Bacon.

An immensely experienced officer, the tall, well-dressed detective had seen more than his share of horror in a long and distinguished police career, especially with the Homicide Squad.

The crew-cut detective had joined the Victoria Police as a cadet in 1973 and graduated from the Glen Waverley Police Academy the following year. His first postings were in Melbourne's CBD, at the then Russell Street headquarters and then in Flinders Lane, before working as a uniformed officer at various inner Melbourne stations.

Maher was promoted to the rank of Detective Constable after four years' service, working mainly in inner suburbs. He later joined the Tactical Investigation Group and, when promoted to Detective Senior Sergeant worked with the Licensing, Gaming and Vice Squad. Finally, as a Detective Senior Sergeant, he applied to join the Homicide Squad and, since 1994, has investigated more than 130 murder cases and several police shootings.

Thorough to the point of being determined to find any needle in any haystack, Maher investigated the Salt Nightclub murders of July 8, 2002, in which a mob chased and hacked to death 19-year-old James Huynh with a sword, with his cousins, 21-year-old Nam Huynh and 25-year-old Viet Huynh drowning in the Yarra after leaping into the river to escape their pursuers. Seven men were convicted, although three later won appeals.

Maher also led the investigation into the killing of housewife Julie Ramage by husband James Ramage and the shooting death of Senior Constable Tony Clarke. The Ramage killing was particularly notorious because James Stuart Ramage claimed at his trial that he was provoked. Ramage had bashed and strangled his wife of 23 years at the family home on July 21, 2003, and dumped her body in a shallow grave near Kinglake, north of Melbourne. The 45-year-old said he had reacted after his wife told him that sex with him repulsed her. He was found not guilty of murder and, instead, was convicted of manslaughter and sentenced to 11 years' jail, with a minimum of eight years.

Senior Constable Clarke was on police traffic patrol near Launching Place along Victoria's Warburton Highway on the night of April 24, 2005, when he pulled over a car driven by 27-year-old Mark Bailey, a man with a history of mental illness. Bailey somehow managed to get hold of the police officer's service revolver from its holster and fired at Clarke as he tried to take cover. He then forced Clarke on to the ground and shot him in the back of the head before driving off and later shooting himself dead.

As a Homicide Squad officer, Maher had seen more horror than anything imaginable outside a war zone, although he admitted he "somehow got used to it" because of the responsibility of the task in hand in any given case. "I don't necessarily look at the horror of what has occurred but, instead, I try to look at a body as a piece of evidence. I just have to let the emotion wash over me so that I look at everything objectively. It is all about professionalism and being alert and ready to take everything into account without worrying about what is in front of you."

A family man with many and varied interests, Maher likes nothing better than to push the more ghastly aspects of his job to the back of his mind by going bush, to ski, fish or just camp in the open.

He also loves his sport and, in particular, Australian football. A devoted Essendon supporter, he is a grand-nephew of one of the club's most decorated players, Frank Maher. A brilliant rover, Frank Maher played 137 games with Essendon from 1921-28, captained the club over the 1925-27 seasons and later coached Fitzroy and Carlton.

Although the grand-nephew of this great football champion had seen the bloodied bodies of many gunshot, stabbing and other homicide victims, the Nicole Patterson stabbing and mutilation was as bad as it got. He recalled: "I took a call from D24 just after 7pm after an initial report that the woman, Nicole Patterson, might have committed suicide. However, it was obvious as soon as I walked into the room where she died that this was not the case and that this would be a murder investigation.

"It was a very confronting scene, even for someone who had dealt with death and murder many times. Here was a young woman who had been cut down in her prime and her body horribly mutilated. The style of killing left us all stunned but we just had to focus as quickly as possible. When we get to these types of scenes we are facing the unknown and we knew in the first minutes of the investigations that we would have to cast a very wide net.

"We started from absolute scratch and the first thing we had to do, apart from the formalities, was to learn of Nicole Patterson's background and for what purpose she used the room in which we found her body. We had to contact friends, relatives and virtually anyone who knew her. In this way we quickly learned Nicole was trying to establish a psychotherapy business."

Officers from the Crime Scene Unit of the Victoria Forensic Science Centre (VFSC) made an extraordinarily thorough examination of the murder scene and surrounding areas from 8.40pm until well into the next morning. Senior Constable Robert Huygen of the VFSC said in his statement: "The address contained a single fronted weatherboard house on the western side of the road behind a low brick fence and a small front garden with shrubs and small trees.

"A driveway led to the front of the house along the southern side of the property and a footpath ran along the northern side of the property, also to the front of the building. There was no access from either the driveway or the footpath to the side or back yards. A large dog was in the rear and side yards, which were secured by high fences. Access to the rear yards was available only via the backdoor located in the laundry at the western end of the house. The back door was locked. All of the house windows were locked and there appeared to be no recent tampering to them or the entry doors.

"A verandah was attached to the front of the building. It was over the front door, which opened to a hallway and also over a window of the front room in the house. At the ends of the verandah were the driveway and the footpath. The door was close to the footpath."

There had been no forced entry to the humble cottage and this later convinced police that the man they particularly wanted to interview was the mysterious "Malcolm", the man with the 9am appointment with Nicole.

Senior Constable Huygen and the forensic team found what appeared to be bloodstains near the middle of the outside face of the front door and collected swabs of these bloodstains. Further swabs were taken from the knob of a lock inside the front door and from an area outside the wire door above the exterior handles. Swabs also were taken from bloodstains found on the southern wall of the hallway and on an interior doorjamb. It was obvious that Nicole's killer had traipsed through the house and left smatterings of blood along the way.

One of the most chilling aspects of the crime was that small amounts of blood were found in Nicole's bedroom. The killer had walked through the house and any vivid imagination could conjure an image of what might have occurred. Did the killer parade in front of a mirror with the severed breasts? Did the killer wear any of

Nicole's clothes as he performed a goulish ritual of imagining himself as the dead girl whose body he had just mutilated in almost the most horrific manner imaginable? Anything was possible as the killer certainly wasn't looking for items to steal. He was a killer, pure and simple, and a cold-hearted, remorseless one at that — someone who had preyed on a lone woman.

In the room where Nicole had been murdered and mutilated so savagely, Senior Constable Huygen noted that Nicole's body could easily be seen from the open front door and it was immediately obvious that the unfortunate woman's breasts had been sliced from her body.

He said in his statement: "Blood smears were on the carpet near the deceased with a blood-soaked area near to her left side. The blood to the left of the deceased and her body position indicated she had at one time been lying further to her left and had apparently been rolled on to her back." The inference from this is that the killer had done this so as to remove the breasts, which were never recovered and obviously were taken as "souvenirs".

Senior Constable Huygen collected the silver neckband, fibre and carpet samples, hairs (from the dog in the back yard), a scarf and other items of particular interest. Meticulous in the extreme, the police officer noted every detail of the room of death. He stated: "The front room with the deceased appeared to be a sitting room. It contained numerous ornaments, a desk with a chair, a bookshelf with books, two lounge chairs and another chair. The light in this room was on.

"On the floor beyond the deceased's feet were a pillow and a clean, brown coloured drink mug. A lounge chair was to the left of the deceased. On the floor in front of the lounge chair was a round serving tray containing a second clean mug, a bowl with sugar, a jug with milk and a tipped over coffee pot. Contents from the pot were in the tray and on the floor. A pair of 'Candy' brand slip-on shoes and a box of tissues were next to the tray. One shoe was on the tray's edge. Another used drink mug was on the desk in the room." Senior Constable Huygen collected and removed the mugs, the tray and contents and the shoes.

The most significant part of Senior Constable Huygen's statement concerned what he found in the lounge room. He said: "The lounge room contained neatly arranged furniture and contents. The light for the room was on and the radio was on. A telephone was on the floor next to the entry doorway from the hall and beside the phone was a case with a telephone answering machine, pens and notes. A couch was next to the case with the answering machine."

Then, highly significantly, there was the following vital clue: "Amongst items on the couch was a turquoise-coloured diary. The diary contained an entry at 9am, Monday, April 19, which read 'Malcolm — 0417037312'." Dupas, after killing Nicole, had searched the house for items which could incriminate him and, had he turned over the couch, he might have found the diary which was to play an important, but not necessarily decisive part in his arrest and conviction.

Nicole had taken the mobile number of the man known only as "Malcolm" at this stage of the police investigation. Could this be the killer's number? It all seemed too easy, too convenient. The killer obviously planned this murder in great detail, so why should he give his victim his phone number to write down?

Meanwhile, Nicole's body was taken to the Coronial Services Centre (morgue) at Southbank. Pathologist Dr Matthew Lynch performed an autopsy the following day.

He wrote in his report: "At approximately 2200 hours on April 19, 1999, I was notified by the office of the State Coroner of the discovery of a deceased woman with evidence of a chest injury at a premise in Northcote. I attended at the scene where I was met by (Senior Sergeant) Geoff (sic) Maher of the Homicide Squad. There I observed the deceased young adult Caucasian female lying supine.

She had evidence of chest injuries and the breasts had been removed. She was naked from the waist down although there was a pair of blue underpants present about the left ankle. The body was cold to touch and rigor was well established. An ambient temperature at 0100 hours on April 20, 1999, was 16 degrees Celsius and rectal temperature was 24 degrees Celsius. A rectal swab was taken prior to taking a rectal temperature. It was arranged for the body to be transported to the Victorian Institute of Forensic Medicine, where a postmortem examination commenced at 0900 hours on April 20, 1999."

Dr Lynch then wrote: "The order in which the injuries are described are in no way intended to indicate the order in which they are sustained." He then noted that the body weighed 59 kilograms and measured 167 centimetres. Nicole had been a well-proportioned, even if petite, young woman.

Dr Lynch also noted there were bloodstains on a white brassiere and blue long-sleeved T-shirt, white camisole (partly cut open at the front) and on a navy blue cardigan. Significantly, there were "elliptical defects" on the back of the cardigan, suggesting Nicole had been stabbed from behind, among other terrible injuries. The preliminary examination was meticulous and Dr Lynch even noted that the blonde Nicole had painted her toenails purple and that she had a tattoo of a tiger, with outstretched claws, high on her right buttock.

The autopsy revealed Nicole had been stabbed 13 times to the back, chest and limbs, with damage to both lungs and her heart, and that both breasts had been removed. There were injuries to her right thigh, right wrist and thumb and index finger. Nicole obviously had fought for her life and Dr Lynch noted: "The incised injuries to both hands are classic examples of defence-type injuries." The right pleural cavity contained about 200ml of blood and the right ventricle leading to her heart had been cut. Large amounts of blood were found in both lungs but, significantly, the hyoid bone and thyroid cartilage both were intact. This meant Nicole had not been strangled. Nicole, horrendously mutilated, had been in good health.

It was around the time that Dr Lynch arrived in Harper Street that Nicole's mother was told of her daughter's death. Mrs O'Donnell recalled: "I took a call at 10.15pm from our son-in-law John (married to Nicole's sister Kylie). He asked if he could speak with my husband Brian. I didn't recognise John's voice, so I just handed the phone to Brian. He looked shocked and this, in turn, frightened me. Brian then had to break the news to me that Nicole was dead, but I insisted it could not be true.

"I had always thought that if anything like this happened there would be police officers at the door. This didn't happen and I later discovered that Nicole's friend Rena had contacted her mother who, in turn, contacted my son Andrew, who then rang his father. John later brought Kylie and their two daughters to our house and I kept thinking that it must have been someone else and there had been a mistake.

"I rang police headquarters and asked to speak to the Homicide Squad and after they gave me Jeff Maher's number he at first did not fully believe I was Nicole's mother. Then, when he realised the truth, he apologised and explained that he often had to deal with a lot of dirty tricks when people are trying to get information. By this time it was early in the morning and I went into a state of shock. This sort of thing always happens to someone else. I had to go and see Jeff a couple of days later and it was then that he told me what had happened to Nicole. No one deserved that, no one."

Meanwhile, Senior Sergeant Maher, a detective with bulldog persistence and a strong sense of humour despite his occupation, had few clues. Some proved to be little more than useful, but others were significant and led to Dupas' apprehension and convictions.

The time of Nicole's death was important because of the notes in her diary. Maher correctly and immediately assessed that whoever had made the 9am appointment had killed Nicole and it was significant that two witnesses told police they heard screaming from Nicole's home in Harper Street.

One, 38-year-old neighbour Phillip Omerivic said in a written statement: "I know a woman called Nicky who lives at number 21 Harper St., Westgarth (part of Northcote). She has lived at that address for about four years I think. I do not know her well; I only knew her to say 'hello' when I would pass by her house.

"This morning (April 19), some time after 9am I was walking along Harper Street toward the railway line end of the street. I was on the footpath on the same side as Nicky's house. As I walked past her house I heard a woman's voice yell loudly from the house 'you fucking cunt' and then again I heard the same female voice yell 'you fucking cunt' a second time.

"The female yelled this very loudly; she didn't sound angry but sounded like she was upset at the person she was yelling at. Both times I heard this yelled it all occurred within the time it took me to walk past Nicky's house. I did not look up when I heard it. I did not want to be a sticky beak.

"I could not say for sure whether it was Nicky who was yelling, but I assumed it was her. I don't remember seeing if the door was open and I could not see much because of all the bushes in her front yard.

"I continued walking up the street to my auntie's house. I am not sure of the time, but it was definitely past 9am. I stayed at my auntie's house for about 20 minutes before I started walking back home. I think I crossed over to the opposite side of the road of Nicky's house before I walked past. I do think that I looked over to her place as I passed by. I did not hear anything coming from her place when I walked past on this occasion. I estimate I got home around 10am.

"When I heard the yelling from Nicky's house as I walked past the first time, I assumed it was just a domestic argument. The woman was not calling for help so I did not think that it was anything serious. Later today I heard that a murder had occurred at Nicky's house. Police later knocked on my door and I told them what I had heard."

Omerivic's evidence was similar to that provided by another neighbour, Bruce Thompson, who lived three doors down from Nicole. He said in his statement to police that he was at home on the morning of Nicole's death.

His statement read: "At about 9.30am that day I was on the front verandah of the house having a cigarette. Whilst on the verandah I heard a very brief scream. It sounded like a female voice and it came from further along the street to the left of my house. That is, north from my house. It seemed like someone had been hurt. I glanced up the street, but didn't actually see anything. Everything seemed fairly quiet and normal. I was out on the verandah for a few more minutes. I didn't hear anything else."

Thompson's evidence was more detailed than Omerivic's as he saw a man walking down his street "with a sort of intentness". He said in his statement: "He walked past me towards Westgarth Street. He wasn't running … and as he walked past me, he looked at me. I believe I would have given him a bit of a nod, but he did not seem to respond at all. I cannot recall ever seeing the person before. I am pretty sure he didn't leave in a motor car. He had his hands in his pockets.

"After I finished my cigarette I came inside. I remember after I came back inside I checked the clock in the kitchen next to the stove. The time was about 9.40am and I went outside to hang up the washing. When I finished that I left for work. I left at about 10.15am in my car, which had been parked out the front of the house. I didn't see anybody else in the area. The first time I left the house was when I went to work. I did not leave the house to investigate the scream that I heard.

"The person I saw walk past my house is not anyone I know from around here. I have been asked by police if the person I saw was from the other side of Harper Street. I know the person referred to and can say that it was not the man I saw."

The screams heard by neighbours around 9.30am and the sighting of a stranger in Harper Street soon after the murder further convinced police that Nicole's client "Malcolm", in their language "was a person of interest".

One of the problems confronting police was that no one saw Dupas entering or leaving Nicole's home. Although Thompson saw a man walking towards Westgarth Street, police were unable to determine where the killer had parked his car or, indeed, whether he had arrived by car.

Maher explained: "We did a comprehensive door knock trying to find a witness who might have seen a man leaving the house in Harper Street. This came up with nothing and we could only surmise that the killer parked his car in Westgarth Street or another nearby street and walked up Harper Street to Nicole's home. This was the only direction he could take as Harper Street had a dead end to the north.

"The real problem was that a man walking up or down a street in itself would not have aroused suspicion and the killer, contrary to what many people might have believed, would not have been covered in blood. Stab wounds certainly cause considerable bleeding, but most of the blood is absorbed by clothing, unless an artery is severed in an exposed part of the body, like the neck.

"This was the case with Nicole Patterson and even the removal of her breasts would not have caused much bleeding as this was done after death. Blood did not spray all over the place, although we reasoned that the killer might have had blood on his hands and on some part or parts of his clothing."

Police wasted no time tracking down the registration of the mobile telephone number Nicole had written in her diary. It belonged to 24-year-old La Trobe University student Harbagan Singh Kohli, who had bought the phone on March 14, 1999, soon after he arrived in Australia from India for his Master of Business Administration course.

In a statement to police, Kohli (known as "Harry") explained how he bought the phone: "The first night I stayed at the Glenn College at the La Trobe University and the next day I stayed at the University Lodge for about one month before shifting again to my current address. About one week before this last move I met another Indian man called 'Sonny'. His real name is Pankajpreet Bakshi and he also moved into the same address. There was (sic) already two people living in the house, their names are Petros (known as 'George') and Kim but I don't know their surnames. I think we moved in at the beginning of February.

"On the 14th of March, 1999, I purchased an Ericsson Mobile GF768 phone. I bought it on a $30 flexi plan and because I was new to the country and didn't have any prior dealings with Telstra or history, Petros decided he would sign up the phone in his name for me and that I would pay the bills. One or two days later 'Sonny' did the same thing. The phone number I was given was …. The phone stays in my possession and no one else used it. No one has borrowed my phone to take to their house."

Because the mobile telephone number seemed so significant in the murder investigation, police decided to keep both Kohli and the man known as George under surveillance. Det. Snr-Sgt. Maher explained: "We had to do this because the number seemed to be an important lead. However, it was obvious very early that they led absolutely normal lives and were in no way involved in what we were investigating except that the killer somehow had obtained Harry's mobile telephone number."

Kohli ("Harry") said that on the university's Orientation Day (January 18) he had enrolled with the University Employment Services in search of part-time work and then was told to look at the positions offered on a notice board. He called up to 60 numbers in search of work and, on April 8, came across a notice for a job cleaning, gardening and general labouring work. The name given as reference for this job was "Peter" and Kohli made a call the next day. "Peter" explained that the work would not start until May 12 and asked him to give him his phone number so he could call back. Kohli had given Peter Dupas his phone number.

The Kohli telephone number might have been significant, but it did not directly lead to Dupas. Police, however, discovered another route to Nicole's killer. They checked calls made to Nicole's landline and, through Telstra, discovered that a number of calls had been made through one particular number. A further check revealed that the number was leased to Mr Peter Dupas, of Coane Street, Pascoe Vale. Police had their man, even though they needed further evidence for a conviction.

This was a painstaking part of the investigation and was assigned to a diligent and meticulous detective, Mick Daley, who sat in front of a computer reading links to Nicole's telephone line. She had taken many calls and it was Daley's task to cross-reference these to come up with possible suspects. Det. Snr-Sgt Maher explained: "Mick checked and checked and, after a great deal of diligent work, came up with calls from a telephone landline at a house in Coane Street, Pascoe Vale. He traced the resident, and bingo, the line was rented in the name of Peter Dupas. Imagine how we felt. We knew that a serial violent sex offender who had spent a substantial number of years in jail had contacted Nicole Patterson in the days before she was killed.

"The balloon went up even though Mick was thorough enough to do a double-check before we took any action. But, once we were convinced our information was right, we swung into action. It was then that Detective Senior Constable Paul Scarlett came aboard in the investigation. He was with the Rape Squad and, after providing us with plenty of information on Dupas, he was seconded to Homicide for this investigation."

Scarlett, a tall, quietly spoken police officer with an impeccable reputation for working by the book, had joined the Victoria Police in December, 1989, after waiting three years to achieve his career ambition. He originally had been knocked back because of being partially colour blind but, typical of his determination, he refused to take no for an answer.

After spending four years in uniform, Scarlett became a plainclothes officer at Dandenong — a tough initiation in a tough area. He joined the Rape Squad in 1997 and it was there he first came across Dupas. He was profiling Dupas when Mick Daley visited him during the Nicole Patterson investigation to ask him: "Do you know anything about Peter Dupas?"

Scarlett had a huge file on the convicted rapist and had profiled him so well that Jeff Maher requested that the Rape Squad detective work with him on Nicole's murder. Scarlett then was involved in the search at Dupas' home and the arrest. For Scarlett, a dedicated family man, the invitation to work on a murder investigation was the achievement of a long-held ambition. It was an opportunity he would not waste and, after the arrest and conviction of Dupas for Nicole Patterson's murder, he also was involved in the Margaret Maher and Mersina Halvagis murder investigations.

Scarlett was such an integral member of the investigative teams that he was praised for his work. Dogged in the extreme, he even worked on the Margaret Maher and Mersina Halvagis cases after his brief stint with the Homicide Squad, working on these cases in his own time while with Nunawading Criminal Investigation (CI).

Convinced they were able to make a breakthrough in the Nicole Patterson murder, four Homicide Squad police officers — Snr-Sgt Maher, Detective Sergeant Steve Mitchell and Detective Senior Constables Scarlett and Stuart Cockerell — gathered at the Excelsior Hotel, in Mahoneys Road, Thomastown, about 1pm on April 22, three days after Nicole's gruesome death. They then made their way into a gaming room where they confronted a pudgy, middle-aged man with large spectacles.

Scarlett recalled: "Dupas was wearing a blue cotton-drill work jacket, a type of parka, and was easy to spot as he always looked a loner, even in the gambling room of a pub. He was standing by a gaming machine when he obviously saw us approach him. He didn't look shocked, just a bit surprised. He was totally unemotional, but as we took him by the arm to search him, Jeff (Maher) pointed to the scratches on Dupas' face without making any comment.

"Steve Mitchell did the actual arrest and Jeff told me to run a tape. It ran for seven or eight seconds before seizing. On analysis, the erase head had failed. But, during that very brief conversation, I took notes while Dupas said he knew nothing about any murder and had not been in Harper Street, Northcote, at any time. Under the judge's (Justice Frank Vincent) discretion this brief conversation was admitted as evidence at Dupas' trial and although this was unusual I don't think it had any real influence on the result. It was just a pity that the taping failed."

Scarlett said that Dupas refused to look the police officers in the eye as he was being cautioned. "He looked down and we found this was his normal habit," the officer said. "He just does not look men in the eye. He also came across as shy and introverted. He seemed to cower and stoop and spoke in a very quiet voice. No one could have imagined from looking at Dupas that he could be such a revoltingly cold-blooded killer of women."

In a statement Scarlett made following Dupas' arrest, he said Det-Sgt. Mitchell approached Dupas and asked him: "Are you Peter Norris Dupas?" The wanted man nodded "yes" and then asked: "What's going on?" Det-Sgt. Mitchell then asked Dupas to step away from a gaming machine and took him to the male toilets, where he was searched. The detective cautioned Dupas and then asked him if he knew Nicole Patterson.

"No," Dupas replied.

"Have you ever had anything to do with her at all?"

"No."

Scarlett asked Dupas about the scratches on his face, but was told this was from "working in the shed", with a further explanation when questioned that it was caused by a piece of wood which came out of a machine and hit him on the face.

The detectives then drove Dupas to his home in Pascoe Vale and arrived at 1.42pm, less than an hour after they first approached Dupas in the Thomastown hotel. As Scarlett sat in the police car with Dupas, the other officers went inside. It was there they found more than enough to charge Dupas with murder.

The weatherboard house in which Dupas lived with Iolanda Cruz was crawling with police soon after 1.30pm. Apart from members of the Homicide Squad, there were officers from Search and Rescue, the Force Response Unit and forensic specialists. They went over the house with the proverbial fine tooth comb. They wanted the killer to pay for his crime.

Police not only searched the house, but also a garage Dupas had used for woodworking. They even rummaged through a wheelie bin and came across several items of interest, including a bag with several torn newspaper pieces on which the words NICCI, NORTHCOTE, MACOM (sic), 9.00 and part of a telephone number had been written. The scraps of newspaper appeared to come from the top of an advertising section.

In all, there were 13 scraps of newspaper and they were placed together in an evidence bag. There also was a note with the word "Harry" and a telephone number on the side of a refrigerator in the kitchen. Police, of course, had tracked down the Indian student known as "Harry" and the mobile telephone number matched. The documents later were examined by document and handwriting expert Dr Bryan Found, who was able to piece the fragments together to tell an extremely interesting tale.

On one side of the sheet of newspaper, there was a note that read "Nicci, Mo 9.00". This obviously referred to a meeting with Nicole for a Monday at 9am. There also was an address — 21 Harper Street,

Northcote, with the "h" in the Northcote missing as this scrap of paper had been torn through. But, most informative of all, was the word "Macom" (sic), the name given by the man who had made the appointment with Nicole at almost precisely the time she was killed. The other side of the newspaper had two phone numbers. One was Nicole's home number and the other her mobile number.

Dr Found then compared the writing on these scraps of paper with a sample of Dupas' handwriting. Basically, if a handwriting examiner or expert believes there are similarities between the sample writing and the evidential writing, there is some degree of identification. It is a complex task, but Dr Found was confident enough on the completion of his analysis to say in a statement to police:

"I conducted a handwriting comparison between the questioned handwriting appearing on the reconstructed documents (from the 13 fragments), the note and the handwriting specimens of Peter Dupas. It is my opinion that there are indications that the writer of the Peter Dupas handwriting specimens wrote the questioned handwriting on these documents."

Police also found hairs and other pages with writing and, if this already had reinforced the police view that Dupas undoubtedly was their man, they also found a copy of the *Herald Sun* newspaper of April 21. A photograph of Nicole was featured on the front page and, significantly, there was a rip across the face of the young murder victim. The head and shoulders photograph of Nicole ran underneath the huge splash headline PSYCHO KNIFE KILLER on the front page.

The report read: "A young woman dedicated to helping others was murdered in a savage knife attack in her Northcote home.

"Police are investigating whether Nicole Amanda Patterson knew her killer.

"The body of the 28-year-old psychotherapist, a crisis counsellor who gave advice to some clients at her home, was found in a pool of blood after an attack that shocked police."

Det. Snr-Sgt Maher would not give reporters details of Nicole's injuries except to say they were "inflicted in a frenzied knife attack". A neighbour told the *Herald Sun:* "I'm shaking, I'm shaking … it's a horrible thing. She was a lovely, happy girl."

Other significant items taken from the Dupas house included yellow PVC and cellophane tape, a blue jumper, overalls, shoes, a blue jacket and a bloodstained green jacket with a black balaclava in one of the pockets. These items then were examined for possible forensic evidence, eventually adding to the probability of Dupas' guilt.

Apart from the murder of Nicole, one of the most chilling aspects of the case was that Dupas lived with an exceptionally intelligent woman who had absolutely no idea she was sharing her life with such an evil monster. Iolanda Cruz was a decent, hard-working woman who deserved much better.

Dupas was taken to Homicide Squad headquarters in St Kilda Road and interviewed by Det-Sgt Mitchell in the presence of Det. Snr-Sgt Maher. After stating the time as 5.30pm on April 22, the taped interview was based on a question-answer format. This interview is important as it reveals that Dupas was shown extreme courtesy and, on legal advice, he refused to comment. The detectives who interviewed Dupas obviously were patient and even used his Christian name when asking him questions. The following is the full text:

Q: What is your full name and address?

A: Peter Norris Dupas.

Q: What is your age and date of birth?

A: 6.7.53

Q: Can you speak up, please, Peter?
A: 6.7.53

Q: And keep your voice up.
A: Righteo.

Q: What is your current residential address?
A: Coane Street, Pascoe Vale.

Q: Right. What is your occupation at the moment?
A: I'm a — factory hand.

Q: Righteo. And you're employed with? Are you currently working?
A: I'm, I'm d…, doin' work — worker's compensation.

Q: Righteo, Peter. I intend to interview you in relation to the offence of murder. Before continuing, I must inform you that you're not obliged to say anything or do anything, but anything you say — you say or do may be given in evidence. Do you understand that?
A: Yes.

Q: I must also inform you of the following rights. You may communicate with, or attempt to communicate, with a friend or relative to inform that person of your whereabouts. You may communicate with, or attempt to communicate with, a legal practitioner. Do you understand these rights?
A: Yes.

Q: Do you wish to exercise any of these rights before the interview proceeds?
A: Yes?

Q: Which of the rights would you like to exercise?
A: I'd like to ring a practitioner and a friend.

Q: All right. You'd like to contact both of those people if I continue to question you.

Det. Snr-Sgt. Maher then asked: Is it true, Peter, that this afternoon you did speak to a legal practitioner?

A: Yes.

Q: Would you like to speak to the same legal practitioner?

A: Yes.

Q: And if that's not possible, another legal practitioner?

A: Yes.

Q: All right then. What relative or friend would you like to be contacted.

A: Pat O'Brien (a retired priest who first met Dupas when the sex offender served a term in Ararat prison years earlier).

Q: Yes, we've got his name down here. Have you got a contact number for Pat O'Brien?

*Dupas gave the detectives Father O'Brien's number.*

Q: Right. Are you an Australian citizen?

A: Yes.

Q: Right. What I intend to do now is suspend the interview.

A: Can I …?

Q: Yes.

A: Can I also say …?

Q: Yes.

A: …That I've been told already that I should have somebody from the Public Advocate's Officer here …

Q: Yes.

A: With me.

Q: Yes.

A: I've been told this by a solicitor. The solicitor who told me was from Legal Aid, Robyn Mills. I'm supposed to have an independent person during my interview.

Q: Righteo. We'll try and contact these people for you. I'll suspend the interview so we can try and keep contact with these people. Do you agree with me that the time now is 5.33pm?

A: Yes.

Q: We'll suspend the interview at that time

The interview was suspended, with a resumption after a break of just over two hours. Det. Snr-Sgt. Maher and Det-Sgt. Mitchell again went through the ritual of asking Dupas his name, address and age, also informing him of his rights a second time. The interview continued, with Det-Sgt Mitchell asking the questions:

Q: Do you wish to exercise any of these rights before the interview proceeds?

A: I've already done that.

Q: Righteo. Let's just discuss that for a moment. You earlier, prior to arriving at St Kilda Road — arriving at the Homicide Squad offices — you had a conversation on a mobile phone to solicitor, Mr Michael Young — de Young. Is that correct?

A: Yes.

Q: And since arriving back here, can you tell us what conversations you've had with — with any other persons other than police personnel?

A: I've also phoned a friend.

Q: Who was the friend you phoned?

A: Pat O'Brien.

Q: And have you spoken to anyone else here at the Homicide Squad offices?

A: No.

Q: Have you spoken to solicitor Mr Michael de Young here?

A: Yes. Mr de Young has — I suggested it — is use my rights to make no comment statements.

Q: Righteo. I understand that. I intend asking you some — some questions and invite you to reply anyway. Let me first indicate to you that the offence of murder that I'm talking about relates to a young lady by the name of Nicky Patterson, who was allegedly murdered on Monday, the 19th of April, 1999, in Northcote. Do you understand that?

A: Yes.

Q: Righteo. Do you agree with me that — that earlier today, myself and other detectives initially spoke to you at the — a hotel in Thomastown?

*No comment.*

Q: Righteo. I was just attempting to clarify the fact that, at that time, I detailed you — the — caution that I've detailed to you there and your rights at the time of your arrest earlier today. Do you understand that? I was going to invite — I was going to ask you, and I do ask you now whether or not you agree that I detailed to you that the murder I wanted to speak to you about was the murder of Nicky Patterson. Do you remember that I detailed to you that the murder that I wanted to speak to you about was the murder of Nicky Patterson?

A: Yes.

Q: And do you remember that I also gave you a full caution which was almost exact — was exactly that I — same as the one that I've detailed then?

A: Yeah.

Q: And gave you your rights?
A: Yeah.

Q: Do you agree that earlier you told me that you were on Workcare at the moment?
*No comment.*

Q: Who do you live with at the moment?
*No comment.*

Q: Is — I understand that your solicitor's given you certain advice and they're your rights, of course. Right? What I — it's a matter that — that you've been arrested in relation to the murder of Nicky Patterson on Monday, and I'm inviting you to — to answer my questions. If there's anything you've got to say for yourself in response to allegations that you're responsible for the murder. Do you understand, Peter?
*No comment.*

Q: (To Det Snr-Sgt Maher) — Is there anything at the moment, Senior Sergeant, prior to …

Det Snr-Sgt Maher then asked Dupas: How long have you lived at the address in Pascoe Vale, Peter?
*No comment.*

Det-Sgt Mitchell then said: "Well, what I might do at the moment, given the circumstances, I might — we might suspend the interview for a short time, while we are making some further enquiries. You seem to be shivering at the moment, Peter. Is there some reason you're shivering?
*No comment.*

Det-Sgt. Mitchell therefore ended the interview, with the time recorded as 7.52pm. This interview, in which Dupas refused to make any comment about the murder of Nicole, lasted just seven minutes.

The interview was suspended for almost an hour and a half and, during this time, Dupas spoke with Father O'Brien and Ms Mary Wright (a friend).

After the usual caution, the interview proceeded with Det.Sgt Mitchell asking the questions:

Q: Peter, earlier today, after we arrested you at the — at the hotel in Thomastown, we conveyed you back to your home premises. Do you agree that I handed you a — well, in fact, Senior Sergeant Maher, handed you a copy of the search warrant in relation to your premises?

*No comment.*

Q: Have you got a copy of that with you at the moment? Do you want to open it up? Open it up, Peter, have a look at it. Is that the — is that the copy of the warrant that was handed to you — to you before your premises was entered today, by Senior Sergeant Maher?

*No comment.*

Q: Do you know Nicky Patterson?

*No comment*

Q: Earlier today, I had a conversation with you outside the hotel, after I cautioned you and gave you your rights. You agree that I gave you — that I cautioned you and gave you your rights earlier tonight. In the conversation in the car (on the way to the Homicide Squad offices) that I had with you, do you agree that you told me that you didn't know Nicky Patterson and had no contact with her?

*No comment*

Q: Have you ever spoken to her?

*No comment.*

Q: Have you ever been to number 21 Harper Street in Northcote?

*No comment.*

Q: Can you tell me, Peter, what you did last Monday — Monday morning — Monday just gone. Monday, the 19th of April, 1999?

*No comment.*

Q: Peter, on your face I can see what appears to me to be a scratch mark. Can you explain that to me?

*No comment.*

Q: Do you agree with me that you've earlier told me that — again in the car outside the hotel in Thomastown — that you received that scratch — that mark — should I say — from a piece of timber when you were doing some woodwork in your garage?

*No comment.*

Q: Peter, will you consent — will you — will you agree to participate in an identity parade?

A: No.

Q: Will you provide me with a sample of your handwriting?

A: No.

Q: Do you agree to provide me with a copy of your — with a set of your fingerprints?

A: No.

Q: Right. I haven't got the actual proper writing of that, but I don't think that you've got a lot of say in the matter, actually, Peter. I think that we can take your fingerprints in — in the circumstances, here, when you're suspected of an offence of murder, we — we've got the power to take your prints. Do you understand that?

A: Yes.

Q: Will you — do — will you consent to undergo a forensic procedure? No, by that, I mean we would like to take a sample of your blood. We would like to take a sample of your hair. And …"

Det. Snr-Sgt Maher then added: "physical examination … and — and a physical examination of your body and your injuries. Will you consent to that procedure?"

A: No.

Q: Righteo. Peter, you are going to be charged with the murder of Nicky Patterson. You are not obliged to say or do anything unless you wish to do so, but whatever you say or do may be recorded and given in evidence. Do you understand that?

A: Yes.

Q: Do you wish to say anything in answer to the charge?

*No comment.*

Q: The interview will be concluded. The time is now 9.26pm. Do you agree that it's 9.26pm, Peter?

A: Yes.

With that, the tape recorder was switched off and the interview ended.

Dupas was taken from the interview room and, just under two hours later, was subjected to a medical examination. This was performed by the highly qualified Dr Stephen Jelbert, a founding member in 1985 of the Association of Australasian and Pacific Area Police Medical Officers. And Dupas would have been most unhappy with Dr Jelbert's description of him in the statement he made to police. Dr Jelbert described Dupas as "an anxious, timid looking man wearing bifocals." He stated that Dupas was obese and noted that he had "prominent deposits of fat over the pector muscles which had the appearance of female breasts." In other words, Dupas had large "man-boobs".

The examination, according to Dr Jelbert's statement, also revealed:

There was a bluish-yellow bruise near the top of Dupas' thigh and it appeared to be "some days old".

There were two small curved scratches or abrasions down the centre of his left cheek that also appeared to have been caused several days earlier. Significantly, Dr Jelbert noted that the two marks were typical of one caused by a fingernail scratch. He added: "The injury does not appear to be that type of injury that might be caused in such a way as Dupas described."

There was a bruise under the nail of the left index finger and a superficial scratch on Dupas' left hand.

Dr Jelbert took fingernail clippings and scraping for analysis, as well as blood samples. Also, blood samples taken from the jacket taken from Dupas' home provided a perfect DNA match with Nicole's blood. Analyst Nigel Hall, the Senior Forensic Scientist at VFSC, indicated that the chances of the blood stains on Dupas' jacket not matching Nicole's DNA profile were 6.53 billion to one — an astronomical figure that later caused Dupas enormous concern in the Mersina Halvagis murder.

Police were meticulous in preparing their case against Dupas and compiled one piece of evidence after another to make sure the monster could not escape justice. In addition to the DNA samples, the telephone links and witness statements they also, as already indicated, had his handwriting analysed to prove there was a match with notes found at Dupas' home. Police also had the tapes taken from Dupas' home analysed for a match with those found at Nicole's home.

Det-Snr-Sgt Maher, before informing the media of the Dupas arrest, contacted Mrs O'Donnell to tell her the news. She recalled: "Jeff told me they had arrested a serial rapist in relation to Nicole's murder. I obviously wanted to know about the man who had been charged with killing my daughter, but not too much."

Dupas' arrest was big news in Melbourne, with the *Herald Sun* running the huge headline MURDER CHARGE on the front page of its April 23 edition. The report read in part:

"A man was charged overnight with the frenzied stabbing murder of a young psychotherapist in her Northcote home.

"Homicide Squad detectives last night arrested Peter Norris Dubas (sic) and took him to their St Kilda Rd offices for questioning over the slaying of Nicole Amanda Patterson 28.

"After the interview, detectives charged Mr Dubas (sic), 45, of Coane St, Pascoe Vale, with her murder.

"He was remanded in custody by a bail justice at an out-of-sessions court hearing at midnight and was due to appear in Melbourne Magistrates' Court today.

"The arrest came three days after Ms Patterson's body was discovered in a pool of blood inside her Harper St home by a female friend."

The following day, Friday, April 23, family and friends paid tribute to Nicole at what her mother described as "a truly beautiful" funeral service at the Ampitheatre, Fairfield. Mrs O'Donnell, an eloquent woman with an eye for detail, recalled:

"Kylie and I gave great thought to where the service should be held as we needed room for what we thought would be about 300 people. We decided on the Ampitheatre because it was in the open and Nicole loved walking the banks of the nearby Yarra. It was an area she loved.

"The days leading up to the funeral were wet and sombre and Kylie and I were worried about the possibility of poor weather. As Nicole would have said, 'have faith'. It turned out to be a glorious day, with the sun shining and fluffy clouds drifting across the sky. Ducks quacked on the river and the setting could not have been better. It was a beautiful, beautiful ceremony in front of 700 people.

"We had a large portrait of Nicky on an easel and the sun shone on it until it was taken away. It looked as if we had ordered the sun to reflect on her just for the occasion and it made me feel as if Nicky had something to do with it."

Nicole's remains were cremated and her ashes contained in a wall plaque at the Warrandyte Cemetery, close to the babies section and a water feature. Peace, perfect peace after such a tragic and senseless death.

# CHAPTER FOUR

# R v Dupas

The pale-faced, overweight Dupas faced trial in the Victorian Supreme Court from Monday, August 7, 2000. The judge was Mr Justice Frank Vincent, with Mr Geoffrey Horgan, a Rumpolesque barrister as prosecutor and Mr David Brustman, a tall, bespectacled barrister with a great love of aviation, particularly gliding, as defence counsel. The trial opened with the mealy-mouthed Dupas, quiet as a mouse and in a barely audible voice, squeaking a plea of not guilty.

The tall and elegant Justice Vincent had been elevated to the bench as a judge of the Victorian Supreme Court in 1985 after more than 25 years as a barrister and 200 murder cases, believed to be a record unlikely to be equalled. Renowned for his compassion, Justice Vincent probably developed his sense of justice from seeing society from all angles.

Highly successful in his chosen profession, he came from humble origins. The son of a wharf labourer, he grew up in Port Melbourne and, after his father's death, his mother worked in a factory and as a florist. Educated in Middle Park and later in East Melbourne, he entered the University of Melbourne law school on a Commonwealth Government Scholarship and, after graduation, joined the bar in 1961.

The trial, after the usual legal necessities, opened with Mr Brustman telling the court that Dupas' de facto, Iolanda Cruz, was seriously ill and although she would not be able to give evidence, would tender two statements. These statements merely told the court of her activities on the day Nicole Patterson was murdered, on April 19, 1999. Her statements were neither accusatory nor beneficial to Dupas as the accused. They were statements made by a good honest women who, to her absolute horror, had been living with a monster without even a hint of his past or what levels of depravity he could reach.

These preliminaries were followed by brief comments about the lack of evidence regarding any sexual penetration during the attack on Nicole. Mr Horgan told the judge: "Your Honour, in my opinion it is just incredible that this was other than a sexual type of murder because of the obvious features about the mutilation. I simply say, or am proposing to say to the jury what I have said; it is not possible to say whether or not sex took place, and that is not possible because it could have happened. If sex did take place, it happened post-mortem and if condoms were used, there would be no trace. So it is not possible to determine the question. Mr Horgan said this matter was "unresolved and unresolvable".

The Crown called several witnesses to give evidence relating to the screams outside Nicole's house, the telephone calls — both to the mobile number and to Nicole's home, forensics and, most critical of all, the DNA sample taken from the "greeny-coloured" jacket found tucked at the back of a workshop at Dupas' home. The jacket had blood on it and the court was told that the chances of this being any other person's blood was 6.53 billion to one. It was devastating evidence, but so too was much of the evidence presented by the Crown. Det. Snr-Sgt. Maher and his team had been meticulous in their collection of evidence and it was obvious Dupas' defence would struggle.

The DNA evidence from Dupas' jacket was hugely important for the prosecution and so too could have been any evidence given by handwriting expert Dr Bryan Found. Although Dr Found was listed by the prosecution to give evidence, he was told while waiting outside the Supreme Court that he would not be needed.

This might have seemed unusual, but jurors normally easily understand handwriting evidence and any defence lawyer would be foolish to challenge the evidence and make matters worse for the accused. Instead, Dupas admitted that he had written the note and had made the appointment, but there was nothing wrong with all this and that this did not mean he had killed Nicole.

Det. Snr-Sgt. Maher, in giving evidence, said he had the overall supervision and conduct of the investigation into Nicole's death and was asked by Mr Horgan whether he supervised "the police processes" at the house in Harper Street. He said he had and then was asked whether the police had found Nicole's driver's licence. The detective said the licence "never turned up", despite a "comprehensive search of the entire premises". The inference was that this might have been taken as a "souvenir".

Mr Brustman, in cross-examination, asked Det. Snr-Sgt. Maher which police officers had found various items at Dupas' home. He admitted he did not know which officer had found the copy of the *Herald Sun* and added that he "thought" it was a Grant Keithley who found the green jacket. These questions prompted Mr Horgan, in re-examination, to ask the detective: "Did you instruct the police, Mr Maher, to plant evidence on the accused at the accused's premises?"

Det.Snr-Sgt. Maher replied: "No."

At the completion of the case for the prosecution, Mr Justice Vincent asked Mr Horgan: "What is your position?" He told the judge that the only witness he would call would be the accused himself, Peter Norris Dupas.

Mr Brustman then addressed the jury: "Mr Foreman and ladies and gentlemen of the jury, the Crown has now closed its case. You have the evidence now to consider what the Crown has put before you from that witness box.

"It is not by any means in all cases that an accused person himself, or herself for that matter, gives evidence, but in this case you, Mr Foreman and ladies and gentlemen, will have the opportunity of hearing his side of the story from his lips. I will obviously have more to say about this after when we get to give our final addresses, which will probably be tomorrow.

"The ambit of this case, as is quite obvious, and by agreement is, in fact, of very, very short compass. The events, therefore, ladies and gentlemen, of April 19, 1999, and to a lesser extent the 22nd day of April, 1999, the day as you, of course, now know when Mr Dupas was arrested and when, among other things, a jacket, a newspaper and various other items were found in particular positions at his house, occurred.

"It is not for me to give evidence, but for me to tell you just what he will say. You will hear soon his story, how he was in a relationship with a Ms Cruz, Iolanda Cruz. Her evidence by way of it being read is already before you. Their relationship, you will hear from him, had a couple of problems. Primarily, the problem had to do with gambling. You will hear some detail, not a huge amount, but some detail about that gambling problem from him.

"He will tell you that from a newspaper advertisement, in other words, as the Crown case puts it, that from a newspaper advertisement in a local paper he got the name of the deceased. She advertised her services and he will tell you that he rang her up. You will recall — I don't ask you to look at it now — that there are a number of phone calls, two or three, of more than a minute duration, though not much more. The others of seconds' duration. He will tell you he made those phone calls. As I said to you at the outset of this trial, it is not in dispute, there were a couple of conversations, two, possibly three with her.

"The other conversations were not conversations, but were simply an answering machine, which would explain the 20 seconds or 15 seconds as the case may be. He will say to you, in any event, he had some discussion with her. What that discussion with her is about he will tell you in some detail, but essentially it is not much more than a discussion about what problem he wished to see her for and what arrangements would be made.

"He will say to you that an appointment was suggested by her for Monday, the 19th day of April of last year. He will say to you that he had second thoughts about that appointment, it having been made, and rang her up and cancelled it. But that the appointment, by her, was left open, although he said he wanted, and rang her, to cancel it. That piece of background evidence will be given in much more detail — I am just opening it very briefly to you — by him.

"He will tell you what he did on the weekend before April 19. Without going in any way to the detail of that, essentially that involved as, of course, you have already heard, a trip with three other persons, his lady friend — the woman he lived with (Iolanda Cruz) and two others, Mr (Pat) O'Brien and Mr O'Brien's female partner, as you have heard, to Wilson's Promontory. He will say they came back and that after they came back he had quite a number of clothes, camping gear and so forth of O'Briens. I will call them the O'Briens, probably Mr O'Brien and other name.

"On Monday, the 19th of April, the day Miss Patterson was killed, he will say, and tell you, he did not keep the appointment he had cancelled at all. He will tell you what he did. Those events essentially concerned seeing his partner, Iolanda, off to work, getting petrol, having breakfast, attending to domestic chores in and around the house, washing a large amount of clothes, camping gear and so forth, attending to that camping gear left over from the weekend before, having problems with one of his motor vehicles, doing something about that motor vehicle, speaking to Ms Cruz at lunchtime, speaking to Mr O'Brien a little later that day, and otherwise working at his workshop on, I think a cocktail cabinet. It might be another piece of furniture, but working in his workshop doing woodwork. He will tell you he didn't go anywhere near the premises of the deceased and obviously that he did not kill her.

"On the 22nd day of April, three days later, he will say to you, Mr Foreman and ladies and gentlemen, that he was arrested as you have heard on the afternoon of that day in a hotel gambling, doing that which he had initially sought help for from Miss Patterson. The events of April 22, he will tell you, were that he was arrested, he was brought back, ultimately to the police station, nothing particularly in dispute as between the Crown and him, but what I tell you he will say to you is this: At no stage did he say to any policeman or did he say to any doctor that the scratch which he will tell you came from a piece of wood or timber, or piece of wood flying up from a lathe in his workshop. He will tell you, indeed, that he doesn't have and never had a lathe in his workshop. He will say to you how he got that scratch. That scratch was got from a piece of wood while he was working. The point, however, is that he will tell you at no stage did he or volunteer that to any police or doctor because it didn't happen.

"The jacket: Mr Foreman and ladies and gentlemen, Mr Dupas will tell you that the green khaki, whatever it is, is his. He will tell you that that jacket was a jacket used for working and for fishing. A pretty knock-about jacket. He will say to you that in all probability to the best of his recollection he had it on, on April 19. He will tell you that it must have been in the shed after that because that is where it was ordinarily kept. He will say to you, as the police have said to you, that that jacket was at his premises on the 22nd when it was seized.

"He will tell you, Mr Foreman and ladies and gentlemen, that he does not know how Miss Patterson's blood, or bits of it, got on the jacket. That they are on the jacket is a fact. He will tell you that they could not have got on to that jacket by virtue of that jacket coming into contact with Miss Patterson because he had never, as I have said, been to the premises of Miss Patterson. How that blood got on the jacket is a matter of argument about which we have said something and we will say something later on, but Mr Dupas will tell you his story in his evidence."

Mr Justice Vincent then asked the ashen-faced Dupas to step forward. In a barely audible voice he tried to tell the court his name, but could barely be heard. Mr Brustman asked him to speak up and Dupas' voice lifted a decibel or so, but only to the point of just being heard. He was asked to speak up later in his evidence. After giving his name, address and occupation, Dupas admitted he had a gambling problem and this had caused friction with Ms Cruz. His counsel then asked him: "Did you seek to do something about that, did you seek to get some help for this?"

Dupas: "I didn't want to. I kept putting it off and, yes, I did."

Mr Brustman: "Did you make a number of telephone calls to the deceased?"

Dupas: "Yes, I did."

Mr Brustman then asked Mr Justice Vincent if he could hand an exhibit to Dupas; it was a list of phone calls made from Dupas' home number in March and April, 1999.

Mr Brustman: "You made these calls. Is that right?"

Dupas: "Yes."

Mr Brustman (after asking Dupas to return the list to him): "Why did you make these calls?"

Dupas: "I saw an article in a newspaper and it mentioned there could be help for relationships and anxiety and I think stress, and I wanted to try and straighten it up because I didn't want to lose my relationship with Iolanda."

Mr Brustman then asked Dupas about the duration of the calls, with some lasting just 20 seconds. He asked him: "What sort of calls were they? Did you actually speak to Miss Patterson?"

Dupas: "It was an answering machine and I didn't put any message on it."

Mr Brustman: "There are three calls in excess of that, and I will take you to each of them, Mr Dupas. On March 3 a call of two minutes and 10 seconds, very soon after two very short-second calls, and then much later on the 12th of April, of two and three quarter, and one and a half minutes, all right?"

Dupas: "Yes."

Mr Brustman: "The phone calls on March 3 which were seconds after one another, one of seconds, and a couple of minutes after, another one of seconds, what do you say about that? Was that the first time he (Dupas) spoke to Miss Patterson?"

Dupas: "Very briefly, because she was with someone."

Mr Brustman: "As briefly as you can, can you tell ladies and gentlemen what that call was about?"

Dupas: "I was basically asking what sort of help she could do for anyone. I recognised my problem with her, I didn't go into any detail. I said I had a gambling problem and was scared of my relationship breaking up and I told her a few things about my relationship with Iolanda."

Mr Brustman: "Did she make an appointment on that day for you to see her?"

Dupas: "That is, what, the first phone call? No."

Mr Brustman: "Between the 3rd of March and the 12th of April you made a number of other calls which are of only seconds, and you tell us that you didn't speak to her on these occasions?"

Dupas: "I didn't speak to her."

Mr Brustman: "Did you want to speak to her?"

Dupas: "Part of me did, part of me didn't. When you have got a problem you always think that you can have the big win the next time and it will be over with."

Mr Brustman: "On the 12th day of April, 1999, at about 8.47am and then at 8.52am you spoke to her first for two and three quarter minutes, and then for one and a half minutes. Correct?

Dupas: "Yes, yes."

Mr Brustman: "These were actual phone calls in which you spoke to her?"

Dupas: "Yes."

Mr Brustman: "What were they about?"

Dupas: "The first phone call was, I told her who I was again, and she remembered my first phone call, and I told her what had happened since and that my gambling had not improved and I felt if Iolanda found out I had been gambling I would lose her and I said that was causing me stress and I didn't like hiding it from her because she was pretty open."

Mr Brustman then questioned Dupas on the vital question of making an appointment to see Nicole.

Mr Brustman: "Was an appointment made?"

Dupas: "Yes."

Mr Brustman: "Was that appointment, if I can lead that, for Monday, April 19?"

Dupas: "Yes."

Mr Brustman: "At what time?"

Dupas: "Nine o'clock."

Mr Brustman: "Was that appointment made in the first phone call at 8.47 or in the second phone call at 8.52?"

Dupas: "The first phone call."

Mr Brustman: "Why the second phone call, Mr Dupas?"

Dupas: "Even while she was talking to me I didn't think I would be able to go through with it, being able to talk to someone about it (his gambling), and after I got off the phone … I thought about it and I thought, no, I don't want to, I can beat this by myself, and I was scared that something might get back to Iolanda."

Mr Brustman: "Did you cancel the phone appointment or what?"

Dupas: "Yes, I explained to her the way I was feeling and she said she understood and I cancelled the appointment. I said I would not be going."

Mr Brustman: "What did she say when you cancelled the appointment?"

Dupas: "If you need to contact me, contact me."

Mr Brustman: "There has been evidence put before this court in this case about two things — first that you gave a name not yours — 'Malcolm'?"

Dupas: "Yes."

Mr Brustman: "Secondly, that in making the appointment and speaking to Miss Patterson you gave false phone numbers; in other words, false forwarding details. Do you say that is true, that is what you did?"

Dupas: "Yes."

Mr Brustman: "Why, Mr Dupas, first of all, did you give the name 'Malcolm', which is clearly not yours, and why did you give details of a forwarding number to Miss Patterson which clearly was not yours?"

Dupas: "The first phone call that I made before she didn't ask me any time or anything and I was not actually expecting it. On the second phone call when she asked me my name I panicked because I thought if I gave my name to her she might contact me, and I didn't want Iolanda picking up a phone message or anything. That is why."

Mr Brustman: Where did you get 'Malcolm' from?"

Dupas: "This is just a name I thought of quickly. I don't know why 'Malcolm'. No particular reason."

Mr Brustman: "The telephone number you gave was a real number but someone else's?"

Dupas: "It was written down in front of me next to the phone."

Mr Brustman: "How did that come to be?"

Dupas: "That was someone who was going to do a job for me and it was sitting by the phone and I read it off."

Mr Brustman: "Just going back a bit, when you made the phone call, did you write on a piece of paper details of your appointment as were put before this jury?"

Dupas: "I had the newspaper when I was ringing and I wrote it on the top of the newspaper."

Mr Brustman: "Mr Dupas, that was on the 12th. Did you have anything at all to do with Miss Patterson after that day?"

Dupas: "No, nothing at all."

Mr Brustman: "Did you ring her?"

Dupas: "No."

Mr Brustman: "Did you speak to her?"

Dupas: "No."

Mr Brustman: "Were you ever in her presence after that time?"

Dupas: "I have never been in her presence at any time."

Mr Brustman: "After the 12th were you ever aware of being in her presence?"

Dupas: "No."

Mr Brustman: "Have you ever been in her presence?"

Dupas: "No."

Mr Brustman, in attempting to break down the prosecution case, then turned his attention to the day of Nicole's murder, April 19.

Mr Brustman: "What time did you get up?"

Dupas: "It would be about eight."

Mr Brustman: "Ms Cruz has told us through the prosecutor that she left early in the morning and went to work; is that right?"

Dupas: "Yes."

Mr Brustman then turned his attention to Dupas buying petrol that morning.

Mr Brustman: "Had she (Ms Cruz) said anything to you before leaving about petrol?"

Dupas: "Yes, she said she wanted me to fill the car up with petrol because she wanted to use it."

Mr Brustman: "We have heard evidence that a transaction was effected at a service station close to you. Did you effect that transaction?"

Dupas: "Yes, I did."

Mr Brustman: "When approximately was that?"

Dupas: "It would have been about a quarter to eight."

Mr Brustman: "Right. Before you went to get the petrol did you realise something else was missing at home?"

Dupas: "Yes, the main reason I went to get petrol at that time was that at that time I didn't have any milk for my breakfast, my morning coffee, so I thought I would go and get the milk on the way."

Mr Brustman: "You got dressed, I presume?"

Dupas: "Yes."

Mr Brustman: "Do you know what you were wearing?"

Dupas: "I am not completely sure, no."

Mr Brustman: "Did you leave your house?"

Dupas: "Yes."

Mr Brustman: "What time?"

Dupas: "Eight or something."

Mr Brustman: "Where did you go?"

Dupas: "Drove down Cumberland Road to the milk bar, bought the milk, then straight to the petrol station and filled up with petrol."

Mr Brustman then briefly turned to the greenish jacket police found tucked away at the bottom of a shelf in Dupas' workshop.

Mr Brustman: "The jacket. We all know what we are talking about. Unless there is some problem with it. The jacket, did you wear that jacket that morning?"

Dupas: "I'm not sure. I may have."

Mr Brustman: "All right. Just tell us what that jacket was. What did you use it for?"

Dupas: "My work jacket, and I was working that morning going to work."

Mr Brustman: "How long had you had that jacket?"

Dupas: "Couple of years, and it was secondhand when I bought it at an op shop."

Mr Brustman: "Was it also kept in the shed?"

Dupas: "Yes, it was, yes. It was only a work jacket."

Mr Brustman: "Was it kept in that bottom shelf where it was said to have been found?"

Dupas: "No, it wasn't."

Mr Brustman: "Where would you ordinarily keep it?"

Dupas: "It was three lots of cupboards there, in the end cupboard there is a space where I kept my overalls and my jacket; it was always in there."

The clear inference was that the police might have planted the jacket, with its bloodstains, in the shed. This, however, did not offend the police and Det. Snr-Sgt. Maher explained later: "The defence barrister was only acting on Dupas' instructions. He obviously was the one who came up with this possible defence and Mr Brustman therefore had to raise it. We thought the raising of this suggestion by Dupas represented disgraceful conduct, absolutely reprehensible. However, it was a ridiculous claim for a number of reasons, especially as Dupas inferred I had carried a vial of Nicole's blood in my pocket for when I found an appropriate item.

"What he did not know was that blood of that nature has coagulant chemicals and the blood found on his jacket did not have these coagulated chemicals. Besides, I would have had to obtain the blood and place it in a vial during the autopsy and I was not part of the autopsy. Besides, I didn't know it was THE jacket he was wearing until afterwards, when we examined the video surveillance tape at the garage where he bought petrol.

"Dupas' defence theory in this regard therefore was ridiculous and the 6.5 billion to one odds of the blood being other than Nicole's were extremely telling. No wonder Dupas had to come up with some way to try and discredit this. The evidence was so overwhelming, and not only with the jacket and the bloodstains, that he had to try and counter it in any way possible, but his claims obviously did not fool the jury.

Following these questions about the jacket and where it was found, Mr Brustman returned to the matter of Dupas buying petrol.

Mr Brustman: "You drove out to get milk and petrol; is that right?"

Dupas: "Yes."

Mr Brustman: "Again, I can lead this I think. You went to the service station on the corner of Cumberland Road and Bell Street; is that right?"

Dupas: "Yes."

Mr Brustman: "A couple of intersections down from your house?"

Dupas: "Yes."

Mr Brustman: "Did you go to a milk bar also?"

Dupas: "Yes, I went to the milk bar first."

Mr Brustman: "Where was the milk bar?"

Dupas: "That was just before Gaffney Street."

Mr Brustman then asked Dupas what he did after buying the milk and petrol and Dupas told him he returned home, at about 8.20am. Dupas then said in evidence that he did three or four loads of washing and explained that he didn't regard his activities that morning as being out of the ordinary and that he even had his normal morning cup of coffee.

He said the only problem he encountered that morning was a faulty car alarm. Dupas told the court the alarm kept going off and could recall that he noted that it went off at both nine and 10 o'clock. He added that he spent a "fair bit of time" on the clock. Significantly, Dupas also told the court that the alarm went off while he was on the phone to a security firm. This was at 10.56 am and, just minutes earlier, he had called a mobile number to speak with a contractor who was going to do some work for Dupas and Ms Cruz. Telephone records backed Dupas on this evidence.

In other words, Dupas claimed that on the morning of Nicole's murder he had had a very ordinary few hours, except for the troublesome car alarm, had been out only to get milk and petrol and had spent much of his time doing the washing. Dupas was trying to prove that, far from travelling to and from Northcote to kill Nicole Patterson, he had spent that morning attending to innocent domestic chores. Just a normal morning, so he claimed.

Dupas, continuing his evidence, told the court of how he had found a broken torch on the floor of a room and decided to put it in a rubbish or wheelie bin.

Mr Brustman: "Did you find anything there while you were doing this particular thing?"

Dupas: "Yes, my old runners."

Mr Brustman: "Your old runners."

Dupas then was handed the runners, as a court exhibit.

Mr Brustman: "Are they the runners you are talking about?"

Dupas: "They certainly are."

Mr Brustman: "You found those. What did you think when you found those?"

Dupas: "That they're certainly not serviceable, as people have been saying."

Mr Brustman: "What did you decide to do with them?"

Dupas: "I threw them out in the rubbish bin."

Mr Brustman: "You threw them out. You threw them in a wheelie bin, didn't you?"

Dupas: "Yes, I did."

Mr Brustman: "Why did you throw them in the wheelie bin?"

Dupas: "Because I wouldn't wear them any more. They hurt your feet for a start. They're right through to the ground, and they stink."

Mr Brustman: "When was the last time you had worn those runners?"

Dupas: "About three months previously."

Police thoroughly examined the sneakers through forensic testing, but could find no direct link with the Nicole Patterson killing. However, the sneakers were important because they indicated that Dupas probably thought they bore traces, unseen to the naked eye, to the murder scene. For example, he might have thought there were tiny specks of blood, giving police a direct DNA link.

Dupas, continuing his evidence, said that after buying the milk and petrol he did not leave his house again until about 11.15am, to do some shopping at a Safeway store in nearby Hadfield. He said this took him about 20 minutes and, at about 1pm, his friend Pat

O'Brien visited him. Dupas said he stayed at home all afternoon until he drove to collect Ms Cruz from a railway station about 6pm.

Mr Brustman: "Did you leave that house at any other time for any other purpose?"

Dupas: "No, I didn't."

Mr Brustman: "On that day, Mr Dupas, or any other day, but on that day, did you have any contact with the deceased, Miss Patterson?"

Dupas: "No, I didn't".

Mr Brustman: "Did you go anywhere near where she lived?"

Dupas: "No."

Mr Brustman: "Did you kill her?"

Dupas: "No, I did not."

Det. Snr-Sgt. Maher knew Dupas would reply in the negative and said the killer's complete denial of any of the facts presented at the trial compounded the belief that Dupas was totally remorseless. "He did not admit to anything and it was ridiculous for him to suggest he did not even go anywhere near where Nicole lived," he said.

After dealing with the events on April 19, the day Nicole was murdered, Mr Brustman again turned his attention to April 22, the day Dupas was arrested. After asking Dupas about where he was in the hotel when he was arrested and Dupas replying that he was in the gaming room, Mr Brustman turned his attention to the scratches found on Dupas' face.

Mr Brustman: "It has been said that following your arrest you were asked a couple of questions and reference was made to a scratch or to two scratches on your face, right?"

Dupas: "Yes."

Mr Brustman: "Did you have those scratches on your face?"

Dupas: "Yes, I did."

Mr Brustman: "How did you get those scratches on your face?"

Dupas: "When I was working on my cocktail cabinet I got them."

Mr Brustman: "Do you know when you got those scratches on your face?"

Dupas: "I do."

Mr Brustman: "When?"

Dupas: "Just before Pat (O'Brien) arrived."

Mr Brustman: "On what day?"

Dupas: "On the 19th."

Mr Brustman: "On the 19th?"

Dupas: "Yes."

Mr Brustman: "There are some machines, obviously working machines in your house, right?"

Dupas: "Yes, I've got a saw and a sander."

Mr Brustman then asked Dupas how he got the scratches on his face.

Dupas: "Carelessness really."

Mr Brustman: "Don't worry whether it was careless or not. How did you get them?"

Dupas: "The cocktail cabinet I was making has got a — I would have to go into a bit of detail here. I made it. It's got a frame. It was beside the bench where I had all my wood stacked to go on the frame itself. I was working down, screwing down the main part that was going to hold the fridge underneath it. I got up off balance and as I got up I just grazed my head against the pole, wood that was on the side of the bench. Didn't pay any notice to it, just a normal — just felt a touch like that (demonstrating). See, I just wiped it and kept working. I didn't notice it until I just went inside to check the washing machine, put a bit of Savlon on it and that was the last I thought of it."

Mr Brustman then asked Dupas if he had told police that the scratches were caused by a piece of flying wood, and he replied: "Definitely not." Mr Brustman also asked Dupas if he had told Dr Jelbert the scratches came from a lathe or a machine flying up and hitting him in the face and Dupas gave the identical answer of "definitely not".

The defence counsel then moved on to the question of newspapers found at his house.

Mr Brustman: "There were some local newspapers in the bottom of the aperture … underneath the laundry?"

Dupas: "In the laundry trough, yes."

Mr Brustman: "Were those local newspapers yours?"

Dupas: "Yes, and Iolanda's as well."

Mr Brustman: "Sorry?"

Dupas: "Yes, Iolanda's; ours, yes."

Mr Brustman: "What has been said in evidence in this court in the last few days is that there was a *Herald Sun* depicting or relating to the murder of Miss Patterson underneath your laundry trough on top of the local newspapers. You've heard that?"

Dupas: "I've heard that."

Mr Brustman: "Was that newspaper, Mr Dupas, yours?"

Dupas: "No, we've never bought it. I've never seen it before."

Mr Brustman: "Have you ever seen it before?"

Dupas: "No, I haven't."

Mr Brustman: "Do you and Iolanda have papers such as the *Herald Sun* or *The Age* or *The Australian*, that is, the dailies, at home?"

Dupas: "Yes, the only papers — those papers we ever bought were on the weekend for the TV guide. The *Herald Sun* we used to buy on Sunday. We didn't that weekend (April 18) because we were at

Wilson's Promontory. Pat (O'Brien) gave us his, and that was the paper that was in the toilet area, yes."

Mr Brustman: "Other than the *Herald Sun* which you and Iolanda get for its TV guide on the weekend, do you as a couple, or either of you, get and keep at home or store when you're finished the *Herald Sun, The Age* or *The Australian*?"

Dupas: "*The Age* — we had it at one stage because when we were looking for a house we had it, but I don't know whether they were still there or not or thrown out."

Mr Brustman: "The first time you say you'd ever seen that *Herald Sun*?"

Dupas: "Yes, definitely."

Again, Dupas inferred that the newspaper had been placed at his house. Again, Maher found this an outrageous suggestion, but could not blame the defence as Dupas had given the instructions.

Mr Brustman asked Dupas again about the greenish jacket. This jacket went to the crux of the prosecution case as Nicole's blood had been found on it and Dupas had to contend with the prosecution evidence that the chances of it being someone else's blood on that jacket were 6.5 billion to one. These, of course, were enormous odds and this DNA evidence represented the Dupas defence's biggest hurdle.

Mr Brustman: "And would you tell us again whether or not — or what's your memory of whether you wore it on the 19th?"

Dupas: "I'm not sure. It was a cold morning and it's — possibly I did have it on in the workshop, yes."

Mr Brustman: "Did you have that (jacket), in fact, on April 21?"

Dupas: "Yes."

Mr Brustman: "Where did you have that jacket?"

Dupas: "In the cupboard where it belonged."

Mr Brustman: "And which cupboard was that?"

Dupas: "The third cupboard in the workshop."

Mr Brustman: "Down the bottom where …?"

Dupas: "No, on the third shelf."

Mr Brustman: "Police say they found it?"

Dupas: "No, on the third shelf."

Mr Brustman: "On the third shelf?"

Dupas: "Yes. My overalls were there as well."

Mr Brustman: "Had you always kept that jacket there on the third shelf?"

Dupas: "Yes."

Mr Brustman: "Had you always kept that jacket there on the third shelf with your overalls?"

Dupas: "Yes."

Mr Brustman: "Did you hide that jacket on the bottom shelf and stuff a yellow box and some material or fabric in front of it?"

Dupas: "No, I didn't."

Mr Brustman: "Had that jacket ever been there, put by you there or by anyone else before this day?"

Dupas: "Well, it certainly wasn't put there by me."

Dupas' counsel then questioned him about the number of police who searched his house on the day of the arrest and Mr Brustman suggested to him that it was "like a small army". Dupas also said he was never in the shed on the day of the search, April 22. Mr Brustman then focused on the blood found on the jacket in question.

Mr Brustman: "Mr Dupas, do you know how there are some stains, a number of small stains, on that jacket which contain blood not yours?"

Dupas: "No, I've no idea."

Mr Brustman: "Did they come in any way by virtue of you wearing that jacket in proximity to anyone else?"

Dupas: "No."

Mr Brustman: "When was the first time, Mr Dupas, that you saw those stains?"

Dupas: "First time I saw them was when the photo was showed to me."

Mr Brustman: "After your arrest?"

Dupas: "After my arrest."

Mr Brustman: "Mr Dupas, finally, on April 19 of last year did you go to an address in Northcote of Miss Patterson and kill her?"

Dupas: "No."

After Mr Brustman said "I have no further questions", Mr Horgan cross-examined Dupas and started with the appointment the accused had made with Nicole.

Mr Horgan: "Mr Dupas, you made an appointment, did you, on April 12 with Nicky Patterson?"

Dupas: "The exact day, if it's (the) 12th, yes."

Mr Horgan: "You made an appointment with her?"

Dupas: "Yes."

Mr Horgan then had Dupas agree that he knew that Nicole was the person offering counselling services and had introduced herself to him. Dupas also agreed that he contacted her through the advertisement in the *Leader* newspaper and wanted to speak with her about his gambling addiction because he feared it would damage his relationship with Ms Cruz. After Dupas agreed that he knew Nicole was based in Northcote, Mr Horgan honed in with several particularly pointed questions.

Mr Horgan: "And that (Northcote) is a fair way, isn't it, from Pascoe Vale?"

Dupas (in a barely audible voice): "I believe so."

Mr Horgan: "Sorry?"

Dupas: "I believe so, yes."

Mr Horgan: "What do you mean, you believe so? Is it, or is it not?"

Dupas: "It's a fair way, yes."

Mr Horgan: "How long does it take to get there?"

Dupas (warily): "I don't know. I've never been there."

Mr Horgan: "Did you think about that?"

Dupas: "Not really, because I looked in the other local papers and I hadn't seen anybody advertising like that in any of the others."

Mr Horgan: "But you knew when you spoke to her in March that she was some distance away?"

Dupas: "Well, yes, some distance."

Mr Horgan: "Why did you ring her?"

Dupas: "Because …"

Mr Horgan: "And not anyone else?"

Dupas: "There wasn't any other ads, sir, in the paper."

Mr Horgan: "Mr Dupas, you don't mean to tell the court that you couldn't find anyone who was capable of dealing with the gambling problem in any other way than the *Northcote Leader* newspaper, do you?"

Dupas: "As I've said to you, it wasn't just a gambling problem."

Mr Horgan: "Well, what else was it then?"

Dupas: "It was my feelings of Iolanda being — wearing the pants in the family and I wanted to be able to talk about that to somebody, yes."

Mr Horgan pressed Dupas on "Iolanda wearing the pants" and the accused told the court he wanted "to feel more secure in my relationship" and felt he wasn't the bread-winner in the family. Mr Horgan then returned to the question of why Dupas sought counselling from someone who lived about half an hour's drive from his home.

Mr Horgan: "Why in these circumstances seek a counsellor, a long distance from where you lived at Pascoe Vale who advertised in the *Northcote Leader* newspaper?"

Dupas: "A long distance? I don't see that as a long distance. It's not that long."

Mr Horgan, after further questions about the time it would take to drive from Dupas' home to Northcote, asked the accused: "Why did you think Nicky Patterson or that number or that counsellor who advertised would have any knowledge at all or any expertise in dealing with a gambling problem?"

Dupas: "I didn't at the time."

Mr Horgan: "Why did you select her to get in touch with?"

Dupas: "Because, of course, the ads had said about relationships."

Mr Horgan: "Did the ads say anything about gambling?"

Dupas: "No."

Later, Mr Horgan asked Dupas: "I want to know why you got in touch with somebody in Northcote half an hour's journey away who doesn't advertise any expertise in gambling?"

Dupas: "No, but advertises in relationships."

Mr Horgan also asked Dupas if he had drug or sexuality problems for which he needed counselling, but Dupas said "no" to both.

Dupas, under Mr Horgan's cross-examination, said he made an appointment with Nicole for 9am on April 19, but cancelled this appointment five minutes later and said: "I thought about it and I thought no, I don't want to go through with this and I rang straight back and I told her."

Mr Horgan also questioned Dupas about the earlier phone calls he had made to Nicole and specifically about the one he made for the April 19 appointment and Dupas admitted he didn't want to give her his real name. Dupas told the court: "She said — asked me my name and I panicked. I didn't want to give her my full — proper name because I was scared she might ring back on the answering machine (and) would get Iolanda. So I gave her the name of Malcolm." Dupas also admitted he gave Nicole a false number.

Mr Horgan: "I don't understand why you did that."

Dupas: "Because I didn't want anyone contacting our answering machine and ringing when I wasn't there."

Dupas told the court he "panicked" in giving Nicole the name Malcolm, but Mr Horgan suggested this was a lie.

Dupas: "No, it's not."

Mr Horgan: "Tell me this: If it's not a lie, Mr Dupas, how does it come to be written on a piece of paper (the top of page 26 of the *Northcote Leader)*. 'Malcolm, nine o'clock, Nicky Patterson', with her address?"

Dupas: "Because I was writing down at the same time. I had the paper next to the phone bench. There is a phone bench where the phone was."

Yet, when Mr Horgan further questioned Dupas on why he wrote down the details, the accused could only reply "it was just something I did".

Mr Horgan persisted with his questions about why Dupas wrote down the appointment details, but without getting a full and satisfactory reply. The prosecuting counsel then asked Dupas: "You must have been shocked, were you, Mr Dupas, when you heard of her death, Nicky Patterson's death?"

Dupas: "I didn't really know much about the death until the police …"

Mr Horgan: "I will ask you the question again: You must have been shocked when you heard about her death?"

Dupas: "I didn't know much about it. I'd heard something on the — about someone being killed in that area until the police sort of came upon me."

Mr Horgan: "You didn't realise, you didn't put two and two together and think that's my counsellor or my would-be counsellor?"

Dupas: "No, didn't know."

Mr Horgan (unable to hear Dupas): "Sorry?"

Dupas: "No, didn't know."

Mr Horgan: "Didn't pick up the name, didn't pick up the name Nicole Patterson?"

Dupas: "No, I didn't."

Mr Horgan: "Didn't know the name, but heard someone in Northcote had been killed in a brutal way?"

Dupas: "Yes, I had heard."

Dupas then admitted he had telephoned Nicole, but did not know her and added: "I talked to someone for a matter of two or three minutes on a phone call. Now, to me, that's not knowing somebody." He then made the extraordinary claim that the police attacked him when he was apprehended at the Thomastown hotel.

Mr Horgan: "So the police come up to see you in the hotel and they attack you?"

Dupas then retracted significantly in his suggestion of being "attacked" and claimed that what he meant was that his hands were held against a gaming machine. Following further questions about whether Dupas knew Nicole Patterson or who she was, the case was adjourned to the following day, with Dupas returning to the witness box. Mr Horgan almost immediately asked Dupas about the runners found discarded at the Pascoe Vale home.

Dupas: "Well, I had them for that long. I'd worn them to work for about a year or so. They were only $20 runners and they were just worn out."

Mr Horgan: "What was worn out?"

Dupas: "And smelly."

Dupas added that the runners also were not a good fit and that the soles were not comfortable. Mr Horgan, however, asked Dupas to explain why they were so worn if they were so uncomfortable to wear. Following further questions about the runners Dupas so inexplicably discarded, Mr Horgan asked him: "Mr Dupas, you murdered Nicole Patterson?" Dupas denied this, but Mr Horgan continued pressing Dupas.

Mr Horgan: "Do you say, do you, that it's just a cruel series of coincidences that point to my (Dupas') guilt?"

Dupas: "I'm not guilty."

Mr Horgan then went through what he described as "those circumstances" surrounding Nicole's murder, starting with the appointment Dupas made with Nicole for 9am on April 19, 1999.

Mr Horgan: "That's unfortunate because you understand the evidence to be that she was killed at about that time?"

Dupas: "I understand that, yes."

Mr Horgan: "So that's a very unfortunate coincidence? The very time, the very day, the very time that you make an appointment to see her she happens to be killed. It's a bad coincidence, isn't it?"

Dupas: "It is."

Mr Horgan: "And there is another bad coincidence. We know from the pathologist that she fought back before she was killed and on the very day you just happen to get scratches on your face that look … just like fingernail scratches. That's a bad coincidence, too, isn't it?"

Dupas: "They weren't fingernail scratches."

Mr Horgan pressed Dupas on the matter of these scratches and Dupas, still insisting they were not fingernail scratches, admitted to Mr Horgan's suggestion that this was a "bad coincidence" for him.

Mr Horgan: "And it's just bad luck and an unfortunate thing for you that you happen to have made the appointment to see Nicky Patterson in a false name, because that looks bad?"

Dupas: "Yes."

Mr Horgan: "And that's just another piece of bad luck you've had?"

Dupas: "Yes."

Mr Horgan then turned to the bloodstained jacket police found at Dupas' house as this arguably was the most crucial evidence against the accused.

Mr Horgan: "And it's just bad luck too, isn't it, that the jacket you say you were probably wearing on that morning happens to have the deceased's blood in it?"

Dupas: "I don't know how that blood got there."

Mr Horgan: "I know you say that, but that's bad luck too, isn't it? It is a cruel turn of fate?"

Dupas: "I don't think it's bad luck, no."

Mr Horgan: "For you it's bad luck?"

Dupas: "For me it is, yes."

Mr Horgan: "What do you mean you don't think it's bad luck? What's that mean?"

Dupas: "I don't know how it got there."

Mr Horgan: "You don't know how it got there. No idea. Can't think of a reason?"

Dupas: "No, I can't."

Again, Dupas could hardly be heard in his reply and Mr Horgan had to repeat the same question, with the same reply.

Mr Horgan: "Not by stretching your imagination to its wildest extremities can you think of a reason how that blood got there?"

Dupas: "What are you asking me?"

Mr Horgan: "What are you smiling for?"

Dupas: "Stretching it to my wildest imagination."

Mr Horgan: "Pardon?"

Dupas: "I believe it was put there by somebody."

Mr Horgan: "You believe it was put there by somebody?"

Dupas: "Yes."

Mr Horgan: "Who do you believe it was put there by?"

Dupas: "I can't say. I wasn't there when it was done."

Mr Horgan: "Who do you think it was put there by?"

Dupas: "The police."

Mr Horgan: "The police? Anyway, you were wearing that jacket that morning, weren't you?"

Dupas: "Yes, I think so."

Dupas might have sounded doubtful about this, but Mr Horgan pointed out that there was a video of Dupas wearing the jacket when he bought petrol that terrible morning. Dupas could not possibly deny that the jacket had Nicole's blood on it and his explanation that the police must have tampered with the evidence was preposterous.

Mr Horgan then turned his attention to the note reading "Malcolm, 9 o'clock, Nicky Patterson" found in a wheelie bin at Dupas' house, all screwed and torn up.

"Mr Horgan: "That's bad luck too, isn't it, because that looks bad?"

Dupas: "It was thrown out in the rubbish, yes."

Mr Horgan: "It looks bad though, doesn't it?"

Dupas: "To you it does, yes."

Mr Horgan: "What about to you?"

Dupas: "It's just something I did. Wasn't bad intent."

Mr Horgan: "It wasn't what?"

Dupas: "Bad intent."

Mr Horgan: "Don't drop your voice. I am losing it every now and again."

Dupas: "It wasn't bad intent."

Mr Horgan: "So these are unfortunate things that have happened at that point to you, but they are just a combination of misfortune, bad luck, or in your gambling terms, a bad run of luck?"

Dupas: "Yes."

Mr Horgan: "It's unbelievable, isn't it?"

Dupas: "No."

Mr Horgan: "It's incredible?"

Dupas: "No."

Mr Horgan: "And it's incredible, Mr Dupas, because you are the murderer, aren't you?"

Dupas: "I am not."

Mr Horgan moved on to the evidence the police painstakingly had produced suggesting Dupas had driven in a triangle from his Pascoe Vale home to buying petrol and then on to Nicole's home in Northcote. Dupas denied emphatically that he had been to Northcote and said he didn't even know the area well, even though he conceded he had been through the area and knew the main streets. Mr Horgan then returned to the vital evidence regarding Dupas' jacket.

Mr Horgan: "It's an amazing coincidence also, isn't it, that the police happen to sprinkle with the deceased's blood a jacket you just happened to have been wearing at eight o'clock on April 19?" The point Mr Horgan was making was that the jacket was taken from Dupas' house on April 22, well before they inspected the video from the petrol station which showed Dupas wearing that particular jacket.

Dupas asked Mr Horgan to repeat the question and after the prosecuting counsel obliged, replied: "I don't know why?"

Mr Horgan: "The jacket's photographed at the house in the living room or the dining room of your house; you've seen the photos?"

Dupas: "Yes."

Mr Horgan: "On brown paper and it shows blood on it?"

Dupas: "Yes."

Mr Horgan: "That means the blood must have been put there by the police before they left the place at 11, 11.30 that evening, that night?"

Dupas: "I presume so."

Mr Horgan: "That means, doesn't it, Mr Dupas, your case must be that the police have carried around a vial of the deceased's uncongealed blood to be able to sprinkle it on a jacket that they might find at your place?"

Dupas: "I don't know."

Even when pressed Dupas could not answer this question satisfactorily because, in essence, it was impossible for the police to have planted this evidence. Dupas could offer only the feeble response: "I don't know the exact method that was used."

Dupas also suggested that the police had planted the newspaper with the photograph of Nicole and, when Mr Horgan asked him if this was "to make you look guilty?" he replied "yes".

Mr Horgan: "So they (the police) have falsely set about fabricating evidence against you to make you look guilty?"

Dupas: "I believe so."

Mr Horgan kept pressing Dupas on "these unfortunate experiences", the coincidences that pointed to guilt and Dupas' replies were far from convincing. The prosecuting counsel eventually turned to the gruesome question of Nicole's mutilated breasts.

Mr Horgan: "Mr Dupas, I only have one further thing I want to ask of you and it is this: Where have you hidden your trophies, the breast (sic) you cut off the deceased, her driver's licence and her purse?"

Dupas: "I don't know what you're talking about. That's not true."

Mr Horgan: "Where have you hidden the murder weapon?"

Dupas: "I did not kill Nicole Patterson."

Mr Horgan: "Mr Dupas, I suggest to you that is a lie and you have been lying as often and whenever it is suited you in your evidence in cross-examination and in-chief?"

Dupas: "That is not true."

Although Mr Brustman re-examined Dupas, an acquittal appeared to be a forlorn hope.

On August 22, 2000, on the morning Mr Justice Vincent was to hand down his sentence, the *Herald Sun* ran a tremendously moving news item under the huge headline AMY'S PLEA. The "Amy" referred to was Nicole Patterson's eight-year-old niece, whom the *Herald Sun* said was "broken-hearted" over the death of her aunt 16 months earlier. A kicker line above the headline read: "I used to be happy but now I'm sad because Nicky's dead. She's in heaven with God and you can't see her any more."

Amy, daughter of Nicole's sister Kylie, had even drawn an image of herself with Nicole. It read, in a childlike scrawl: "Nicky and me. I miss Nicky." Amy drew Nicky with a flower on her head and with a flower sprouting from a heart between herself and her aunt. The *Herald Sun* published this drawing, along with a photograph of Kylie, Amy and younger sister Alisha.

The news item read in part: "Amy's diary was handed to Justice Frank Vincent yesterday as Nicole's family sought to express the impact of Nicole's death.

"Amy's mother, Kylie, said the diary contained 'lots of stuff about how much she misses Nicky' and more than 50 photographs of Amy and her aunt.

"It included a story Amy wrote about 'My Favourite Person', six months after Ms Patterson's death and a drawing of a cracked and broken heart."

Kylie told the *Herald Sun*: "It was something she did herself. It just breaks my heart every time I read it."

The *Herald Sun* also interviewed Nicole's boyfriend Richard Smith under the "Amy's Diary" banner headline. The sub-head read: "There are some people who are untreatable." Underneath there was another headline which read "Dupas should be put down, says boyfriend." Smith was quoted as saying that he believed no punishment fitted Dupas' crime. He added: "I am now at a point where my grief has turned to anger and all I want is revenge. I discussed the death penalty with my best friend this morning. He's anti it, but in this case I'm for it."

When Justice Vincent sentenced Dupas to life imprisonment without any possibility of parole there were cries of both anguish and jubilation — anguish over Nicole's terrible death, and jubilation over what the judge told the murderous monster.

Nicole's mother, Mrs O'Donnell said: "It helps to know he is not going to be out there doing it again. If he were to walk free he would kill again."

Her former husband, Bill Patterson, added: "It (Nicole's murder) will never be closed but hopefully we can get on with our lives now." Mr Patterson then pleaded with Dupas to supply police with information on other murders in which he was a prime suspect. "I hope there's a part of him that can find something in himself the capability of letting go some of the dark secrets he has in his mind. It's not just our daughter. We know that. He's going to go to his grave with a lot of secrets."

Mr Justice Vincent told him in that sentencing on August 22, 1990:

"Miss Patterson, who was 28 years of age at the time (of her murder), carried on practice as a qualified psychotherapist and youth counsellor. She worked at the Ardoch Centre, an organisation which endeavours to assist homeless or disadvantaged young people, and she also assisted in activities associated with the Australian Drug Foundation.

"However, she had an ambition to develop her own private practice. To this end, she inserted an advertisement in a local newspaper circulated in the Northcote area in which she lived. It indicated that Miss Patterson engaged in the counselling of persons with respect to relationship and sexuality problems. The advertisement also made clear that strict confidentiality concerning any disclosures made by clients would be maintained. I suspect, but do not find, that your interest was excited by these references as you are a secretive individual with very disturbed sexuality.

"When and how you learned that the person who inserted the advertisement was an extremely attractive young woman is unknown. Perhaps, as the prosecutor suggested to you in cross-examination, you saw a photograph of Miss Patterson which appeared in a local newspaper, although you denied this was the case.

"However your attention was attracted to her, it is evident that you must have selected her as a potential victim some time before her death. Without initially appreciating the significance of the answer in the course of cross-examination, you made the startling admission that you first attempted to contact her by calling her on a public telephone a day or so before March 3, 1999, that is, approximately six weeks before she was killed.

"You claimed that you are unable to recall where the particular telephone was located and you were evasive when asked about your reason for adopting this course, rather than ringing her from your home. It is highly likely that you were already seriously contemplating the possibility of attacking her at that time.

"I doubt that we will ever learn how you went about the task of gaining the information that you required to assess the extent of her vulnerability so that you could feel confident about the safety of proceeding further, including the need to ensure that Miss Patterson would be alone and unsuspecting at the time that you chose to put your intentions into effect.

"Although you had obtained her mobile telephone number and would probably have experienced little difficulty in speaking to her had you really wished to do so, for some unexplained reason you made a number of telephone calls to her home between March 3 and April 12 when the appointment for you to see her was made. There is, in the circumstances, force in the prosecutor's contention that you were stalking Miss Patterson trying to ascertain her movement patterns and endeavouring to determine whether there was anyone else present in the house in which she lived and conducted her practice.

"It is also clear from the history of your earlier offences that you posses the ability to present yourself as quite inoffensive to those who may be described as your targets, so that your unsuspecting victims are caught unawares when you strike. I have little doubt that on the occasions on which you did speak to Miss Patterson you adopted the same approach, exercising significant skills in manipulation.

"Ultimately, on the morning of April 19, 1999, and not long after your partner, Miss Cruz, with whom you were living in a house in Pascoe Vale, left for work, you set out for your victim's home. She was, it appears, expecting a client named Malcolm who was suffering from depression, as those words were found on a note in her handwriting that was subsequently found by police.

"One of the relatively few statements that you had made in the witness box which I accept is that you indicated in the telephone conversation which led to the appointment being made that you were experiencing problems in your relationship with your partner arising from a low level of self-esteem. You stated in your evidence that she was nice to you and responded to your concerns. This would have been exactly the situation which you were hoping to achieve.

"I have no doubt Miss Patterson experienced no sense of danger as she prepared for an appointment with a client who had presented such issues and who was to see her at the innocent hour of nine o'clock on a Monday morning. She almost certainly felt comfortable and secure in the safety of her own home in a normal suburban street at that hour and on an ordinary working day.

"We are unlikely ever to know precisely what took place upon your arrival or for how long you were present in the house before you commenced a savage attack upon Miss Patterson. The terror experienced by her at that moment, which you had contemplated in your perverted imagination and for which you had carefully planned, now became a terrible reality. You struck at her again and again, using a knife capable of inflicting deep wounds. The weapon has never been found.

"Defensive injuries to her hands provide silent evidence of her unsuccessful attempts to defend herself against what must have been a sustained and determined assault. Altogether, Miss Patterson received 27 stab wounds. Her breasts were completely cut from her body, probably, but not necessarily, after death in a depraved act of contempt. They were never located and it appears likely that in a further act of obscenity they were taken as a kind of trophy.

"After checking the house that there was nothing left which might incriminate you, and collecting her handbag and driver's licence, also presumably as trophies, you returned to your home where you resumed your normal daily activities as if nothing had occurred and with your urge to kill, at least temporarily, sated.

"At that stage, you must have felt reasonably confident that you were safe from detection. But you had made two mistakes. First, although you had given the false name of Malcolm and had provided Miss Patterson with a false telephone number, the number was, in fact, that of a student who you had engaged to do labouring work for you.

"Second, although you appear to have partially searched the premises, you had not seen Miss Patterson's diary which was underneath some other items on a couch in the living room. It contained a reference to the appointment and, importantly, the incriminating telephone number. Not surprisingly, when the investigating police members became aware of your possible connection with that number, you quickly came under suspicion. You were arrested and a search of your house was conducted, in the course of which important evidence that led to your arrest was found.

"As this summary suggests, there is much that is unknown concerning the selection of your victim, the preparations which you undertook to gain access to her and exactly what took place when you arrived at her home.

"However, the information that has emerged enables the finding to be made beyond reasonable doubt, in my opinion, that you regarded Nicole Patterson as nothing more than prey to be entrapped and killed. Her life, youth and personal qualities assumed importance in your mind only by reason of the sense of satisfaction and power which you experienced in taking them from her.

"For the normal decent members of the community, it is difficult to comprehend that anyone could have acted as you did. There is absolutely nothing in the circumstances which could conceivably be regarded as extenuating in any possible way. You are reasonably intelligent and cannot be described as suffering any mental illness as that term is currently understood. You did not act impulsively or in a state of high emotions, whether engendered by some external incident or otherwise, or whilst you were affected by alcohol or drugs. Rather, you carried out your crime with remorseless deliberation and after careful manipulation of the situation, in full understanding of the significance of your actions. Your level of personal culpability must be regarded, accordingly, as extremely high.

"Viewed from the perspective of the community, which this Court represents, your offence constitutes a profoundly serious example of the most serious crime known to our society. That degree of seriousness and the unequivocal denunciation of conduct of the kind in which you engaged must be reflected in the response of this Court.

"You have breached the most fundamental principle upon which any decent society must be based; the sanctity of the life of each of those who dwell peacefully in it. In doing so, I have no doubt that you have increased significantly the regrettably understandable level of fear experienced, I would suggest, by almost every woman in this society, that she may become the victim of sexual violence. The Court in a case such as the present one must, through the sentences that it imposes, assert commitment to this principle and make it perfectly clear that such behaviour will not be tolerated. The courts must endeavour to deter those who may be inclined to act in this way."

Justice Vincent then said he had read the victim-impact statements made by Nicole's friends and family and found himself "deeply saddened". The judge also referred to Dupas' criminal past, involving "repeated acts of sexual violence". Significantly, he told Dupas:

"All of the offences were sexually related or motivated. A number of them involved physical violence and use of a knife. On three separate appearances you were sentenced to terms of imprisonment for the commission of rape, aggravated rape or assault with intent to rape. On the second and third of those occasions you committed your offences within a very short time of your release from custody. It appears that the only periods during which you were at large in the community without committing offences were two periods of approximately 12 months each during which you were subject to strict parole conditions following your release from prison in 1992 and 1996. However, it was not long after that form of control was lifted by the expiration of the sentence to which it was related that you reverted to your usual type of criminal behaviour."

Just before announcing the sentence, Justice Vincent told Dupas: "You are now 47 years with a deeply entrenched desire to engage in sexually violent behaviour ... There is absolutely nothing in the material before the Court to suggest that the serious risk which you pose would diminish rather than perhaps as a consequence of physical infirmity associated with age. Setting to one side your categorisation under the law as a serious sexual offender and the obligation imposed by legislation to regard the protection of the public as the paramount sentencing consideration in your situation, common sense would dictate that this must be the case.

"You have not responded in anything remotely approaching an appropriate fashion to sentences of imprisonment, psychiatric treatment or community supervision. Realistically considered, the prospects of your eventual rehabilitation must be regarded as close to hopeless that they can be effectively discounted. There is no indication whatever that you have experienced any sense of remorse for what you have done, and I doubt that you are capable of any such human response.

"I have had regard to the sentences which have been imposed by the Court over recent years upon persons who have committed the crime of murder in circumstances of sexually motivated violence ... When regard is had to the seriousness of the crime which you committed and the other sentencing considerations to which I have adverted, including your high level of culpability, the nature of the offence which you committed, the need to protect the community from the risk that you will continue to present for the foreseeable future, the total lack of remorse and the absence of any significant prospect of rehabilitation, only one course can sensibly be seen to remain.

"You must as a consequence of the commission of the terrible crime which has brought you before this Court be removed permanently from the society upon whose female members you have preyed for over 30 years. I do not consider that it would be appropriate to fix a minimum term in your case.

"The sentence of the Court is that you be imprisoned for the rest of your natural life and without the possibility for release on parole."

Police involved in the investigation were ecstatic, as Maher explained: "There was absolute elation for two reasons. Firstly, he had been found guilty and this made us all feel good about a job well done, that a killer had been caught and convicted and, secondly, the sentence of a life term with no possibility of parole meant Dupas would never again rape or kill."

Dupas, a cold and heartless killer, showed no emotion at the sentencing and was led away to spend the rest of his days behind bars. The jury then was called to stand before Justice Vincent while as associate read Dupas' prior convictions. This could not be done during the trial because of the possibility of swaying the jury but, as Dupas' litany of foul sexual crimes was detailed, some members of the jury wept openly. They now knew with certainty they had made the right decision and that a monster had been removed from society.

Nicole's family, naturally, was ecstatic. Mrs O'Donnell described the trial as "an exhausting process" and the two hours the jury was out were particularly harrowing. "We all were anxious and didn't really know what to expect. Of course, the evidence was overwhelming, but it was difficult to read the jurors' faces. In a way, the elation was mingled with relief. As Justice Vincent sentenced him (Mrs O'Donnell sometimes finds it difficult to mention Dupas by name), my ex-husband said 'you bastard'."

"Nicole's killer had been sentenced, but there also was sympathy for George (Halvagis) as police were still working on his daughter's case. George was a rock for us and we also wanted his daughter's killer brought to justice."

The Dupas sentencing was huge news in Melbourne and, indeed, around Australia. It was the lead item on all television news that night and the newspapers the following day splashed the case across their front pages. The *Herald Sun* blared TIME TO CONFESS. Its report reads, in part:

"Killer Peter Dupas has been urged to confess to any dark secrets he may hold about the violent deaths of two other women.

"The plea was made after Dupas, 47, was sentenced to spend the rest of his life in prison.

"The evil predator stalked, murdered and then mutilated psychotherapist Nicole Patterson, as part of a 30-year campaign of terror against women ...

"...He is the prime suspect in the murders of Mersina Halvagis, who was stabbed laying flowers on her grandmother's grave, and of prostitute Margaret Maher."

The *Herald Sun* even ran the following editorial, under the heading JUSTICE DONE AT LAST:

*"'You regarded Nicole Patterson as nothing more than prey, to be trapped and killed.' - Justice Frank Vincent*

"The justice system yesterday finally caught up with Peter Norris Dupas. Victorians everywhere breathed a heartfelt sigh of relief.

"But many demand an answer to the question: why did the system take to so long to recognise the deadly threat he posed and lock him away?

"If the system had not failed, 28-year-old Nicole Patterson's family and friends would not be mourning her today.

"Supreme Court judge Justice Frank Vincent yesterday reflected community sentiment when he sentenced Dupas to serve the rest of his life in jail for the mutilation murder of Nicole.

"Justice Vincent told the serial rapist his only course was to ensure that Dupas be 'permanently removed from society'.

"The judge was right. Dealing with Dupas was never a question of revenge punishment or deterring others.

"Very early in his depraved career, the priority should have been always to ensure that this monster was denied the opportunity to stalk our streets.

"Heaven knows, it was obvious enough. His awful record began when he stabbed a woman neighbour while still at school.

"Over the years he preyed on a succession of women armed with a knife, raping and stabbing.

"Police recognised his potential to kill back in 1974 when they first charged him with rape. No one listened to them.

"It bears repeating that, though this violent sex offender was sentenced to a maximum of 31 years' jail for various offences against women, thanks to the parole system, he did not even serve the minimum of 21 years set by various courts.

"It was classic 'revolving door' justice.

"Police want to question Dupas about the murder of another woman, but he has refused their request for an interview.

"This anomaly, along with a number of others spotlit by the system's failure to deal with Dupas, must be given urgent attention by the Bracks Government.

"There must be no repeat."

The Nicole Patterson case and the suggestion that Dupas was responsible for other murders sparked public outrage and the *Herald Sun* ran several letters, accompanied by the bare-torso photo of the mutilating monster shown on the front cover of this book.

One reader wrote: "The rage and frustration that the broad community feels about the treatment and record of Peter Dupas is a manifestation and reflection on the attitude that is constantly highlighted throughout our courts. Surely the people who constantly read his record of atrocities and released him time and time again need to be accountable for their repeated misjudgement of a fiendish mind. Who can say to all the grieving relatives, 'I'm sorry but I made another mistake'? It's too late for the community to do anything except demand retribution."

Another wrote: "No justice! To allow a man with Peter Dupas' record to be released from jail so early and so easily is a criminal act in itself. Our legal system is very much at fault. A complete overhaul is needed so that those violating the laws are dealt with more realistically and real justice is done."

The president of the Crime Victims Support Association, Noel McNamara, wrote: "After the trial of Peter Dupas for murdering Nicole Patterson, again we hear victims' families complaining about a system weighted heavily in favour of the offender. Dupas has forfeited all his rights as a human being. The fact that he has the right to refuse to be interviewed by police about other homicide matters is a disgrace to our legal system. The laws, as they stand today, forget the victims and favour the criminal. In this case, the legal system has got it horribly wrong."

Standing outside the Supreme Court the day Dupas was sentenced was a silver-haired, middle-aged man in an open-neck shirt. George Halvagis took particular interest in the Nicole Patterson murder case as he knew in his father's heart that Dupas also had killed his beloved daughter Mersina. And he would never rest until Dupas again had been brought to justice.

## CHAPTER FIVE

# The Monster Appeals

Despite the overwhelming evidence presented in court over little more than a week in the Nicole Patterson murder trial, Dupas sought leave to appeal both the verdict and the sentence. The matter went to the Court of Appeal, with Justice John Winneke presiding, with Justices Phillips and Batt. The hearing was heard on June 12, 2001, and the court's decision was handed down less than two months later, on August 3.

Basically, Dupas appealed on four grounds: (1) The verdict of the jury was unsafe and unsatisfactory, (2) The judge erred in his direction, (3) The judge erred in his directions concerning the evidence given by pathologist Dr Jelbert in cross-examination and

(4) The judge erred in admitting into evidence part of an untaped conversation between police and Dupas at the time of his arrest.

The appeal involved considerable legal and factual matters and, in judgement, Justice Winneke said: "It follows that in my view none of the grounds relied upon by the applicant (Dupas) in support of his application for leave to appeal against conviction has been made out...

"... This was, in my view, a case where the evidence against the applicant was so overwhelming as to lead me to the satisfaction that no actual miscarriage of justice has occurred in the sense that the applicant has thereby lost a chance that was fairly open to him of being acquitted. On the disputed evidence in this case, it was clear that the deceased was killed by a person whom she was expecting and, according to her appointment book, was expecting a person described as 'Malcolm', being the ficticious name used by the applicant.

"The jury must have rejected the applicant's explanation that he had cancelled the appointment, a conclusion unaffected by any of the deficiencies in the charge relied upon in this Court and, in any event, consistent with the details in the deceased's 'appointment book' ...

"More significantly, it was not disputed that the deceased's blood was found on the applicant's jacket which he conceded he was wearing on that day. The jury must have rejected the proposition mounted on the applicant's behalf that the blood of the deceased was placed on the jacket by the police, again a matter which was not the subject of any of the deficiencies in the charge raised in this Court. It was not disputed that the applicant was wearing that jacket on the morning of April 19 and, once the jury had concluded that the blood was on that jacket otherwise than through outside interference, it was inevitable that they would conclude that he was her assailant."

In regards to the sentence of life imprisonment without the possibility of parole, Justice Winneke said:

"It was not suggested that his Honour (Justice Vincent) was in error in imposing the maximum sentence of life imprisonment. The only ground was that his Honour should have fixed a non-parole date. In this respect, it is significant to note that the applicant was, at the time of the trial, 47 years of age. Section 11, sub-section one of the Sentencing Act 1991 provides: 'If a court sentences an offender to be imprisoned in respect to an offence for (a) the term of his natural life ... the court must, as part of the sentence, fix a period during which the offender is not eligible to be released on parole unless it considers that the nature of the offence or the past history of the offender make the fixing of such a period inappropriate.'

"The trial judge considered that it would be inappropriate, having regard to the nature of the offence and the applicant's antecedents, to fix a non-parole period. He said: 'When regard is to be had to the seriousness of the crime which you have committed and the other sentencing considerations to which I have adverted, including your high level of culpability, the nature of the offence ... the need to protect the community from the risk which you will continue to present in the foreseeable future, the total lack of remorse and the absence of any significant prospect of rehabilitation, only one course can be seen sensibly to remain. You must as a consequence of the terrible crime which has brought you before this court be removed permanently from the society upon whose female members you have preyed for over 30 years. I do not consider that it would be appropriate to fix a minimum term in your case.'

"In fixing such a sentence, his Honour had taken into consideration the submission made by the Crown that it was, in the circumstances, the only sentence which could be sensibly be passed, and the submission made by trial counsel for the applicant in which it had been conceded that a head sentence of 'life imprisonment' was the only appropriate head sentence but that the court should fix a non-parole period although 'an extremely lengthy one'."

Justice Winneke pointed out that it was argued on Dupas' behalf that it was "exceptionally rare" to decline to fix non-parole periods in Victoria, even for multiple killings and that even though Dupas' chances of rehabilitation were slim, the fixing of a non-parole period was inappropriate, especially as Dupas was likely to serve his entire sentence "in protection".

However, Justice Winneke said: "For my own part, I can find no error in the exercise of his Honour's sentencing discretion. It is pointless, I think, to compare degrees of gravity between crimes like this one of gross inhumanity. It suffices to say that this was a brutal and callous crime committed against a carefully selected target in the sanctuary of her own home. The mutilation of the victim's body, and the manner in which it was accomplished, demonstrated the applicant's utter contempt for his victim and for those who loved her and cherished her memory. It was a crime which was carefully planned and the nature and number of the phone calls made to the victim's home prior to the commission of the offence suggest that the applicant was 'staking out' the movements of his intended victim and the fact that she would be alone in her home at the time which the applicant had appointed for the commission of the crime.

"Furthermore, the antecedents of the applicant, combined with the nature of his crime, amply warranted, to my mind, the view formed by his Honour that the fixing of a non-parole period would be inappropriate. Those antecedents demonstrate, as his Honour noted, that the applicant has 'an appalling criminal history' which has involved repeated acts of sexual violence against women extending over a period of approximately 30 years.

"That criminal history, admitted by the applicant, revealed 16 prior convictions involving six court appearances between March 27, 1972, and November 11, 1994. Those convictions included convictions for rape of women in their own homes, assault with intent to rape and malicious wounding, aggravated rape and false imprisonment.

"They had brought with them terms of imprisonment of nine years in 1974, six and a half years in 1980, 12 years in 1985 and three years and nine months in 1994. The trial judge appended to his sentencing remarks the remarks of three of the judges who had previously sentenced the applicant. Those remarks demonstrate the capacity of the applicant to seek female targets, to worm his way into their confidence, to gain access to their homes and, having done so, to violently sexually assault them, generally with the aid of a knife.

"That criminal history justified, in my view, the trial judge's comment that the applicant, at the age of 47 years, still had 'a deeply entrenched desire to engage in sexually violent behaviour'. Indeed, the behaviour had commenced in 1964, when the applicant was only 14 years of age, at which time he entered the house of a female neighbour and attacked and wounded her with a knife. That matter was dealt with in the Children's Court and, because of legislation, did not form part of his recorded criminal history. The fact is that the applicant has spent, because of the convictions and sentences to which I have referred, most of his adult life in confinement. However, the danger which he presents to the community (as the trial judge said) is due in part to his innate intelligence and his capacity to pass himself off to female members of the community as a 'decent man'.

"Indeed, his Honour had before him a victim impact statement from Ms Cruz, who was living with the applicant at the time of his crime, in which she contemplated that she, too, had been the victim of the applicant, his family and friends as a consequence of their 'hiding Peter's horrendous criminal past from me'. As she said:

"**My belief that I was a good judge of character has been destroyed because I have been completely fooled by a monster into believing that he was a caring and gentle man.**"

"This 'Jekyll and Hyde' personality of the applicant reflects, in his Honour's words, 'an ability to exercise a considerable degree of control over your underlying impulses which were then released when you considered that it was safe to do so and they emphasise your resistance to any rehabilitation endeavour'.

" … In the light of the material which was before his Honour it is my opinion that the findings which he made and the conclusion to which he came were amply warranted. This was 'a terrible crime' in the sense that it was a crime of very great heinousness unattended by any factors of mitigation. In that sense it falls within the 'worst category' of offences of murder …

"Having regard to the nature of the offence and the past history of the applicant to which I have referred, it seems to me to have been well open to his Honour to have imposed the sentence which he did. I would, accordingly, dismiss the application for leave to appeal against sentence."

Justices Phillips and Batt concurred and the monster then must have come to the realisation that he would spend the rest of his life behind bars, probably in fear of his own safety, and, indeed, his life because of the unbelievably abhorrent manner in which he killed and mutilated Nicole Patterson.

Meanwhile, Dupas not only was found guilty of murdering Nicole Patterson and had his application for leave to appeal dismissed, but his depravity helped police solve a murder committed 18 months before Nicole was slaughtered and mutilated so sadistically. Police turned their attention to the murder of Margaret Maher in October, 1997. It then was George Halvagis' turn to savour justice.

## FOOTNOTE

The removal of a victim's breast(s) during or after a murder is extremely rare and few instances have been reported around the world. However, the death of Nicole Patterson has strikingly eerie comparisons with a horrific murder near Montreal, Canada, in 1992.

A woman called in to see her married sister, Chantal Briere, and was horrified to see her shot dead and mutilated. The dead woman's breasts had been removed and police had little evidence — until they realised the killer had stolen the dead woman's credit card and used it at a convenience store 10 kilometres away. They tracked the killer down through surveillance cameras at the store and he eventually broke down and confessed to THREE murders. The killer, Serge Archambault, first killed seven years earlier and, after mutilating and then dissecting the body, he buried the remains in various countryside areas.

Archambault killed another woman four years later, but his third killing was the one which bore so many similarities to the Patterson case. Archambault, like Dupas, found a way to be invited into his victim's house and then took her completely by surprise. In the Archambault case, he pretended to be interested in buying the woman's home and she ushered him inside believing his call was genuine — just like Patterson did with Dupas. Although Archambault shot his victim and Dupas knifed Nicole Patterson to death, the breasts were removed in both cases and never found.

Although Archambault confessed to three murders, Dupas always has maintained his innocence, despite the overwhelming evidence. Both have been described as sexual sadists and the sentencing judge in Archambault's case described him as "diabolically perverted", a term anyone could apply to describe Dupas. Archambault, like Dupas, was sentenced to life imprisonment, but with some possibility of parole. Like Dupas, Archambault was a loner who had had overwhelming sexual, sadistic tendencies from his early teens. He claimed after his arrest that he was "the victim of moods I cannot control". Dupas has never made any such admission, but he certainly was unable to control his sexual perversions.

Archambault's crimes were so horrific Canadians nicknamed him "the Butcher of St Eustache" (the area where he killed Briere) and although Dupas has never been given a similar soubriquet, he always will be known as a mutilating monster.

Archambault's crimes were so notorious in Canada that his killings inspired forensic pathologist Kathy Reichs to write crime fiction from the viewpoint of a pathologist. Now one of the world's most celebrated crime novelists, Dr Reichs admitted in an interview that she wrote her first novel *Deja Dead* after being involved in the Archembault investigations.

Dr Reichs, forensic anthropologist for the Office of the Chief Medical Examiner, North Carolina, and for the Laboratoire et de Medecine Legale, Quebec, said in this interview: "In the case of Serge Archambault … I helped with the identity in the dismemberment case. It was quite unique and showed a lot of skill going directly into the joints. I was able to say you're looking for someone who knows something about anatomy — an orthopaedic surgeon or butcher. And it turned out he was a butcher. I had just finished the case and he had just been convicted of three counts of first degree murder when I started *Deja Dead* and I drew on that."

## CHAPTER SIX

# Dead in a Ditch

Margaret Josephine Maher might have been a prostitute and drug addict, but no woman deserved her fate at the hands of the mutilating monster, Peter Norris Dupas. Although Margaret was just 40 when she was murdered in the early hours of October 4, 1997, she looked considerably older. She had abused heroin, amphetamines, cannabis and other substances for years and prostituted herself to support her habit.

Regarded by police and social workers as a "harmless, hopeless case", she plied her trade along the Hume Highway, not far from where she lived in the outer northern Melbourne suburb of Craigieburn. She lived in a flat on the highway and therefore did not have far to go in search of work for the cash she needed to live and to pay for her drugs.

Margaret Maher, born on June 14, 1957, lived by herself, although schoolgirl daughter Natasha often visited and occasionally stayed with her. Her rented home might not have been Shangri La, but it was comfortable, even if crowded. There were the usual comforts of a small television set, solid furniture, a tiny, but neat kitchen and a multitude of potted indoor plants. As at Nicole Patterson's home, there were dolls and toy bears, reminders of childhood. Margaret, despite her precarious occupation and drug habit, kept her home neat and tidy.

Her personal appearance was not quite as meticulous and her dress, demeanour and facial appearance indicated she had lived a hard life. Although she once would have been pretty, Margaret had a shock of untidy dyed blonde hair which showed dark roots. She also had numerous tattoos, on her breasts, on her right upper arm, her right hip and foot and a small one with a man's name on her right wrist. Slightly plump with a pot belly, Margaret probably had a striking figure when young. At 40, her best times were behind her, and tragically, she had no future when she left home early on the night of October 3, 1997 — 18 months before Nicole Patterson was murdered.

Margaret was well known in the area where she lived, and not only because of her habit of hitch-hiking along the Hume Highway looking for customers — often truck drivers. Local shopkeepers knew her well and she often was seen at the Broadmeadows Town Shopping Centre or the Bi-Lo Supermarket in Gaffney Street, Pascoe Vale. Margaret also bought second-hand clothes from the Recycled Clothing shop in Gaffney Street.

Dressed in dark grey tracksuit-type slacks, a pink blouse and light purple top, Margaret left home about 7.15pm on October 3 and called into a newsagency in Barry Road, Campbellfield, where she bought a packet of cigarettes and a "scratchie" gaming card. Margaret's daughter had left the home 15 minutes earlier and later told police her mother was desperate for drugs as she was in dispute with one of her dealers and seemed intent on trying to find someone who would sell her some amphetamines.

Soon after, Margaret knocked on a neighbour's door along the Hume Highway and indicated that she had inadvertently locked herself out of her home and that her daughter had the keys. She asked for help but the neighbours, Coral Payne and Raymond Williams, said they could not help her as they did not have the necessary tools.

About 7.45pm, a woman saw Margaret hitch-hiking towards the city on the Hume Highway near the Campbellfield McDonald's restaurant. The woman, Christine Jackel, later told police she saw Margaret get into a late model "green/blue" Falcon and that the driver headed off towards the city.

This turned out to be correct but, at 8.05pm, Margaret called in at a pharmacy in Gaffney Street and collected her methadone, which was part of her treatment for drug addiction. Margaret told the pharmacist, Santino Grasso, that she had been given a lift to Gaffney Street by a man who lived at her former address in Craigieburn.

From there, Margaret was seen in the Safeway store at the Broadmeadows Town Centre shopping complex. She was there several hours and the last person to see her in the store was a woman (Marina Henne), who saw her walking across the car park in the direction of Pascoe Vale Road at about 12.15am. Margaret was carrying shopping bags which contained a few items, but the bags and their contents were never seen again. It also was the last public sighting of Margaret Maher.

Police later presumed Margaret had started to hitch-hike, but there has never been any evidence of this. Then, at 1.45pm on October 4, an elderly group, a man and two women, who were collecting aluminium cans in Cliffords Road, Somerton, came across a sight they will never forget. It was Margaret Maher's bloodied and battered body lying in a ditch. Her slacks had been pulled half-way down to the middle of her thighs, exposing a tattoo of a star on her left hip. The light purple jacket was pulled up to her waist and there was a terrible wound on the woman's chest. In fact, the left breast had been sliced off and later was found in Margaret's mouth. At the back, the dead woman's buttocks were exposed.

The man and two women who made this gruesome discovery were Ronald McDonald, wife Mauriel and sister-in-law Elaine Westely. In a statement Mr McDonald later gave police, he said:

"My name is Ronald McDonald and I reside at an address known to the police. On Saturday, the fourth of October, I was at my home address. With me were my wife Mauriel McDonald and my sister-in-law Elaine Westely. We decided to go for a drive along the back roads of Craigieburn and Somerton. We do this about once a week and the main reason for doing this is that we drive along the back roads and see if any person had dumped aluminium cans, pots or pans and other assorted junk. We hand in what we find and gain a little extra cash to off-set the pension.

"We set off at about 1.15pm. I was driving, my wife and sister-in-law were also in the vehicle. I drive a 1973 Holden station wagon which is orange in colour." He then gave police the registration number before continuing:

"We went from Broadmeadows to Roxburgh Park, (where) they were having a boot sale and we stopped off to have a look. The car boot sale was held in a reserve off Somerton Road. From there we continued on along Somerton Road and turned left on to Cliffords Road. We travelled north along Cliffords Road. When we were about halfway between Somerton Road and a set of railway tracks which head into the Martin Bright Steel Factory, I saw a pile of rubbish to the right of me by the side of the road. It seemed like someone had dumped computer parts on the side of the road. I pulled the vehicle over to the left-hand side of the road and stopped directly opposite the pile of rubbish which was on the other side of the road.

"We all got out of the vehicle to rummage through the pile of rubbish. I moved a sheet of cardboard and saw that some of the computer circuits moved with it. Once I did this I noticed what I thought was a body. I saw a hand with rings on the fingers and a chain bracelet on the wrist. The body was not completely exposed and some parts were covered. I could see the lower back region; there was a graze on it, lower down on the leg I could see a tattoo of some sort. We stood back and looked. My wife said that it looked like a shop dummy, but once I saw the rings and the tattoo I knew that it was the body of a person."

In her statement, Mrs McDonald said: "We saw some rubbish on the right hand side of the road. My husband stopped the car and we all got out to see if there were some aluminium cans which we collect to supplement our pensions. As I was walking towards the rubbish I saw some boxes and some type of electrical circuit board. My husband moved the box sideways to see if there was anything underneath and I saw bare buttocks and a leg with a black stocking on it. I turned my head away and said to my sister and husband: 'It's only a store dummy. Let's not get involved, it's only a dummy.' My husband then said, 'I don't think so'."

In her statement, Ms Westely said: "My brother-in-law was driving … We went over a railway line and turned left just after the railway line and went down this little bitumen road to just where we go to collect cans. My brother-in-law was driving along the road when he pointed out some boxes on the side of the road to our right.

"I then saw these boxes … My brother-in-law backed up as we thought the box might have been full of cans, which happens quite a lot. All three of us got out of the car. We walked over to the box. I then saw a hand and I said 'look, there's a hand'. My brother-in-law moved the box. I was standing about a metre away from the box. The box would have been about two feet from the side of the road. The grass was about two feet (just over half a metre) tall. My brother-in-law then said, 'oh, what's that?' I thought it was a dummy. I walked up the side of it and saw another hand, rings, bracelets and a head. The body had blonde hair. We all then just walked away. My brother-in-law then said, 'I think I'll phone the police'."

As Mr McDonald had a fitted mobile phone in his car, he contacted police and the three who came across this horrible scene waited in their car for the police to arrive. Meanwhile, they made sure they did not touch the body or contaminate the crime scene in any way.

The first police to arrive on the scene, about 10 minutes after the discovery of Margaret's body, were Sergeants Ralston and Mooney and Constable Riddford, who contained the scene before the arrival of Detective Sergeant Verinder and Detective Senior Constable Ehmer, of the Broadmeadows Criminal Investigation Unit. These detectives took charge until the arrival of the Homicide Squad's Detective Senior Sergeant Ron Iddles.

A police scene examination indicated that Margaret's body was lying on its right side and she was still wearing the clothing she had been seen in the previous night. Items of computer hardware were found near the body and one part appeared to have the name "Jolanta" stamped on it. Significantly, the police also found a black woollen glove which later had enormous ramifications in the identification of Dupas as the killer. There also was a cash register receipt from the Bi-Lo Supermarket, Pascoe Vale, stuck to Margaret's left cheek.

The examination indicated Margaret's pants and underwear had been pulled down, exposing her lower torso and genitals and with her upper clothing pulled up, exposing her chest. There was no indication of sexual penetration, but police did not rule out this possibility. They also determined that Margaret had not been killed in the grassy ditch and that her body had been dumped there. The worst and most disturbing aspect was that not only had Margaret's left breast been sliced off, but it had been stuffed into her mouth, nipple facing out in an incredibly grotesque manner.

Margaret's mutilated body was conveyed to the Coronial Services Centre, Southbank, where a post-mortem was performed by Dr Matthew Lynch, a specialist in forensic medicine and pathology who was employed as a forensic pathologist at the Victorian Institute of Forensic Pathology. Dr Lynch had attended the scene where Margaret's body had been found about 5.45pm, about four hours after its discovery. He noted at that time that there was evidence of a head injury and despite the left breast having been removed, there was "no amount of haemorrhage surrounding the breast injury". First indications were that the breast had been removed after death in some form of sick ritual.

Dr Lynch, after the initial examination, started his post-mortem at the Victorian Institute of Forensic Medicine at 8pm and noted that by this time rigor mortis had set in. After noting that the body was of a middle-aged Caucasian female weighing 71 kilograms and measuring 168 cm in height, Dr Lynch described the clothing Margaret had been wearing — the purple jacket (with the brand inscription Arctic Zone), black leggings and white socks marked "Tommy, the runner". The dead woman also had four bangles on the right wrist, rings on her right index, middle, ring and little fingers, rings on her left ring, middle and index fingers and, finally, two bangles on her left wrist.

Dr Lynch noted some bloodstained frothy material in the nostrils and described a list of injuries to the head, neck, chest, abdomen, arms and legs. He also examined internal organs, removed tissue for examination, performed full toxicology, radiology (which showed no fractures) and took vaginal and rectal swabs. The hyoid bone in the neck was x-rayed separately, but there was no fracture, although there was a small amount of haemorrhage surrounding the larynx.

Injuries included a blunt trauma laceration to the right eyebrow, a cut to the left wrist and, of course, the mutilation of the left breast.

In determining the cause of death, Dr Lynch reported:

"The cause of death in this woman is multifactorial and necessarily complex. She had significant natural disease in the presence of coronary artery atherosclerosis and chronic hepatitis C. The latter is a viral infection commonly occurring in the context of previous intravenous drug use. Toxicological analysis was significant in detecting methadone, methamphetamine ('speed') and benzodiazepines. There was also evidence of some haemorrhage adjacent to the larynx but without any evidence of laryngeal structural damage.

"Individuals with coronary artery disease are at risk of death from cardiac arrhythmia. Pressure applied to the neck may produce evidence of laryngeal haemorrhage and result in death by various mechanisms. The presence of methadone and benzodiazepines may cause respiratory depression. Methamphetamine may cause cardiac arrhythmias.

"A significant finding at autopsy was evidence of blunt trauma in the form of a laceration to the right eyebrow, an incised injury to the left wrist and significantly post-mortem mutilation of the left breast and this had been placed within the mouth of the deceased. There was no evidence of any haemorrhage adjacent to the mastectomy, suggesting the mutilation occurred post-mortem".

Significantly, the last paragraph read: "Post-mortem mutilation of a body is an uncommon and sinister event. The significance of this finding was conveyed to the Homicide Squad." Police therefore were on the hunt for a mutilating monster.

Police, in launching their investigation, asked Margaret's daughter Natasha of her mother's lifestyle and movements before she died. Natasha Maher said she had limited contact with her mother until July, 1997, and then tried to start a relationship with her.

Natasha said: "I stayed with my mother initially for around three weeks and then on and off until the third of October, 1997. My mother is a typical junky. She never planned ahead; she only lived for the day. She had a fixation for needles, using 'speed' (amphetamines) and sometimes heroin if she didn't get her methadone. My mother supported her habit by working as a prostitute. I worried about her because she was my mother and I feared for her safety, because of her lifestyle." Natasha even told of how her mother obtained drugs from a regular supplier and, in return, Margaret sometimes would give him oral sex.

In the final part of her statement, Natasha said that the last time she saw her mother was on Friday, October 3, 1997. She said that after going out in the afternoon, she returned to see her mother desperately searching for any left-over drugs and last saw her about 7pm when Margaret was preparing to go to the pharmacy to get her methadone.

She added: "When I last saw my mother, I would describe her as being in a state of despair and pissed off as she didn't have any drugs. She was wearing a purple overcoat and a purple jumper, which was lighter than the jacket. She was wearing black leggings and white sports socks and runners. I don't know if she was wearing underpants; she usually wears a g-string. She doesn't wear a bra. Mum would wear this attire and sometimes would sleep in clothes when she is out of it from the night before to the morning."

Police also made inquiries about Margaret's drug habits and took a statement from drug and alcohol therapist Anthony Dieine, who worked at a doctor's surgery in Strathmore. He told them: "I first came into contact with Margaret Maher in my professional capacity approximately four years ago. Margaret's situation was much the same as it was at the time of her death. She was on methadone and being overseen by the Austin Hospital.

"Approximately four years ago Margaret transferred from the Austin Hospital program (to the surgery). (When) She first transferred across from the Austin Hospital, she was receiving, I think, 120mg of methadone daily."

This dosage was regarded as "far too high" and was reduced to 100 mg a day and she picked up her methadone from the pharmacy in Gaffney Street, Pascoe Vale. The dosage gradually was reduced to 40mg a day without her knowledge and she did not report that this reduction had any effect on her. However, she discovered the dosage had been reduced, complained and it was boosted to 100mg a day.

Dieine said: "My normal activity with Margaret was to see her every second Friday. I would basically monitor her drug habits and ask her if she had any problems I could help her with. She was such a long-term abuser of drugs that we decided that she was really beyond total rehabilitation. For this reason we maintained her at a level as best we could to prevent her slipping into an uncontrolled system of drug abuse."

Dieine added he was aware Margaret worked in a high-risk occupation as a prostitute from a truck stop on the Hume Highway.

Pharmacy employee Santina Grasso told police that when Margaret obtained her methadone at about 8.05pm, she said she had been picked up by a male acquaintance. Grasso also indicated that Margaret could not pay the $5 for her methadone as she had "not been very busy lately".

Raymond Williams, the neighbour Margaret contacted about being locked out of her home, told police that it was after dark when Margaret knocked on the front door. He said he could not help her and added: "She didn't come back. I wondered what had happened to her and assumed that everything was all right. When I went to bed at 11pm her lounge room light wasn't on." He also told police he could not remember what Margaret was wearing that night.

Housewife Christine Jackel told police that she, her husband and children drove to the Coles supermarket in Glenroy before stopping off at the McDonald's restaurant on the Hume Highway on the way to see friends at Wallan. While sitting in the car waiting for her husband to return with their order, Jackel saw a woman on the other side of the highway. She said this woman was wearing a "pinky-mauve coloured jumper, probably a white skivvy, black leggings, with socks and joggers which I think were white". She added: "I recognised this woman as I had seen her on several prior occasions. I often saw her at McDonald's as we often stopped there on the way to Wallan."

This sighting of the woman believed to be Margaret was about 8pm and Jackel said the woman "seemed to be a person who led a difficult life". She added: "For these reasons she stood out and I remember her."

Jackel also said in the statement she gave to police: "As I watched her, she first appeared to be intending to cross the road as she was looking around at the traffic. However, she made no attempt to cross the road and continued to walk in the direction of the city on the opposite side of the Hume Highway. As she walked along she was walking very close to the edge of the road and she was slightly holding her right arm out from her body. For this reason I thought she may have been hitch-hiking but she also may have been just walking that way."

Jackel said she then saw a "greenie-blue or dark teal-coloured" Ford stop suddenly without its blinkers being applied. She said: "I got the impression by the way that the car stopped that the driver was just responding to her as a hitch-hiker rather than someone who was expecting to pick her up. I think this vehicle contained only a driver. I did not notice anyone in the back and the woman seemed to get into the car fairly quickly. She got into the front passenger seat. After the woman got into the car, it drove off almost straight away. It had stopped in the left lane and when it drove off, it just continued out of my sight."

Assuming this woman was Margaret Maher, police were able to deduce that she had been picked up on the Hume Highway and driven to the pharmacy by her male acquaintance. Jackel's evidence was important in helping track Margaret's movements and the housewife came forward after reading of the body's discovery in the October 6 edition of the *Herald Sun*.

Another witness, chef Anthony Marinelli, came forward after reading that a body had been dumped in Cliffords Road. He said in his statement to police:

"When I finished work (at the Epping Hotel), I left in my vehicle heading back to Broadmeadows. I travelled my normal route which includes driving along Somerton Road, then turn left into Pascoe Vale Road. At approximately 10.30 to 10.45pm I was travelling along Somerton Road. I passed Cliffords Road on my right and the nursery on my right, when I noticed a car with its headlights on. I noticed this car as I was approaching the V-line level crossing which crosses Somerton Road.

"The vehicle I noticed was to my right on the north side of Somerton Road. It was travelling along the V-line track which runs parallel to the train track. It was travelling in a southerly direction towards Somerton Road with its lights on, and was about 40 metres north of Somerton Road.

"In relation to the car, I can say it was a large '80s model white car. I can say that it was quite wide. I cannot recall anything distinctive about the car, except that it may have had tinted windows. I could not see the driver or other occupants of the car. I remember thinking this was unusual as the only other vehicles I have seen on this track have been V-line four-wheel drives and trucks. I was able to clearly see the vehicle as the area is well lit with security lights ... In the days following, I became aware that a body had been dumped in Cliffords Road around the same time as I saw the white Ford." This car was not Dupas', but police were determined to track down all leads, regardless of how insignificant they might have seemed.

Police, determined to retrace Margaret's movements on the night she died, also received information from a shop assistant at Safeway's, Broadmeadows. Matthew Blake told police Margaret was well known to those working on the store's afternoon shift as she was

*Nicole Patterson, in primary school uniform, was a bright, happy little girl.*

*Pretty Nicole Patterson was just starting a psychotherapy practice when "client" Peter Dupas killed and mutilated her.*

*Life was good for Nicole Patterson when she was bridesmaid at sister Kylie's wedding.*

*Nicole Patterson adored nieces Amy and Alisha.*

*This black and white photograph of Nicole Patterson
was taken just before she was killed.*

The monster struck in a front room at this house in Harper Street, Northcote.

The driveway of Nicole Patterson's rented house in Harper Street.

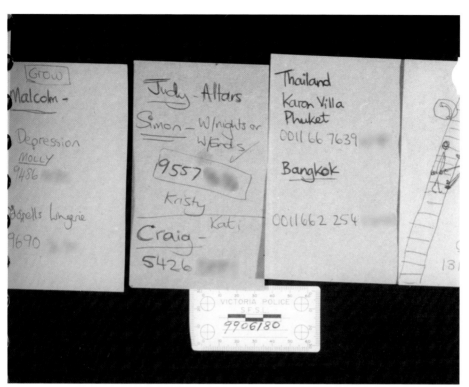

The note on the left, found at Nicole Patterson's Northcote home, clearly has the name "Malcolm" written at the top.

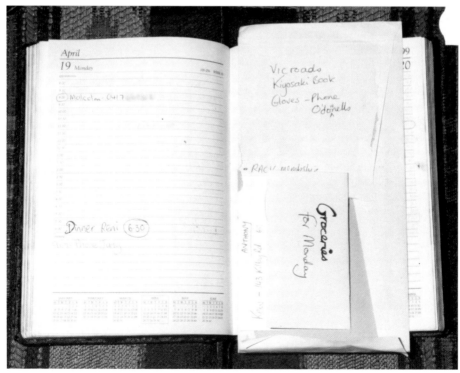

An appointment with death – the name "Malcolm" is written on the top left page of this diary.

*Margaret Maher might have led a hard life, but she was harmless and did not deserve her fate at the hands of Dupas.*

*Margaret Maher's mutilated body was found near where this police car stands.*

*Margaret Maher's body was dumped on the verge of this lonely road.*

*These computer parts, in a cardboard "California Pistachios" box and marked "strawberry custard" in red on the inside of one flap, was found near Margaret Maher's body.*

*Quiet, hard-working Mersina Halvagis had graduated from La Trobe University.*

*An aerial view of part of the Greek section
at the Fawkner Cemetery, off Box Forest Road.*

The red car Mersinia Halvagis drove to the Fawkner
Cemetery is the only vehicle in the car park.

Mersina Halvagis' grief-stricken father George prays
near where his daughter was so savagely murdered.

*Detective Senior Constable Paul Scarlett (left) and
Detective Senior Sergeant Jeff Maher in the row of graves
where Mersina Halvagis was attacked and murdered.*

*Detective Senior Sergeant Jeff Maher played a major role in the Dupas investigations.*

*Detective Senior Constable Paul Scarlett worked tirelessly, often in his own time, to bring Dupas to justice for the murder of Mersina Halvagis.*

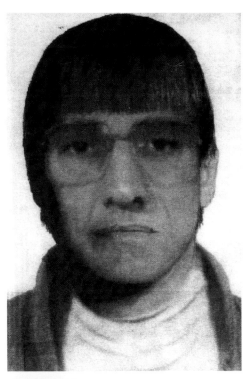

*This police computer image, released in 1998 in the Mersina Halvagis investigation, was based on a witness description of a man seen at Fawkner Cemetery just before Mersina Halvagis was murdered.*

*An artist's sketch of Dupas, with victims (from top to bottom on the left) Margaret Maher, Mersina Halvagis and Nicole Patterson. The illustration depicts Dupas in hell and is titled "Poor Little Pugsley".*

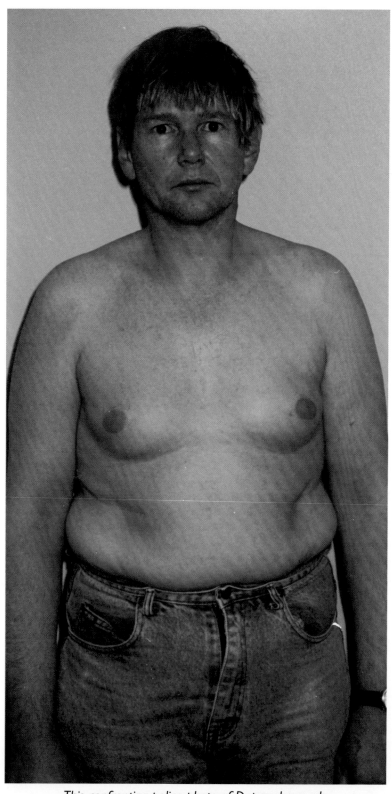

*This confronting police photo of Dupas shows why
he has been described as a killer with "man-boobs".*

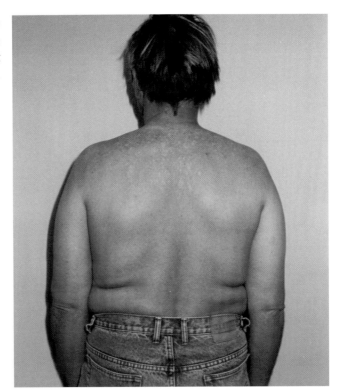

The pudgy Dupas from the back in this police photo, rolls of fat bulging over his jeans.

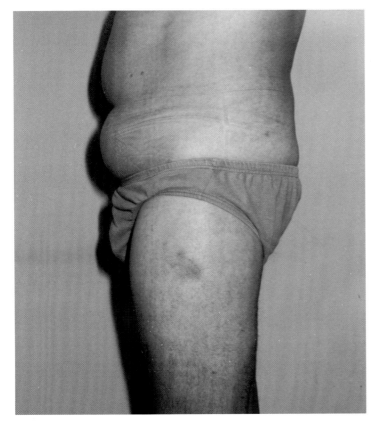

The overweight Dupas stripped down to his underpants, with a bruise on his thigh. This photo was taken by police three days after the Nicole Patterson killing.

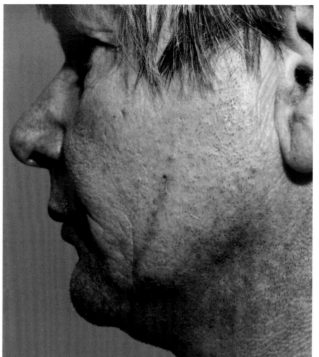

*Nicole Patterson managed to scratch Dupas before he killed her. This police photo also was taken three days after Nicole was killed.*

*Dupas arrives at the Supreme Court of Victoria during his trial for the murder of Nicole Patterson. He might look mild and meek, but is a remorseless monster.*

a regular customer. He told them: "Margaret would rarely be seen at the store prior to 8.30pm. She would often come and shop for hours on end. She would never really bother anyone.

"On Friday, October 3, 1997, I was working from 3pm until midnight. I recall seeing Margaret around 10.30 to 11pm between aisles one and two. Aisles one and two contain shampoo and hygiene, or health and beauty. I then saw Margaret again as I was leaving at midnight. Margaret was being served at number four by a girl named Nadia. Nadia was filling in that night but at that time was a casual worker at the store ...

"On this night Margaret was wearing blue-coloured leggings and she had her black handbag. I cannot remember what colour top she had on. She was buying an 'Impulse' deodorant can and a couple of other items which I am not sure of. I walked out the store and continued on home. I did not see where Margaret went after that. Margaret was also known to me and the rest of the staff as 'Blondie' because of her bleached blonde hair. Margaret would often bring a lot of items to the register but only purchase a small amount of items."

This sighting of Margaret was extremely strong evidence that she was still alive at midnight as she was so well known to Blake and other Safeway staff that it would have been most unlikely to have been a case of mistaken identity.

The Bi-Lo receipt found on Margaret's left cheek indicated she had made purchases at the supermarket at 6.17pm and was issued from the store's cash register number 0005. Checkout assistant Beverley Bride indicated to police that this was the cash register on which she was working at that time, but had no memory of the woman who had made the purchase.

Police also asked friends and neighbours if they could fill them in on Margaret and the precarious life she led. They were told Margaret charged $30 for a "screw" or $40 for "a head-job and screw". Police also learned that Margaret once had led a very ordinary life working at a bank but, after being introduced to heroin, her life became what she described as "a roller coaster ride".

Despite every police effort, there was no significant breakthrough. A special group, the Mikado Task Force, was formed to investigate the Maher and other murders, with seven officers involved in sifting through a mountain of evidence, statements and leads. The special task force spent 11 long and tiring months in trying to solve the Maher and other murders and, although it eventually was closed down and the officers returned to their respective squads, several officers continued to pursue leads in their own time. These officers included Paul Scarlett, who refused to concede he and the others had reached a dead-end.

An inquest into Margaret Maher's death was held at the Coroner's Court, Melbourne, from April 18, 2000, with the Homicide Squad's Detective Sergeant Gordon Hynd as the first witness and Senior Constable Wayne Kohlman present to assist Coronor Mr Ian West.

Kohlman opened the inquest by asking Hynd whether he had prepared a summary "outlining the circumstances" of Margaret's death. He replied "yes" and then gave a detailed account of events leading up to her death and the eventual discovery of her body.

After referring to the post-mortem conducted by Dr Lynch, Hynd said: "The deceased had high levels of drugs of dependence in her system. She was in a poor state of health with coronary disease, and she had some indication of pressure being applied to the neck. The exact nature as to how the deceased died is not able to be taken further at this time. A number of scenarios are possible, and the cause can only be taken further by the person or persons who disposed of the body ...

"She (Margaret) was last seen walking towards Pascoe Vale Road, Broadmeadows, where it is likely she commenced to hitch-hike. It is possible that she was picked up by a person who was later present when she died. If this occurred, it could easily have been by someone who had picked her up before, or equally, someone who had picked her up for the first time.

"The deceased also worked as a prostitute and was well known amongst the interstate truck drivers and other frequent road users in that area. It is possible that Margaret was picked up by one such driver and met her death in his company."

Hynd said the police investigation was ongoing and her death would remain "suspicious until the contrary is determined". He then was asked whether there had been any developments in the police investigation and he replied: "There are still a number of suspects that are yet to be interviewed, so the investigation is still active, yes."

Hynd suggested there were two separate lines of enquiry and later was asked a question directly relating to Dupas without naming him. He was asked: "Are there any cases that you know of in which this type of mutilation has occurred?"

He replied: "There were two other cases — one which we've ruled out as completely different in that it was a domestic type of dispute, and the second one concerns a person who has been charged with a murder that involved that type of mutilation." Hynd suggested that this factor formed one of the two lines of enquiry and added: "There are a couple of circumstances which could be suggestive that he's the offender."

Hynd then was asked: "So, in an official sense he was certainly a suspect and investigations were carried out to see if there was a link between the deceased and this person?"

He replied: "That's right. Obviously this type of mutilation is pretty rare and any person who's been involved in that sort of mutilation must be considered a suspect, and that was certainly done in this case."

The inquest then was adjourned nine days, until April 27. On resumption, Dr Lynch was called to give evidence and Kohlman, in his role in assisting the Coroner, referred to the autopsy report Dr

Lynch had prepared, with the first paragraph stating: "The cause of death in this woman is multi-factorial and necessarily complex."

When asked to comment on this, Dr Lynch replied: "Actually the paragraph I've used to describe the cause of death was combined drug toxicity. There was methamphetamine, methadone and benzodiazepines in a woman with coronary atherosclerosis and subtle signs of neck compression, so essentially the natural disease that Ms Maher had at post-mortem was some heart disease, that is a blockage of the coronary arteries which, in appropriate circumstances, can pre-dispose to sudden death.

"She had various stigmata of chronic intravenous drug use in the form of chronic Hepatitis C, which is a viral infection. It usually occurs in the context of intravenous drug use, although it can less commonly be a result of blood transfusion, but most commonly to intravenous drug use. She had a number of drugs detected in her system. They included methamphetamine, or speed, methadone and then some sedatives in the form of benzodiazepines. Any of these drugs in isolation, given appropriate circumstances, might also explain a sudden unexpected death.

"For example, speed or methamphetamine can produce rhythm disturbances of the heart, so it can result in somebody dying suddenly. Methadone … is usually prescribed in order to assist someone who is usually withdrawing from heroin use. It also can have toxic effects in the form of depression of the respiratory system. The level here exceeds that to which toxicity has been described … so in isolation, once again, the methadone could be a significant contributor to Ms Maher's death."

Dr Lynch then moved to the question of Margaret's neck injuries and said: "She also had very subtle signs of neck injury. They presented in the form of a small area of bruising around the voice box. Now this is very subtle and the reason I've given it probably greater importance in the context of suggesting it might be a contributing factor in her death is because of the single most significant finding in the context of the entire examination, which was the post-mortem mutilation in the form of removal of the left breast.

"So after a post-mortem when I am trying to determine what I think is the cause of death, I'm very heavily relying on the circumstances. In this case obviously the circumstances are incomplete. There is some vital information which is lacking, that is, how she came to be in the position she was found in and how she came to have those injuries inflicted, some before she died and some after.

"So I certainly can't suggest — I certainly won't suggest — that Ms Maher died from natural causes, but given an appropriate version of events, that perhaps mightn't be excluded. Also, I can't exclude the fact she may have suffered some form of neck injury in combination with her natural disease in combination with mixed drug toxicity … it sort of justifies the first part of my comment which said that the cause of death is both complex and multi-factorial."

When pressed, Dr Lynch said he could not provide an opinion as to the precise cause of death, except to say that he "would prefer to have my cause of death recorded as potential combinations of natural diseases, drug toxicity and subtle neck injury".

After Dr Lynch indicated that Margaret's left breast had been removed after her death, he said other injuries "clearly were sustained in life". He added: "She had a bruise and a laceration or a split above her right eyebrow which was associated with bruising. She also had a sharp injury to the region of her left wrist, which has been produced by a knife or something similar that is sharp. That injury was sustained in life."

Asked to summarise, Dr Lynch said: "The determination of a cause of death from the pathology point of view involves a consideration of the circumstances, the autopsy findings, results of toxicology and bringing them all together and, in appropriate circumstances, certainly there was enough natural disease here to explain Ms Maher's death, but I am certainly not suggesting the circumstances are appropriate."

Dr Lynch also said: "I'm certainly prepared to concede that Ms Maher had significant natural disease (but) I certainly would be uncomfortable with suggesting that I think she died from natural causes."

In relation to the "subtle" neck injury, he said: "Any pressure on the neck is potentially life-threatening because it can cause the heart to beat irregularly. Now, I didn't see evidence of significant crushing damage to Ms Maher's neck. I didn't see evidence of the small petechial haemmorhages that often we'd see on the eye in someone who has died from an asphyxial death. However, their absence does not preclude that mechanism of death."

Finally, Dr Lynch said he could not suggest that one part of his findings (drugs, natural disease or the subtle neck injury) was more important and admitted he was "deliberately being vague" on the precise cause of death, but said he needed "a clearer version of what happened in the hours before she died and I think that's the only way to really cover all bases".

The court adjourned, but the Coroner shortly after delivered his finding. Mr West opened by stating: "I find the identity of the deceased was Margaret Josephine Maher and that the death occurred on October 4, 1997, at an unknown place from combined drug toxicity in a woman with coronary artery atherosclerosis and subtle signs of neck compression."

Mr West then outlined the circumstances before concluding: "Where the pathology findings disclose drug toxicity, natural disease and subtle neck injury, further information is needed to either eliminate or give more prominence to any one of these elements that comprise the cause of death statement.

"In these circumstances, it is not possible to make a finding of contribution to the cause of death. The police investigation into the death of Margaret Maher is still ongoing and will remain a suspicious death investigation until such time as the contrary is determined. These are the findings and comments I make having inquired by way of inquest into the death of Margaret Josephine Maher."

# CHAPTER SEVEN

# Drawing a Comparison

Following the mutilation murder of Nicole Patterson, police made the reasonable assumption that the same killer might have murdered Margaret Maher. After all, Nicole had had both breasts removed, while Margaret had had her left breast sliced from her body. This appeared to be an extremely rare ritual, perhaps of a killer taking trophies, so police decided to examine all homicides involving female victims across Australia from 1989 to June 30, 2000.

This research was done in Canberra by Jenny Mouzos, a research analyst through the National Homicide Monitoring Program (NHMP) at the Australian Institute of Criminology, Canberra. The database she researched contained information on 3723 homicides, of which 1378 involved females as victims. She said in a statement: "A review of all these cases in order to determine whether there have been any previous homicide cases that entailed a female having her breast(s) cut off revealed that the only filed case between July, 1989, and June, 2000, involving the removal of the breast was that of the deceased Nicole Patterson, killed on the 19th of April, 1999, in Victoria."

A coincidence? Police did not think so and took an even closer look at Dupas' activities at or around the time Margaret's mutilated body was found in a ditch. They had the black glove and other potential evidence found at the scene and hoped DNA from the glove would give them an undeniable link to Dupas. The glove had been tested for DNA early in the investigation but, fortunately for the police, rapid developments in DNA research allowed them to perform further tests.

Meanwhile, police did a check on telephone calls from Dupas' home while his de facto wife Iolanda Cruz was on holiday in South Africa. They discovered through Telstra records that Dupas had made calls to sex lines and managed to track down the women he had contacted by telephone. These calls proved most revealing. One woman, whose name is not required here, gave police details of how she worked as a sex and fantasy talker and, in particular, of one extremely disturbing call.

The woman said in her statement: "I decided to ring about an advertisement (in the *Herald Sun*) for fantasy phone work. I rang the number advertised and spoke to a person named (name given) ... She gave me a pin number which was my personal pin number. I recorded a message introducing myself. How the system would work was that a caller would call a 1900 number and that would get them through to a switchboard. They could either listen to the recorded messages from employees like myself, punch in my pin number if they knew it from talking to me previously or speak to one of the operators who would put the caller through to me ...

"Calls could only be put through to me if it was logged on to the system. I would do this by ringing and logging on by a set procedure. When I was logged on I could receive phone calls from callers on my home phone ... When I received a call I was to time the length of the call and send an invoice to (the company) and they would pay me. At some stage I had the phone set up so that it had two different rings. One ring would be identified as being from (the company) and the other could be identified as being a personal call. I didn't use my real name ... I never gave out my address or home phone number."

The woman told police she worked for this company for 12-16 months before taking a job with a different sex call company. She said that during her time with this company she had only three callers who worried her. The woman said one of the callers wanted to talk about how he wanted to have sex with his sister and that he watched her in the shower. Then, when he started to give details, she hung up on him. A second caller told the woman how he had had sex with his daughter.

She also told police of a caller who was "horrible". She added: "He was scary ... he talked about his mum and called her a bitch." Then, when the woman told him she was 45, he said he wanted to talk with someone more than 50 and hung up.

He called back some time later and the woman this time told him she was 55 years of age and the conversation, in the woman's statement, went as follows:

Caller: "Do you know what I did to the bitch?"

Woman: "Who?"

Caller: "My mother, the bitch."

The woman told police she was about to say something in reply when the man, whom she described as having a "mean voice" and sounded angry, said something about her (his mother's) neck.

She added: "It was scary. He said something about his hand and pressing on her neck. He also said that he cut down and across the breast. He said he cut across the nipple. I'm sure he never said both breasts and nipples. I don't know if he mentioned which side. At this stage his voice changed and his breathing was different. He liked the blood. You could tell he liked it. When he spoke about the blood he breathed differently and sounded excited, like he was aroused. He said the term 'cut down' twice but I can't remember what it was in relation to this. This made me scared. He then said, 'How does that make you feel?'" The woman hung up.

Terrifyingly, the man called back and told her: "Listen, don't hang up. I know where you live and who you are."

The woman added in her statement: "I was petrified. He said something about me or the house where I lived and he was right. I can't remember what it was but it scared me."

The woman continued: "He said something about her eyes. I don't remember his exact words but he said something about looking at her eyes. Then he said something about putting the steel down her stomach and then he grabbed her hair. When he said he cut her hair he had an angry, hateful tone in his voice. He was talking about pubic hair. I know this because of what he said next. But I don't remember what was said next.

"Any time I tried to speak he got angry and his voice got deeper. He said something about the blood again and was really excited. He said something about blood on him, but I can't remember what he said. The blood was from the nipple. I thought he was getting aroused and masturbating. I thought this because of his voice. He said something about lots of blood. He also said that he fucked her with the blade. He made some comments about the shape of her vagina. I don't remember what term he used but he referred to it as 'pussy'. He said something about her stomach. I don't think he cut her stomach but there was something he said about her stomach and not something he had done to her stomach. This disturbed me; it made her seem like a real person."

Significantly, the woman said in her statement: "He never said the word knife. He either used the word steel or blade. I called him a sick prick and hung up. I picked up the receiver and he was still there. He called me an old cunt." The disgusted and distraught woman then pulled the plug from the wall. She rang the call centre and told them she was not prepared to talk with the caller any more, but was told the man had pre-paid for 30 minutes and that she had to take the call. She refused and the call taker said she would finish the call.

Police also tracked calls Dupas had made to a licensed escort agency which had advertised its services in several newspapers, including the *Northcote Leader*. The proprietor was asked whether she had heard of a Peter Dupas or had taken a booking from him. The woman told police she did not know of a man named Dupas, but when she checked her records there was no doubt bookings had been made from Dupas' home in Pascoe Vale in December, 2000.

There also were calls, from Dupas' home, to a Tarot card reader who had advertised through local newspapers from March to May, 1999. The advertisement said: "If you want to find direction in your life, then call (name and number)." Only one phone number was given, with no address and the woman who advertised took several calls about Tarot card reading, but more women than men.

The woman recalled that she received a call from a male one afternoon and suggested "this male sounded fairly quiet, softly spoken and polite". She added: "He told me he was ringing me about my ad for the Tarot readings and he wanted to know how they could help him. My standard answer was that it could let him know what energies and possibilities are around him so he can make an informed decision about what he wants to do."

This brief explanation led to the caller discussing relationships with women as he had difficulties with these and could she help him. The woman continued in her statement: "I told him that he should be going out and meeting people in a non-threatening environment.

I suggested that he go out with friends and meet women that way." The woman then said the caller gave her his name, but she could not remember it.

She added: "After I suggested he meet women through friends, I thought he started to become insecure in the way he sounded. What made me think this way was the tone of his voice and his obvious persistence in telling me he wanted me to help him meet women. At this stage he began asking me if he can come and talk to me."

This was eerily reminiscent of the Nicole Patterson case in April, 1999, but this time no appointment was made. Instead, the woman said in her statement: "It was around this time that I told him that he should begin counselling if this was such a big issue with him. I began to think that this call was not about Tarot card readings and that this male would be expecting something else from me if he met with me. When I suggested counselling to this man, he told me that he was actually seeing someone already and they weren't helping him or that they weren't giving him what he wanted."

These comments were highly significant as Dupas was willing to change tack to suit his needs. He was trying to manipulate the woman and psychologists contend that one of the traits of psychopaths is the ability to manipulate people to get what they want.

The woman continued: "He then started specifically saying to me that he wanted to be alone with me, and that it was those comments that got me worried. He began telling me that he needed to overcome his fear and nervousness of having a woman touch him." By now the alarm bells were ringing even louder and, wisely, the woman said: "I suggested he go out and get a professional massage for himself." The woman gave him a number and address for a medical clinic and was asked "who it was?" who would give the massage. She replied that she didn't know.

Finally, the woman said: "This man again requested that he come and see me and I told him that I didn't think that a Tarot reading was what he needed. He then asked me if he could call me back if he needed and I told him 'no'. Even though this man never asked for any sexual favours, that was definitely the impression that I got by the way the conversation went. It was about the time that the conversation ended."

Police were able to trace these phone calls to Dupas' home and the call to the sex talker was particularly relevant because the caller talked of mutilating a breast and, as police knew, there were only two recorded breast mutilation murders in Australia over more than a decade — in the killings of Nicole Patterson and Margaret Maher.

Police were trying to learn more of Dupas' private life and, in particular, his sexual drives. They spoke with what normally would be described as friends. In reality, however, Dupas was such a loner that it would be more accurate to describe them as acquaintances.

One of these "friends" was carpenter John Saward, who said he had first met Dupas late in 1996 or early 1997 when he was a supervisor in the carpentry shop of a Salvation Army centre in Brunswick. The workshop was used to help in rehabilitation for people of different backgrounds; they were taught new trades and skills and, hopefully, could return to mainstream society.

No one needed rehabilitation more than Dupas, who had been in and out of jail for most of his adult life through one conviction after another for sexual offences. Dupas had been interviewed in Pentridge about his future and, on release, went to the Salvation Army carpentry shop under Saward's supervision. And he did well, as he liked working with wood and had made children's toys while in Pentridge. Saward also liked making toys and, in his statement to police, said: "We sort of clicked and an association grew."

Dupas spent about nine months under Saward's supervision before finding employment with a furniture manufacturing company in Fairfield and although this job lasted just a few weeks, the sex offender continued his interest in woodwork. After moving into the Coane Street, Pascoe Vale, address with Iolanda Cruz,

Dupas continued making furniture, shelving, CD stands, coffee tables and planter boxes in the garage, often with Saward's help.

Saward, in his statement, told of how Dupas spoke to him about his relationship with Ms Cruz and would say: "Don't you ever say anything to her." Saward then told police that Dupas admitted Ms Cruz knew nothing about his terrible background of sexual offences.

Saward said in the statement: "Peter had never told Iolanda that he had been in jail and he had never told her of his past. I was never fully aware of his past actions, but I did know that he had been in jail for a rape and hostage type thing. I don't know why but I had always thought that the rape Peter had been in prison for related to a split-up with his wife. I thought it was a domestic-type rape."

The carpenter continued: "Apart from spending time together making furniture with Peter, I would spend time with him having a few drinks at his place or he would come to mine. Peter used to drink beer. We had a holiday together at Lake Eppalock one New Year's Eve, which I think was 1998.

"Peter never displayed a real secretiveness but on the other hand he never really told me a great deal about himself or his background. In 1997, (Saward's de facto wife) Margaret (Newman) and I had quite a bit to do with Peter and particularly when Iolanda went overseas to South Africa on a holiday. Peter was a bit more relaxed while she wasn't about because Iolanda was the boss of the partnership.

"On one occasion when Iolanda was away, I was with Margaret and Peter and we were travelling up to the First and Last Hotel in Sydney Road, Fawkner … I remember as we drove past the cemetery Peter said: 'My grandfather is buried in the cemetery somewhere.' I said: 'Do you know where?' He said: 'No, I must look one day.' I said: 'No, you don't have to. You just go to the bloke on the gate and he will look it up in the book.' Whether he did or not, I don't know. I cannot recall any other discussions with Peter about the cemetery."

This brief discussion about the cemetery and Dupas' grandfather being buried there is highly significant in context of the Mersina Halvagis murder there on November 1, 1997.

Saward, in giving police background on the Dupas he knew, told them: "The only other female (apart from Iolanda) that I am aware Peter had a relationship with was a girl who was in Larundel or some other place like that. Her name was Jenny and I had only met her once. I think that it was just a friendly relationship and I don't know whether anything happened between them."

Saward also told police of a discussion he had had with Dupas in the Coane Street house late in 1997 while Iolanda was overseas. And, in light of Margaret Maher's death, it gave some insight to what Dupas was up to around that time. Saward said: "On one occasion Peter mentioned something about taking out a prostitute or some escort girl.

"I didn't really take that much notice at the time, because he was so hyped up about it, that I thought at the time that it was rubbish. He appeared to carry on a bit so I turned off, because it appeared to me as if he was trying to show that he could in fact pull a woman. I turned off.

"About a week later he told us that he had brought some prostitute home to his place and that she was so ugly he had to chew his arm off to get out of bed. This was the terminology he used. I didn't really believe him about that either at the time. On most occasions that I went to Peter's was on a Saturday or Sunday. I am pretty sure that the comments he made about having an ugly prostitute at his house occurred on one Sunday morning."

Saward later told police in a separate statement that Dupas did not specifically mention that the woman he had taken home was a prostitute and had assumed this. He said: "It was more along the lines of him saying 'she could have been a prostitute for all I know'."

Margaret Newman also gave police information about Dupas' everyday life and, in particular, his relationship with Iolanda. She said: "Iolanda was bossy towards Peter and basically laid down the law to him. When we first met Peter, John told me that Peter had been in jail for some hostage type thing. I think Peter told John that it was his wife and it happened as part of or during their separation. It wasn't until quite some time later I found out what really happened. Peter never told Iolanda any of his past.

"Peter always came across as a nice sort of a bloke, even my father liked him and he was always usually a good judge of character. John and Peter spent time building furniture together. Occasionally they would have drinks together and on occasions I was drinking with them …

"Peter never spoke about sex much and I never knew what the relationship between Iolanda and Peter was regarding sex. I can remember that when Iolanda was overseas in 1997, John and I were at Peter's house in Coane Street and a discussion came up about women …

"It was while Iolanda was overseas that Peter started looking up ads in the paper for women. John and I were at his house in Pascoe Vale on one occasion and he asked me to listen to a recorded message of a woman that he looked up in the paper, to see what I thought she sounded like … I listened to the tape and it basically gave a description of herself and what she liked to do. It wasn't a sexual thing; it was more like a dating thing." Ms Newman also told police of the Dupas tale of bringing a woman to his home and having to "chew his arm off" the next morning.

Saward and Margaret Newman moved into a house in Melbourne's outer north-west in September, 1997, and soon after Iolanda's return from overseas stopped seeing Dupas and lost contact with him.

Meanwhile, police had collected several items from where Margaret Maher's body was found and these comprised a length of packing tape, two pieces of white paper, a piece of paper towelling, the front component of a computer, the casing or lid from a computer, a computer case, a white cardboard box containing computer components and circuitry and a piece of cardboard with silver stuck to one side. All these items were tested for fingerprints, but none were developed.

This left other items of interest, including the black glove found alongside Margaret's body and, following the police check of records for women whose breasts had been removed and coming up with only the Nicole Patterson case which involved Dupas, they now were able to subject this glove to further DNA testing.

The original DNA tests proved fruitless but, over the years, scientific research allowed more precision. The inside of the glove was sampled for any trace of DNA and when these tests produced two DNA samples, they were compared with DNA swabs taken from Dupas and a member of the public. The results indicated a mixture of DNA from at least two individuals. One matched the Dupas swab and "could not be excluded as a possible contributor to this mixture". Tests also ruled out the possibility that Margaret had worn the glove.

Forensic scientist Henry Roberts, employed by Victoria Police at the Victoria Forensic Science Centre (VFSC) and a specialist in DNA profiling, reported:

"I have carried out a statistical analysis of the DNA result that was obtained in relation to the glove. In doing so, I have considered two propositions:

"1. The biological material on the glove came from Peter Dupas and an unknown person selected at random from the Victorian Caucasian population.

"2. The biological material on the glove came from two other people selected at random from the Victorian Caucasian population.

"I estimate that the chance of the match would be at least four hundred and fifty thousand (450,000) times greater if the biological material on the glove came from Peter Dupas ... and an unknown person selected at random from the Victorian Caucasian population, than if it came from two other people selected at random from the Victorian Caucasian population."

He concluded:

"In my opinion, this evidence, when considered in isolation from other information, provides very strong support for the proposition that the biological material on the glove came from Peter Dupas ... and an unknown person selected at random from the Victorian Caucasian population."

Bingo! Police again had their man and the DNA evidence pointed to the fact that Dupas, the monster who had murdered and mutilated Nicole Patterson, was the man responsible for killing Margaret Maher.

But police wanted more evidence, and again turned to science, this time having another forensic scientist examine the cuts made to Margaret's clothing and then making a comparison with the clothing worn by Nicole. These examinations were conducted by Jane Taupin, also from the VFSC and a specialist in biological trace evidence. In her statement to police, Ms Taupin said the discipline in which she specialised included analysis of damage to clothing. And that she had won awards for this type of work.

Ms Taupin said in her statement that, on February 27, 2001, she received the clothing Margaret had been wearing on the night she was killed — a jacket, a windcheater, a T-shirt, a pair of leggings or ribbed tights and a pair of socks. She reported that no damage was detected to the jacket, the leggings or the socks, but reported significant damage to the windcheater.

The report indicated: "The windcheater was lilac in colour, fleecy lined and composed of a knitted material. It was heavily stained, predominantly to the upper right and right side. There was a cut that completely severed the centre front of the windcheater. This cut consisted of scissor cut actions that commenced from the neckband and terminated through the hemline. Features of the cuts showed that a pair of sharp, smooth-bladed scissors with medium to long blades produced the severance."

Of the T-shirt Ms Taupin reported almost identical cuts: "The T-shirt was lilac in colour, had short sleeves and was composed of a knitted material. It was heavily stained, predominantly to the upper right and right side. There was a cut that completely severed the centre of the T-shirt. This cut consisted of scissor cut actions that commenced from the neckband and terminated through the hemline. Features of the cuts showed that a pair of sharp, smooth-bladed scissors with medium to long blades produced the severance.

"The cutting of the windcheater and the T-shirt together in the one action by the one implement was considered the most feasible scenario. The approximate alignment of the severed edges, the changes in direction and the neatness of the severed edges supported this proposition."

Ms Taupin, in her statement, then made a comparison with Nicole's clothing and, in her conclusion, reported:

"There were scissor cuts detected to the windcheater and the T-shirt of Margaret Maher. These cuts were similar in profile to the scissor cuts detected in the clothing of Nicole Patterson. All scissor cuts appeared specific in purpose. Directionality of these scissor cuts was similar in both cases. Scissor cuts to the clothing of the deceased are an unusual and outstanding feature. There is little if any peer-reviewed forensic literature on this phenomenon."

Again, bingo! Police now had enough information to question Dupas about the Margaret Maher murder.

But there was more, much more, in the way of comparison. In addition to Ms Taupin's examination of the clothing worn by Nicole Patterson and Margaret Maher, forensic pathologist Dr David Ranson also was asked to review the injury patterns. Detective Senior Constable Scarlett particularly asked him to provide a specialist report examining the injuries present on the bodies of both women. Vastly experienced in forensic pathology Dr Ransom, with multiple credentials and the Deputy Director of the Victorian Institute of Forensic Medicine, had not carried out the original autopsy and was provided with autopsy reports and police photographs.

After describing how Margaret's body was found by the side of the road and noting how her upper clothing was pulled up, he reported, with some biological terminology:

"The most striking pathological feature of this case was the excision of the left breast in its distal part with a series of mixed linear incised and abraded wounds present running horizontally over the upper part of the proximal right breast and lying partly through a tattoo of a butterfly. The excised portion of the left breast was found in the mouth of the deceased and the excised portion of the breast showed an incised injury of L-shaped configuration in the region of the nipple."

Dr Ranson also reported on several "linear and patchy, blotchy abrasions" over the body, with a "moderate number of abrasions over the back of the buttocks". He also commented on the cut to the left wrist and "abraded injuries" to the hands and forearm and marks on the right side of the neck. There also was the wound to the head, just above the right eyebrow and an area of haemorrhage to the right side of the larynx.

In particular relation to the breast injury, Dr Ranson noted: "Examination of the wound edges of the excised portion of left breast and residual breast tissue on the trunk of the body reveals a number of dogged attacks of skin giving the edges of the excised portion of the breast a saw-tooth appearance. This particular feature is very characteristic of excision of skin with the use of a sawing motion of a sharp object such as a knife.

"The series of horizontal incised abraded wounds in the upper part of the residual breast on the left shows characteristics of tentative or initial cuts prior to the main excising actions. The directionality of the skin flaps associated with the horizontal incision abrasions is in keeping with the horizontal nature of the cutting action that removed the breast, which I believe started at the top of the breast and moved downwards through the mid-breast tissue ...

"It is notable that apart from the incised wound to the left nipple in the excision portion of breast that was found within the mouth there are no other obvious injuries to the nipple or central region of the distal left breast. This is in direct contrast to the right breast which has not been excised."

He concluded on his examination of the Margaret Maher injuries: "Whilst the front of the chest may be a region that is subject to injury in a number of assaults where incised weapons are used, the focus on the breasts in particular is a striking feature of this case and the degree of focus of breast damage with specific removal of the breast in a manner and fashion that is unrelated to the probable mechanisms of death in my experience is particularly unusual."

Police interviewed Dupas at their St Kilda Road headquarters on August 6, 2001, just three days after his appeal on his conviction on the Nicole Patterson murder had been dismissed. The interview was conducted by Detective Inspector Greg Hough, Detective Sergeants Philip Shepherd and Michael Daley and, after being cautioned, Dupas was asked why he was shaking, but replied that he was "fine". When asked if he was expecting to be questioned over Margaret's murder, he replied: "Nuh. Nuh." Dupas also was asked whether he had access to the news, on television and in newspapers, and replied that he had heard the news from his solicitor that his appeal had been dismissed. Then, asked if this was a "bit of a kick to you", he answered "yes" and indicated that he might take his case to the High Court of Australia.

Before touching on the Margaret Maher case, detectives asked Dupas about a letter he had written earlier in his life of criminal sexual deviation. The letter in part read: "I feel that I'm not fully confident within myself and there is a possibility that I could re-offend at a later date." It also read: "I have no desire to be launched like a time bomb back into the community uncured. Once again, I can't stress how important it is not only to me, but surely the whole community that this doesn't happen, and I'm given the opportunity to work on my problem."

Dupas said he could not remember writing this and gave no audible reply when asked if the letter was in his handwriting, but admitted he had identified a problem and had sought treatment. Asked if this treatment had helped him, Dupas replied: "I do, yeah."

At this stage of the interview Dupas indicated that he believed Inspector Hough was "beating around the bush" and being sly. The police officer denied this and told Dupas he wanted to be up-front with him and not play games. Dupas replied: "The shit — you know — you know that the questions you're going to ask me, you've got them written down." Inspector Hough indicated he had certain questions he wanted to ask and expressed the hope Dupas would not get anxious.

The interview then turned specifically to events leading up to Margaret's murder and, in particular, phone calls made from Dupas' Pascoe Vale home, but Dupas refused to comment even when asked the simple question of whether a particular phone number was his.

He then was told: "The records indicate that on the 28th of September, 1997, your telephone contacted a telephone number for one minute and 20 seconds. Do you have any knowledge of this?"

"No comment."

Q: "Enquiries conducted reveal that the telephone number was advertised in the adult services section of the *Leader* newspaper distributed in the Pascoe Vale area in 1997. Were you aware of that fact?"

A: "No comment."

Q: "These advertisements stated a female name and it also had a comment similar to: 'Young female, blonde hair' along with a phone number and a PCA number. Are you aware of what a PCA number is?"

A: "No comment."

Q: "The PCA number is a Prostitution Control Authority number allocated to sexual service providers, such as prostitutes. This indicates to me that the advertisement relates to a prostitute. Do you have any comment?"

A: "No comment."

Dupas also was asked whether he had called the relevant number or even called a prostitute, but refused to comment. The detectives then shifted their attention to whether Dupas had shopped at the Bi-Lo supermarket where Margaret had been on the night of her death and whether he had been to Cliffords Road. Again, Dupas refused to comment.

Dupas then was asked: "Do you own any gloves?"

"No comment."

Q: "Do you know a lady by the name of Margaret Maher?"

A: "No comment."

Q: "Have you ever met her?"

A: "No comment."

Q: "Excuse me. The body of Margaret Maher was found on Saturday, the fourth of October, 1997, and she was located laying in Cliffords Road in Somerton. Miss Maher had her breasts (sic) severed in exactly the same manner as Nicole Patterson. Do you have any knowledge of that?"

A: "No comment."

Q: "Now, in regards to Nicole Patterson, she had both her breasts severed of which you've been convicted of her murder and in this case, the breasts (sic) were severed exactly the same. Do you have any knowledge of this murder?"

A: "No comment."

Q: "Have you had any involvement whatsoever in the murder of Margaret Maher?"

A: "No comment."

The interview then was adjourned and Dupas was asked if he would like a cup of tea or go to the toilet. He needed neither and, when the interviews resumed, Dupas again was asked questions about whether he was aware of the Cliffords Road area or whether he had been there. He even was shown a photograph of the area, but still refused to comment.

The interview then turned again to the question of the black glove found near Margaret's body.

Q: "Miss Maher was located in long grass beside the road. Now, located beside her was a glove which isn't — doesn't appear all that well in that photo, so we'll show you the glove that was located beside her and I'll ask you to comment on the glove. That's the glove located beside Miss Maher. Is that your glove?"

A: "No comment."

Q:"Have you ever seen that glove before?"

A: "No comment."

Q: "Have you ever worn that glove before?"

A: "No comment."

Q: "Could you give me any reason why that glove would be located next to Miss Maher's body?"

*No audible reply.*

Q: "Could you give a reason?

A: "No comment."

Q: "Miss Maher was a prostitute and I've obtained statements from associates of yours who have informed me that you commented on one occasion of having a female home to your place which you thought may have been a prostitute. Do you wish to make any comment about that?"

A: "No comment."

Q: "OK. And this — this incident — Margaret Maher's murder occurred a short time after your partner, Iolanda Cruz, left to go to South Africa in 1997. The phone call to the prostitute which I have said occurred within approximately three days from your partner going overseas, and that's the time sequence. Your partner goes on — I think it was the 21st of September. Within a couple of days, you're seeking prostitutes, and within a couple of days Margaret Maher is located murdered in Cliffords Road, Somerton. Can you understand why I believe you're the murderer of Margaret Maher."

A: "No comment."

Q: "The injuries that are inflicted to Margaret, or were inflicted to Margaret, are so similar to the injuries inflicted in the murder of Miss Patterson that a check of records Australia-wide has revealed that they're the only two on record in Australia. Would you like to comment on that?"

A: "No comment."

Q: "Can you understand why just based on that I believe you're the murderer of Margaret Maher?"

A: "No comment."

Dupas then was warned he could be charged with the murder of Margaret Maher and was asked if he wanted to say anything in regards to that issue. He replied "no". Dupas also said he did not wish to make a statement. The interview was adjourned again, with

Dupas being told: "We'll come back in and we'll discuss with you some of the other issues that we want to discuss, OK, and give you the right of option to either participate, as I said from the start, or exercise your rights and say nothing." There was no audible reply.

On resumption of the interview, Dupas said he would like a coffee and, after this was provided, there were further questions, mainly concerning the computer parts found near Margaret's body. He was asked whether his partner, Iolanda, owned a computer and whether he placed the computer parts at the scene where the body was found. Dupas refused to comment and said again that he did not wish to make a statement. Detective Inspector Hough finally told Dupas that the police wanted him to agree to have buccal (saliva) swabs taken. He was asked: "Do you consent to the forensic procedure?" Dupas replied "yes".

The interview was terminated and Dupas was interviewed at police headquarters again, on October 2, 2002. After collecting all the relevant information in the Margaret Maher case, three detectives — Detective Sergeant Michael Daley, Detective Senior Constables Paul Scarlett and Kelvin Gale — collected Dupas from prison and, in an unmarked police car, drove him to the Melbourne Magistrate's Court where they successfully made application for a court order to interview him. This was granted at about 10.55am and Dupas was then taken to St Kilda Road to be interviewed. He was asked whether he wanted to communicate with a legal practitioner, friend or relative and replied "not at this stage".

The police asked several preliminary questions, including age and whether he was an Australian citizen and Dupas answered these questions without any hesitation. Detective Sergeant Daley then asked specific questions about Margaret's murder, starting with the interview on August 6, 2001:

Q: "On that occasion you answered 'no comment' to all the questions put to you?"

A: "No comment."

Q: "All right. We have further information that's come to hand since that date and we intend to further interview you about that today. OK. So, if I could just paint the picture. I'll just let — inform you that on Saturday, the fourth of October, 1997, the body of Margaret Maher was located on the side of the road, at Cliffords Road, Somerton. Are you aware of that location?"

A: "No comment."

Q: "An examination of her body revealed that she's been assaulted prior to her death, and that her left breast had been severed and placed in her mouth. Are you aware of the details of that death?"

A: "No comment."

Q: "Certain items were located at the scene of the location of her body. And one of the item (sic), in particular, which we intend to talk to you about today is the glove. Now, Senior Detective Scarlett is just going to remove that item here now and show it to you. Have you ever seen that glove before?"

A: "No comment."

Q: "Do you know who owns that glove?"

A: "No comment."

Q: "And were you — or, like, in the area of Cliffords Road, Somerton, around October, 1997?"

A: "No comment."

Q: "I'll just ask you again whether you recognise that glove?"

A: "No comment."

Q: "OK, put it away now. Let's get the photos. I'm just going to show a couple of photos, Peter. These photos are taken at the location of the body in Cliffords Road, Somerton. I'll just show you a photo here that depicts the deceased Margaret Maher lying in the grass with some other items lying around next to her. Do you have any comment to make about that?"

A: "No comment."

Q: "I have some close-up views taken from those photos. One you can recognise is the rear buttocks area of the deceased. Sorry, the back area, and — and if you can recognise that, Peter. That's the back of the deceased as they're from a different angle. That computer part or casing, is that there — do you recognise any part of that there?"

A: "No comment."

Q: "I'll just point out to you there, Peter, in the grass is the black woollen glove. Do you have any comment to make about that?"

A: "No comment."

Q: "And I'll just informing (sic) you that that black glove that Detective Scarlett just showed you was actually located at this position, next to the deceased's body. Do you have any comment to make about that?"

A: "No comment."

Dupas' voice was so low and so soft that the detective had to repeat this last question but the reply again was "no comment".

Q: "I'll just show you a different photo taken from a different angle; there's the buttocks area of the deceased, and the glove as well. Do you have any comment to make about that?"

A: "No comment."

Detective Sergeant Daley then moved on to the enormous significance of the DNA tests from this black glove.

Q: "Is it correct, Peter, that on the sixth of August, 2001, you were interviewed by investigators here?"

A: "No comment."

Q: "And on that occasion, you were asked to supply a forensic sample, being a mouth swab. Do you recall that?"

A: "No comment."

Q: "Do you recall that you actually consented to supplying a sample of your saliva and a mouth scraping, for the purpose of analysis?"

A: "No comment."

Q: "And, in fact, on the seventh of August, 2001, investigators attended Port Phillip Prison and spoke to you there. Do you have any comment to make about that?"

A: "No comment."

Q: "And, at that location, you supplied a mouth scraping or a mouth swab. Do you recall that?"

A: "No comment."

Q: "In relation to that mouth swab, Peter, a scientific analysis has been conducted on your — the mouth scraping taken of you. Do you understand that?"

A: "No comment."

Q: "And that DNA was located on that mouth scraping from you. Do you have any comment to make about that?"

A: "No comment."

Q: "I also put it to you, Peter, that the glove that we've spoken about, that was located next to Margaret Maher, has also been scientifically examined. And that traces of DNA were located on that item as well. Do you have any comment to make about this?"

A: "No comment."

Q: "That — that item — I have here in front of me a statement … by Nigel Hall, who is a forensic scientist at the Victorian State Forensic Science Centre, and he has conducted that analysis and located the DNA on the glove. Now, on the glove, there was (sic) two samples of DNA located. Do you have any comment to make about these?"

A: "No comment."

Q: "And Nigel Hall states that, in very basic terms, that he cannot exclude you as one of the DNA sources on that glove. Do you have any comment to make about that?"

A: "No comment."

Q: "Can you explain to me, Peter, how your DNA could come to be on that glove?"

A: "No comment."

Q: "I also have a statement here by a scientist, Henry Roberts, who is also employed at the Victorian Forensic Science Centre. And he has conducted a statistical analysis on the results of Mr Hall's scientific examination. And I'll just inform you that Henry Roberts has concluded that the chance of your DNA and the DNA on the glove is at least 450,000 times greater, sorry, the chance of the DNA on the glove is 450,000 times more likely to be that of yours than if it were to be a person selected randomly from the Victorian Caucasian population. Do you understand what that means?"

A: "No comment."

Q: "I'll just explain it to you, anyway. It's 450,000 times more likely that the DNA on the glove is yours, than any other Caucasian person randomly selected from the Victorian population. Do you have any comment to make on that?"

Dupas' heart must have sunk on this information as the odds were enormous, even if not nearly as great as the 6.53 billion to one in the Nicole Patterson case. Regardless, it was stunning evidence and the stony-faced Dupas merely replied parrot-like "no comment".

Q: "The conclusion of that analysis is that it's more than likely that that DNA on the glove is from you. Do you have any comment on that?"

A: "No comment."

The police at that point suspended the interview and arranged for Dupas to have a coffee. The break was to allow the police to set up a video to show Dupas. The time on resumption was 12.41pm, meaning there was a break of just over a quarter of an hour. The interviewing detectives again reminded Dupas of his rights and continued:

Q: "All right. We just had a short break there where it was arranged for a video playback facility and getting a video tape ready. Do you agree that, in that time, neither myself, Detective Scarlett or any other investigators have interviewed you in relation to any matters whilst the video has been switched off?"

A: "Yes."

The interviewing detective then told Dupas they were playing the crime scene video of when Margaret Maher's body was found.

Q: "That's Cliffords Road, Somerton. Do you recognise that area at all?"

A: "No comment."

Q: "That's the body of Margaret Maher lying on the grass. Do you have any comment to make about that?"

A: "No comment."

Q: "Do you know that woman?"

A: "No comment."

Dupas was shown the glove on video, but refused to comment and, the video completed, the interview concluded. Senior

Detective Scarlett then told Dupas in terms familiar with anyone who has seen a detective thriller on TV or at the movies:

"Peter, you're going to be charged with the murder of Margaret Maher. You are not obliged to say or do anything unless you wish to do so, but whatever you say or do may be recorded and given in evidence. Do you understand that, Peter?"

Dupas merely replied "yes" before being asked: "Do you wish to make a further comment to the charge?" He replied: "Nuh." The interview was wound up at 1.23pm with Dupas on another charge of murder.

Significantly, police deliberately waited until after the coroner's inquest into Margaret Maher's death to charge Dupas with her murder. As Scarlett explained: "We knew before the inquest that we had enough evidence to charge Dupas, but waited because there was so much public interest in Margaret's death that it would have been unfair to him to prejudice any future trial. We played it straight down the line."

# CHAPTER EIGHT

# A Second Murder Trial

A committal hearing was heard in the Melbourne Magistrate's Court late in 2003, but four days later magistrate Mr Phillip Goldberg dismissed the case, indicating there was not enough evidence for Dupas to face trial for Margaret Maher's murder. Prosecutor Michele Williams SC was so upset with this decision she went straight to the office of the Director of Public Prosecutions, Mr Paul Coghlan QC, to suggest Dupas face trial regardless. Mr Coghlan made an almost instant decision in calling his personal assistant to arrange a press conference to announce that Dupas would go to trial a second time on a murder charge.

The *Herald Sun* of September 6 reported: "Magistrate Phillip Goldberg ordered the murder charge against Dupas, 50, be dropped because there was not enough evidence to suggest Ms Maher had been murdered.

"Pathologist Matthew Lynch had told the court he could not separate drug toxicity, heart disease and subtle neck compression as the cause of Maher's death. But the Office of Public Prosecutions will present Dupas directly to the Supreme Court for trial later this year."

Dupas' trial for the murder of Margaret Maher opened in the Victorian Supreme Court on July 26, 2004. It was held before Justice Stephen Kaye, who had been appointed to the bench in December the previous year. A fine legal scholar, he was following a family tradition as his father William (Bill) also had been on the bench. Kaye had been dux of Scotch College in 1968, had graduated from Monash University in 1974 with first class honours and, after being admitted to the bar in 1976, became vastly experienced in civil law, personal injury and medical negligence, commercial law, defamation and criminal law. He was appointed a Queen's Counsel in 1991.

The prosecution remained in the capable hands of Ms Williams, a graduate of Monash University after earlier leaving school at 15 and then studying part-time for her HSC. Ms Williams' path to silk was extraordinary as she had worked in an office on leaving school, was married at 18 and had three children before she even started studying law, at 22.

Ms Williams originally continued her studies in an effort to qualify for a teaching course and, after nominating for 10 tertiary preferences, achieved such high marks that she was eligible to study for a combined law/arts course at Monash. After seeking family advice, Ms Williams decided that studying for a legal career was too good an opportunity to reject, so took a year's leave to have her third child and was breast-feeding between lectures and tutorials in her first year of legal studies.

This remarkable woman then carved a career for herself as a leading barrister before accepting a position as a member of the Department of Public Prosecutions legal team and she now is regarded as one of the bar's most revered counsels.

Dupas' defence counsel was James Montgomery, a vastly experienced barrister who would have found the weight of evidence against his client telling in the extreme.

Ms Williams told the Supreme Court it was the prosecution case that the evidence would indicate the same man had murdered Nicole Patterson and Margaret Maher. "We say the cutting of the breasts is so unique as to effectively be a signature, a stamp," she told the court. "The person who cut off Nicole Patterson's breasts is the same person who cut off the breast of Margaret Maher, and the same person who killed Margaret Maher. They are all one in the same person, and that is Peter Dupas."

Basically, the prosecution case was that Dupas murdered Margaret by grabbing her around the throat and, after her death, removed her left breast and placed it in her mouth. Ms Williams said DNA evidence linked Dupas to both women. In Nicole's case, there was the blood-stained jacket and, in Margaret's case, the glove carrying biological material matching Dupas left next to Margaret's body. She also said it was fanciful to suggest Ms Maher just dropped dead and something was done later to cut off her breast.

The actual cause of death was important as pathologist Dr Matthew Lynch indicated that there were multiple possibilities — strangulation, drug toxicity and heart disease — or a combination of all three.

Dr Lynch indicated there was bruising to Margaret's neck and to muscles adjacent to the thyroid cartilage, caused by pressure. It was critically important to the prosecution case that the pressure on the throat had caused or at least contributed significantly to Margaret's death.

A total of 51 witnesses gave evidence, but Dupas elected not to go into the witness box. Ms Williams later explained this was probably because he "got carved up" in giving evidence in the Nicole Patterson trial. There were few surprises in the trial on the Margaret Maher murder, but Ms Williams felt it necessary to go into many of the specific details when summarising the Crown case.

After reminding the jury that its task represented a "serious duty", Ms Williams explained that each piece of evidence presented by the Crown was relevant. She said: "Each piece of evidence adds up. So it is not a case of looking at one piece of evidence in isolation. This case is effectively what is called a circumstantial case. That is, you look at pieces of evidence as they add up together." Ms Williams then explained that she would go through some of the evidence in her summary, starting with the acts "that caused the death", then the "intention" and, thirdly, about "who did this".

The Crown prosecutor told the jury that the first issue was the "act or acts that caused the death of Margaret Maher". Ms Williams said: "Dr Lynch had said when he gave what is considered the cause of death, he said he couldn't elevate three possible causes of death. You remember he talked about drug toxicity, he talked about heart or natural disease and he talked about the neck compression. His evidence effectively is three possible causes of death and he couldn't elevate one or the other of those."

Ms Williams, after referring to much of the evidence concerning Margaret's last known movements, admitted she could not produce an eye witness who could claim "I saw what happened", but stated the jury had to look at the circumstances in which the body was discovered.

She said: "It is clear that there was human involvement. That is, she is found at the side of the road in long grass … You will recall the evidence of Senior Constable Huygen who said that her body had been placed there, the legs apart, and then rolled over. That was his view because the grass was between her legs … Clearly someone has done this to her; she doesn't get this way herself. It is clear she was dumped, we say, with the computer parts scattered around her and the box put over her. Again, someone has done that to her. That somebody, we say, is Dupas … And the glove, of course, which I shall come to as a separate argument, was there. It was there with the other items."

Ms Williams added that the evidence was overwhelming that the body had been dumped in the long grass and it "defied common sense" that she (Margaret Maher) just dropped dead there … somebody had placed things around her."

The prosecutor also asked the jury to look at the injuries inflicted, starting with the one to the right eyebrow. Ms Williams said: "Clearly that is an injury that has occurred whilst she was alive … well, did she cause it herself? Well, it is not cleaned up, is it? Again, what I am suggesting to you is you don't look at things in isolation; you look at them as all adding up together."

She continued: "The next piece of evidence is the wrist. You will recall the incised injury to the wrist. Dr Lynch said that is consistent with a knife and that injury occurred around the time of death. He wasn't quite sure; he said it was a peri-mortem type injury, around the time of death, again inflicted by somebody.

"Then you look at the neck compression. Again I am saying to you, you add up all these circumstantial pieces of evidence up together. You don't look at them alone, you look at them together; that is what a circumstantial case is.

"Look at the neck compression. Again she has been alive when that was inflicted on her. There was bruising, bleeding. So all of those acts done to her or inflicted upon her, the Crown says, while she is alive. That is what the evidence suggests."

Ms Williams then turned to the breast mutilation when she told the jury: "Then you look at the post-mortem, that is after death, injury; that is, the excision of the left breast. What, does somebody come along after she has dropped dead of a heart attack or drugs and says, 'I can see somebody here and I will take her breast off and I will throw some cartons over her', and so forth. The argument is illogical and it just defies common sense. It is fanciful and that's why I have been submitting to you and urging you — use your common sense."

Ms Williams also told the jury it was "fanciful" and defied common sense to think that the injuries were not done by the same person. Then, after running through much of Dr Lynch's evidence, she continued: "When you look at the whole of the evidence, the substantial cause of death, clearly we say it is a combination of the injuries, but in particular the pressure to the neck."

The prosecuting counsel then moved on to what she termed "the second element of murder" — intent. Ms Williams again insisted that the jury again would be looking at circumstantial evidence and specifically referred to the removal of Margaret's breast.

Ms Williams told the jury: "Cutting off the breast is such a vile, sinister, hostile act that you might well think the person that did that has such a hostile intent that when you consider all the other acts together, in particular the compression of the neck, that that person was intending to kill Margaret Maher or to at the very least inflict very serious injury. It does not bespeak of accident or any other more innocent explanation. The scene itself does not bespeak of an innocent bystander just happening along.

"Again, looking at the chain of reasoning, the acts, when you look at them, the whole of the circumstances, the dumping of the body, the piecing things over, these acts altogether bespeak of an intention to kill or, at the very least, to cause really serious injury, the Crown says. So again, it is from your point, it is analysing the evidence in a practical and common sense way."

Ms Williams again touched on the important question of intent and told the jury: "I understand His Honour will direct you on the lesser charge of manslaughter (the possibility of which the jury had to take into account). I will deal with it now because it is appropriate to do so. But first of all, to get to that stage you would have to be satisfied of the first element, beyond reasonable doubt, that is an act or acts of the accused had caused the death of Margaret Maher.

"If you then, in considering the second element, had a doubt, if you are satisfied it was him that did the acts and so forth but you had a doubt about whether he had an intention to kill or to cause really serious injury, then you might go on to consider the lesser charge of manslaughter."

After telling the jury that the trial judge would give them directions on this, Ms Williams indicated that Justice Kaye had a totally different role to her.

She said: "My argument to you is that it bespeaks of murder because if you are just considering pressure on the neck alone, that might be unlawful and a dangerous act but that is not, in my submission, what you ought do. You ought look at the other acts, the other hostile acts and look at the whole thing together and that has been the emphasis of my argument to you."

Ms Williams also told the jury she had a "third matter or issue", which she described as "identity". She said: "If you are satisfied in terms that someone caused, did an act … that caused the death of Margaret Maher and they had an intention to kill or cause really serious injury, who was this person?

"Now look at the evidence. Again this is now a circumstantial case as to who the person was and by the time I have finished my address to you you will have no doubt, I would suggest, that the person is Peter Dupas.

"First of all, you look at such things as links to Margaret Maher as the accused man — where he lived, where he worked, where he shopped. This alone, of course, is not strong evidence. It simply means that they lived, worked, shopped in close proximity.

"Contrast this with someone who lives miles away. All it means, (is) there has been an opportunity for him to have seen her, been with her in that locality. I can't go further than that because there is no evidence of that". Ms Williams, however, asked the jury to take a close look at a map — exhibit B — giving the various locations in the case.

Ms Williams then moved on to the vital question of the black glove found at the murder scene and told the jury: "Now, the Crown says that the black glove links the accused man to the crime scene and therefore links him to the crime. Where it was located was in close proximity to the body being dumped in such close proximity to the computer parts that were strewn over her and the box and so forth, that is is irresistible, I suggest to you …"

Ms Williams referred to the fact that the glove was found to contain Dupas' DNA or, as she put it, "DNA consistent with the accused man". To simplify matters for the jury, she added: "Now, scientists talk in a particular language and I have to be careful that I don't overstate the matter to you, but just let's have a look at that glove …"

The prosecuting counsel referred to the defence claim that the DNA was "dodgy" but insisted this claim went "absolutely nowhere".

Ms Williams said: "What was the dodginess? What was put? What is the reality about it? You examine the arguments that are made to you and see if they have any weight. We can stand up and shout to the cows come home, but analyse the argument. That glove was taken from the scene. It was located by Senior Constable Huygen. It was lodged and collected, packaged … and so forth. It was lodged at the Victorian Forensic Science Centre on October 6, 1999, at 3.30pm and it stayed there until it was examined by Mr Nigel Hall on August 28, 2000."

Devastatingly to Dupas' defence, Ms Williams asked: "How come Dupas' DNA is in the glove?" She added: "There was a biological mixture of at least two people. Again, deal with what's there, not what's not there or what we don't know. Deal with what we do know. At least two people, one of whom he (Mr Hall) could not exclude as being Peter Dupas …

"My argument to you is clearly it's a strong piece of evidence that links the accused man to the scene and therefore to the crime; that he wore the glove and he wore it for a good reason. He didn't want fingerprints left … My argument about this, and I'm putting it very strongly, is that you might think instead of this being dodgy DNA, that this is a very strong piece of evidence."

Ms Williams also referred to the odds of the DNA result being at least 450,000 times more likely to occur if it came from Dupas and one unknown person selected at random rather than if it came from two unknown people selected at random.

She told the jury: "My argument to you is that … the DNA evidence lends support to the Crown proposition that the accused man was the killer; it lends support for the identity issue."

Ms Williams also referred to what is known legally as "similar fact evidence", but warned the jury that it could not assume that because it had been proven that Dupas had killed and murdered Nicole Patterson it could not be a consequence that he also had murdered and mutilated Margaret Maher. "You are not allowed to reason that way," she said.

Instead, Ms Williams told the jury: "The argument, in a way, is a simple one. The argument goes this way: the removal of a breast post-mortem is such an unusual feature that … it is compelling to say that the person who mutilated Nicole Patterson, being Peter Dupas, is the same person who mutilated Margaret Maher."

Ms Williams went through the evidence relating to the unique features of the mutilations and referred to the expertise of pathologist Professor Ranson, who said the most striking feature in the Margaret Maher case was the position of the left breast. She said: "Now, when he's talking about the focus on the breast he explained the difference between someone who maybe is a person stabbing somebody else or they are injuring them or it's accidental, that sort of thing, as distinct from the direct focus of someone mutilating or excising a breast …

"The removal of a breast is a particularly unusual feature in his experience — a pathologist of many years' standing. And the removal, he said, of a breast after death is a distinctively unusual feature."

Ms Williams continued: "Remember Professor Ranson gave the evidence of them both (the breasts of the two women) being cut off in the same way? The jagged sawtooth edge." In this respect she rejected the defence suggestion of a "copycat" mutilation as having "no basis whatsoever", largely because of one simple fact. Margaret Maher was murdered in 1997, while Nicole Patterson was murdered in 1999 and no details of the removal of Margaret's breast was made public until 2000.

The prosecutor added: "He (Professor Ranson) has been involved as an investigating pathologist in homicide cases in Australia and in the United Kingdom and he's never seen this before." She said the pathologist, as part of his profession, exchanged information with colleagues around the world and "they've never seen it before, apparently".

Ms Williams submitted that the removal of breasts was "a rare and unusual feature" and that, in the 3723 Australian homicide cases from 1989 to 2000 the only filed case involving breast removal was that of Nicole Patterson.

Ms Williams concluded by insisting that Dupas was the one who had mutilated Nicole Patterson after he had killed her and "he is the one who mutilated Margaret Maher in almost identical fashion.

"Mr Foreman, ladies and gentlemen of the jury, I thank you for your time, your concentration and the task that you have ahead of you, and in my submission to you there is only one verdict in this trial, and that is Peter Dupas is guilty of the murder of Margaret Maher. Thank you, Your Honour."

The evidence, both circumstantial and scientific, seemed particularly damning, but Ms Williams later insisted no prosecutor could be confident of which way a jury would react. "The only confidence I felt was that we, as a prosecution team, had done our best in this particular case. We did as much as we could.

"To put this in layman's terms, this was a trial within a trial as we had to present what is known as 'similar fact evidence' and there was considerable reference to the Nicole Patterson case and what had occurred in the severance of breasts."

This particular aspect of the trial was vital, but was so distressing to Nicole's mother, Mrs O'Donnell, she had to leave the court when a video of the Northcote murder scene was played in court. However, she was among those who relished the jury's verdict, on August 11, 2004.

The *Herald Sun* the next day ran the headline RELIEF AS DUPAS IS CONVICTED. The newspaper said the police were "elated and hailed the verdict as an endorsement of the jury system". It also reported that Dupas, when asked by Justice Kaye if he had anything to say, replied: "Yes, it's a kangaroo court."

Margaret Maher's brother Ingo thanked the police for their work in getting the case to court and told the *Herald Sun:* "Margaret lived her life the way she chose and no one had the right to take that life from her."

Mrs O'Donnell told the newspaper she was in court every day of the trial. She said: "I had to be there for Nicky. I'm her mother, where else would I be? Every conviction we can get against him is important to us." Significantly, she added: "I know he's supposed to be in jail for the rest of his life, but I just don't trust the system." Mrs O'Donnell added that her family already felt it had been let down by a legal system that gave Dupas lenient rape sentences, allowing him to be out of jail and able to kill her daughter.

Justice Kaye, in sentencing Dupas to life imprisonment without the possibility of release, told him: "You are already serving a term of life imprisonment, without a non-parole period, imposed on you by order of this Court on August 22, 2000. Notwithstanding that any sentence which I now impose will not have any practical effect on your disposition, nevertheless the process of sentencing you for the murder of Margaret Maher should not be considered to be an academic or futile exercise.

"The functions and purposes of sentencing are not confined to questions of punishment and deterrence of you as the offender. Importantly, they also include the denunciation by this Court of your conduct, and in particular the public condemnation of the intentional taking by you of the life of Margaret Josephine Maher. Secondly, the process of the sentencing involves the imposition by this Court of a just punishment for what is a very serious offence, and the vindication of the rights of the victim, who is deceased, and of those who are left behind to struggle with the grief and trauma occasioned by her violent murder. Thirdly, in a case such as this, the principle of general deterrence is an important consideration in the determination of an appropriate sentence.

"The Crown case against you was circumstantial. It is not therefore possible to draw conclusions as to the precise circumstances in which Margaret Maher met her end. It is clear from the verdict that the jury accepted that Margaret Maher was last seen alive when she departed from the Safeway supermarket at Broadmeadows Town Shopping Centre at 12.20am on October 4, 1997, and was seen walking in the direction of Pascoe Vale Road. The circumstances in which her body was found located by the side of Cliffords Road, Somerton, shortly before 2pm on the same day indicate that you had murdered her at a different location, and then dumped and left her mutilated body where it was found.

"The evidence was that you commenced work on that day at 6.38am. The pathologist who attended the scene and later conducted the autopsy, Dr Lynch, placed the likely time of death between 9pm on October 3 and 7am on October 4. It is therefore apparent that you murdered Margaret Maher in the early hours of October 4 after you either met her or intercepted her, probably while she was travelling along or in the vicinity of the Hume Highway, as she often did.

"The evidence of Dr Lynch was that there were three possible causes of death namely, drug toxicity, advanced coronary artery disease, and the application of compression to the neck. But in its verdict the jury accepted that death resulted from compression of the neck. The jury came to that view based on injuries which were found on the neck, considered in the context of other injuries to the deceased, including a wound caused by blunt trauma over the right eyebrow and lacerations to the right arm. In addition, either shortly before or immediately after her death, there was a stab wound inflicted on the deceased's left wrist with a sharp implement.

"Whatever the precise circumstances, it is clear that the jury accepted that you compressed the deceased's neck with the intention of either to kill her or cause her really serious injury. There has been no suggestion that there was any legal justification for you killing Margaret Maher.

"After you murdered her, you mutilated the deceased's body in the manner which has already been described to the jury, and left it by the side of the road, in a desolate place, as a disgusting display of loathing for the deceased and contempt for her dignity. Not content with what you had done to her in life, you robbed her of her dignity in death. Those actions are, I consider, an eloquent insight into the unmitigated evil which actuated you to kill Margaret Maher and behave as you did.

"The offence for which you have been found guilty is the most serious crime known to our legal system. It involved the intentional deprivation by you of the life of another human being. You have violated the most sacred and unique right any person has, namely, the right to live his or her life as they wish. Margaret Maher had the same right to life as each and every other member of our community. You have taken that from her, and have thereby done the greatest wrong known to our law. Your act has also deprived those who loved her of their daughter, sister and mother. Victim impact statements have been produced to me and I have read them. Those statements are a salutary and specific reminder of the trauma, grief and anguish your actions have caused, and will undoubtedly continue to cause for the indefinite future, to those left struggling with their bereavement for the woman you so cruelly murdered.

"You have an appalling background of previous criminality. The hallmark of your previous convictions involved wanton and despicable acts of violence to defenceless women … they are a chilling account of some of your criminal history." Justice Kaye then detailed this appalling litany of sexual offences committed by Dupas from an early age.

Justice Kaye continued: "As I understand it you were released on parole in 1996. The present offence occurred on October 4, 1997. It occurred in the context of a man who has displayed the abominable and despicable disposition to repeatedly violate the basic rights of women in our community. In so far as the Sentencing Act requires me to take into account your character and background, this is by far the most outstanding and salient feature of it. Secondly, your record of recurrent recidivism over the three decades demonstrates that there is no hope at all for your rehabilitation into society …

"You were further convicted in August, 2000, for the murder of Nicole Patterson on April 19, 1999. You were arrested for that crime on April 22, 1999. In the present trial some of the evidence given in your previous trial was adduced again. The murder of Nicole Patterson was brutal and cold-blooded. You had planned it for some time. You murdered her in her own home, when she had no prospect at all of defending herself.

"The evidence relating to that offence was adduced because of the striking similarity between the mutilation of Margaret Maher after her death and the mutilation which was inflicted on Nicole Patterson after you murdered her. The evidence of your further offending, and your conviction for it, although not a subsequent and not a previous conviction, is relevant to your character …

"It is also relevant because it cannot be said that, notwithstanding, your previous violent path, the present murder for which I now sentence you was in some way or other a 'diversion' from your usual conduct. In addition, the murder by you of Nicole Patterson, only 18 months after you had murdered Margaret Maher, makes it plain that you lacked the slightest recognition of the enormity of what you had done to Margaret Maher, yet alone feel even the faintest twinge of remorse for it.

"In view of your appalling criminal history, and in view of the particularly serious nature of the crime for which you have been convicted, it is only appropriate that you be sentenced to life imprisonment. Even if the murder of Nicole Patterson had never occurred, I would have no hesitation in imposing a term of life imprisonment upon you."

Quoting recent cases in which no minimum terms were fixed, Justice Kaye continued: "It is clear, both in the present case and from your previous convictions for rape and like offences, that your offending is connected with a need by you to vindicate a perverted and sadistic hatred of women and a contempt for them and their right to live. As such the present offence must be characterised as being in the most serious categories of murders which come before this Court.

"You intentionally killed a harmless, defenceless woman who, like all your other victims, had no prospect of protecting herself against you. At the time you committed that offence, you had, over almost three decades, terrorised women in this state. You have repeatedly violated a central norm of a decent civilised society. Your conduct in the present case is without mitigation or palliation. There has been no recognition by you of your wrongdoing. Rather, you repeated the same offence, with even more brutality, 18 months after murdering Margaret Maher.

"Based on your repeated violent offences, and on the gravity of this offence, there is no prospect of your rehabilitation. Nothing was advanced on your behalf to reflect that there is even the faintest glimmer of hope for you. Even if there were, any considerations of rehabilitation must, in this case, be subordinated to the gravity of your offending, the need for the imposition of a just punishment, and the principle of general deterrence. All those circumstances combine, in my view, not only to justify, but also require that I do not fix a minimum term …

"The sentence of the Court is that, for the murder of Margaret Josephine Maher at Somerton on October 4, 1997, you be imprisoned for the rest of your natural life and without the opportunity for release on parole. Accordingly, the Court sentences Peter Norris Dupas to be imprisoned for the rest of his natural life and without the opportunity for release on parole."

Outside the court, Nicole's sister Kylie said Dupas should not have been free to commit the two murders and that he should have been "kept inside" following his multiple convictions for rape. Kylie described Dupas as "the most evil predator, a psychopath, a true evil predatory, cunning repulsive person" and added: "It's such a rare evil that comes into this world that's destroyed these women and our lives. We're just praying that this man is accountable for everything he has done."

Also outside the court after the sentencing was Mersina Halvagis' father, George, who had attended every day of the trial knowing that Dupas was suspected of killing his daughter. He told reporters that he was happy with the verdict and said: "Margaret has got justice." And so too would Mersina and her family, thanks to police determination and persistence.

Dupas' second life sentence without the possibility of parole normally would have been front-page news, but August 17, 2004, was a huge news day for the *Herald Sun* as it was in the middle of the Athens Olympic Games. The *Herald Sun* front page that day paid tribute to two Australian gold medallists, 118km cycle road race winner Sara Carrigan and 100metre butterfly winner Petria Thomas under the banner headline WOMEN OF STEEL. At the top of this there was a line telling readers that underworld identity Carl Williams, of *Underbelly* notoriety, had been charged with murder.

The Dupas sentencing was reported on page two, with a spill to page 15. The small page two item carried the headline DUPAS JAILED FOR LIFE … AGAIN, while the main report on page 15 ran under the headline RAPIST SHOULD NOT HAVE BEEN LET OUT.

The report led with Nicole Patterson's mother, Pam O'Donnell, calling for mandatory minimum sentences for repeat sex offenders and her argument that a serial rapist such as Dupas should never have been free to kill.

It said that Mrs O'Donnell was bitter that nothing had been done to improve sentencing of serial offenders. Mrs O'Donnell told the newspaper that more than 10,000 people had written or telephoned the Attorney-General about lenient sentencing, but that nothing had changed.

The report continued: "Mrs O'Donnell said her daughter and Margaret Maher had paid the ultimate price for lenient treatment of Dupas, who had three convictions for rape before his first murder." Mrs O'Donnell also told the *Herald Sun:* "Dupas should never have been able to kill my daughter and Ms Maher."

Mrs O'Donnell, through the *Herald Sun*, thanked the Director of Public Prosecutions, Paul Coghlan QC, for "having the gumption to take Margaret's case to trial". She added: "I'm just so thankful the DPP could see how evil Dupas was" and, finally, asked: "But why was he even out there to kill our girls?"

The *Herald Sun* of August 18 ran this editorial under the headline PROTECTING THE COMMUNITY:

"Peter Dupas is evil; he is a savage predator who for 30 years was too often free to walk the streets.

"This week a judge sentenced Dupas to life imprisonment without parole for the 1997 mutilation murder of Margaret Maher.

"He was already serving a life term with no release for murdering Nicole Patterson in 1999.

"In August, 2000, before he was sentenced for the 1999 murder, the *Herald Sun* said in an editorial that the Dupas saga was 'a chilling indictment of the Victorian justice system, which so far has failed to fulfil its obligation to protect the public'.

"We recalled that the danger signs had been evident from the moment in 1968 when, while still at school, Dupas repeatedly stabbed a female next-door neighbour.

"There followed a pattern of preying on women while armed with a knife, raping and stabbing.

"All told, he served only 23 years of the possible maximum of 31 years' jail he received for various crimes. For three rapes, he served less than 18 years.

"When he was freed from jail after serving two of his sentences, he committed the murders that brought the life sentences that finally acknowledged him as an unacceptable risk to society.

"Dupas is a vile reminder that in such cases the priority is not punishment or deterrence, but protection of the public."

In an amazing coincidence, an article by Attorney-General Rob Hulls featured alongside this editorial. Hulls wrote: "It would be foolish for anyone, especially any politician, to suggest that our justice system is perfect.

"However, what we must all do, especially politicians, is to make it as perfect as we possibly can.

"To do this we must get the fundamentals right. We must have a judiciary that is fearless, independent and given the discretion to decide cases on their individual merits."

Mr Hulls wrote of the Victorian Law Reform Commission interim report recommendations of toughening rape laws and of how the government wanted "smarter sentencing". He also wrote of the setting up of a Victims Register to give victims the right to make submissions to the Adult Parole Board before it determined whether to make a parole order.

He concluded: "As a government we will continue to do all we can to make our justice system as perfect as possible. The community expects no less."

But, of course, this was all too late for Nicole Patterson, Margaret Maher and Mersina Halvagis.

Meanwhile, "life" truly meant "life" for Dupas for a second time but, as in the Nicole Patterson case, he appealled, principally against the admission by Justice Kaye of "similar fact evidence". Dupas' application for leave to appeal also was based on the trial judge's directions to the jury relating to that similar facts evidence was flawed and, in fact, these two grounds flowed into the more general ground that they led to a miscarriage of justice and that the verdict should be set aside.

Chief Justice Warren, in his judgement dismissing the application for leave to appeal, said: "Although the potential of a miscarriage of justice as a consequence of the admissibility of propensity evidence is always present, it is ultimately a question for the trial judge to determine the degree of risk and the appropriate manner in which it should be addressed depending on the facts of a given case."

He added: "The applicant fails to make out any error on the part of the trial judge with respect to the assessment of prejudice compared to the given probative force of the evidence in question."

Justice Nettle concurred and, in his judgement, referred in considerable detail to the "similarity" evidence presented at the trial and said:

"The Crown contended that the evidence concerning Nicole Patterson was admissible as similar fact evidence pursuant to section 398A of the Crimes Act, 1958. It argued that the similarities between her death and mutilation of Margaret Maher were so striking as to lead ineluctably to the inference that the applicant murdered and mutilated Margaret Maher.

"Alternatively, the Crown submitted that the evidence that the applicant mutilated Nicole Patterson after death was admissible on the more limited basis that similarities between the mutilation of both women were so striking as to yield the inference that it was the applicant who mutilated both women and hence the applicant who murdered Margaret Maher.

"The judge rejected the first of those contentions but accepted the second. In his Honour's opinion, the first was tantamount to saying that the appellant had a propensity to murder and mutilate women and therefore that it was likely it was he who had murdered and mutilated Margaret Maher. His Honour considered that it was impermissible to reason in that fashion because the two women were killed in different ways and because there was not a great deal of similarity between the circumstances in which each was killed.

"Nicole Patterson was killed and left in her home after the applicant responded to an advertisement that Nicole Patterson had placed in a local newspaper in respect of her services as a psychotherapist. Margaret Maher was a prostitute working the Hume Highway. Her body was left at the side of the roadway.

"The judge accepted, however, that the similarity between the way in which each woman had been mutilated was so striking as to enable a jury to infer that the same man had mutilated each woman. It followed in his Honour's opinion that it would be open to infer that the applicant was both violently disposed towards Margaret Maher and with her or at about the time of her death. It followed in turn that the evidence concerning Nicole Patterson was circumstantial evidence which, in conjunction with proof of other facts, was capable of supporting the conclusion that the appellant killed Margaret Maher."

Justice Nettle also said: "The applicant's principal intention in support of his application for leave to appeal is that the judge erred in holding that differences between the circumstances in which each woman died were 'of limited relevance'. Counsel for the applicant (Mr C.B. Boyce and Mr L.C. Carter) submitted that it was necessary to look at the mutilation of each woman in context and that when viewed in context there were significant differences between them. Counsel argued that the extent of the differences was such that it would plainly not be 'an affront to common sense' to exclude the evidence concerning the mutilation of Nicole Patterson.

"I do not accept the argument … despite such differences as there may have been between the circumstances surrounding the mutilations of Nicole Patterson and Margaret Maher, I consider that the judge was right to conclude that there was underlying unity in the extraordinary nature of the method and incidence of the mutilation of each woman."

Justice Harper, concurring with Justices Warren and Nettle that the application be rejected, said he did not differ "in any material respect from either" and gave what he described as "a third perspective".

He said: "The differences (in the two murders) were many. The most significant was that the former (Nicole) suffered multiple stab wounds from which she died, whereas Ms Maher's injuries were relatively slight; and her attacker — if she was attacked — did not use a knife. The striking similarity in the post-mortem dealings with each body (the removals of breasts) could not properly be extended so as to overwhelm the differences in the manner of the two deaths.

"His Honour (the trial judge) was at pains to make this clear. He correctly informed the jury that they should not consider the 'Patterson' evidence at all, but rather put it out of their minds, unless and until they were satisfied beyond reasonable doubt that Ms Maher had died at the hands of someone who intended to kill her, or cause her really serious injury …

"When the members of the jury retired to consider their verdict, the Patterson evidence was nevertheless before them. It could not have but made a deep impression. They could not have divorced themselves from it. And its prejudicial effect would have been at its most powerful when the jury came to decide whether they were satisfied beyond reasonable doubt that Ms Maher's death was caused by a person, and, if so, whether that person intended to kill her.

"This was the weakest aspect of the case against the applicant. It would have been tempting for the jury to throw aside a doubt they might otherwise have had on the basis that, if they were satisfied that the applicant murdered Ms Patterson, then they could accept without rigorous analysis that he also murdered Ms Maher. He was that kind of man …

"Once the jury were satisfied that Ms Maher was murdered, the question of the identity of the murderer became the sole remaining issue. I agree with his Honour that the inference that the man who mutilated the body of Nicole Patterson was the same person who had earlier mutilated the body of Margaret Maher is supported by the underlying unity in the extraordinary nature of the method and incidents surrounding the two cases. Thus supported, the inference becomes so strong as to be capable of removing any reasonable doubt. It already having been established that Ms Maher was murdered, the conclusion that the mutilator was also her murderer then was inevitable … I would refuse the application for leave to appeal."

There was a sad sequel to the Margaret Maher murder as her daughter Natasha died of a drug overdose on March 22, 2007. Although no one will ever know, it seems likely that her mother's horrific death after years of drug addiction affected her tremendously. Natasha Maher's funeral service was held at the Star of the Sea school chapel in the bayside Melbourne suburb of Brighton.

Paul Scarlett, who was one of the pall-bearers, described the funeral as "heart-rending" as the 60 or so mourners knew Natasha had been crushed by her mother's death. The detective said: "Her family was distraught, especially as they had gone through enormous mental anguish over Margaret's death. This was yet another terrible blow and, for example, her grandfather was extremely distressed. A very solid family, they mourned as one, deeply and unconditionally."

Margaret Maher's life might not have been exemplary after she succumbed to a drug habit, but her death brought untold misery and grief. The circumstances surrounding her death were horrific in the extreme and those who had worked on the case felt Dupas was among the worst of the worst. Scarlett described him as "the very personification of evil", while prosecutor Ms Williams suggested he was a man "without conscience and incapable of normal human feelings".

Yet there were even worse revelations to come, thanks to the diligence of Scarlett and other police officers. They long had come to the conclusion that Dupas had murdered Mersina Halvagis and were deteremined to prove it. The dead woman's father might have had some satisfaction from Dupas' convictions and sentencing for the Nicole Patterson and Margaret Maher murders, but desperately wanted some closure for the almost everwhelming grief he and his family felt over the death of his beloved daughter. He prayed for a conviction and these prayers eventually were answered.

# CHAPTER NINE

# Death in a Cemetery

Any parent would have been proud to have a daughter as bright, polite and kind-hearted as bank accountant Mersina Halvagis. Born into a tight-knit Greek family on February 17, 1972, she was employed in the Group Accounting section at the head office of the ANZ Bank in Melbourne and enjoyed a life of quiet domesticity with her parents and siblings in the bayside suburb of Mentone. Mersina had graduated from La Trobe University and, at a university ball in 1992, met a young man she believed would be her soul mate for many decades. She and Angelo Gorgievski became engaged after almost five years of going out together, but their dream of a married life was ended late on the afternoon of November 1, 1997.

Mersina had spent the Friday night at the home of Angelo's parents in Mill Park and, after her fiancé went to work at the Bunning's hardware store in Epping the following day, Mersina decided she would make one of her regular visits to her grandmother's grave at the Fawkner Cemetery. She borrowed her fiance's car, a red Ford Telstar, drove to the cemetery, parked within the cemetery grounds and bought blue and white statis flowers at 3.47pm. The woman who sold her the flowers, plus two bottles of Sprite soft drink, was the last person to see Mersina alive.

Mersina left the cemetery kiosk and walked about 50 metres to her grandmother's grave, which was located in Row M of the Greek Orthodox Section. She was placing the flowers in a vase when she was attacked, suffering terrible stab wounds. Her killer attacked her from behind and Mersina would have reacted in absolute horror at the sight of the huge blade that was to slice her life so savagely short. Several visitors to the cemetery heard screams, but thought nothing of them at the time. Mersina was left dead between two headstones and no one knew what had happened until early the next morning.

When Gorgievski returned home about 6.45pm from his job at the hardware store, there was no sign of Mersina. He therefore started a search for her and contacted police. Knowing Mersina was going to visit her grandmother's grave, Angelo and police went to the Fawkner Cemetery. About 4am, Angelo made the most terrible discovery of his life. His fiancée was dead, sprawled near her grandmother's grave and on the ground of an empty plot. The area immediately was zoned off for a homicide investigation.

Daylight revealed a horrific sight. Mersina's bloodied body was between a brown marble headstone to her right and a black one to her left, with her head touching this monument. He left foot was pointing to a black monument, with the right leg bent at a 45-degree angle. There were no shoes on her feet, but there were bloodstains on both legs and both white socks. Even more horrific, the top right of her grey trousers was heavily bloodstained, with obvious gashes over her abdomen. There also were deep gashes to the little and ring fingers of her left hand, clear indications that she had put up a fight and had even grabbed at her killer's knife.

Mersina's right foot was alongside an overturned pot plant and it was obvious from this, and other evidence, that she desperately tried to fend off her attacker. Behind her head, the Perspex cover to a brown marble prayer box was wide open and, to the right, there was a container of water. There also was a bottle of Sprite lemonade on top of the prayer box, which featured a small crucifix.

The brown, blue and white long-sleeved shirt she was wearing also was heavily bloodstained and pulled down from her left shoulder, exposing a white bra. Mersina's black shoes were found next to pot plants and obviously had been thrown away by the killer. In Mersina's long and carefully groomed nails were pieces of gravel and a tuft of hair. Her spectacles were found between her legs and police also retrieved cigarette butts and a glass jar with a cork stopper.

The statis flowers were scattered on the ground, near a standing and half-full bottle of olive oil. The flower stems had been cut and, nearby, were pieces of twine and a rubber band. Mersina obviously had undone the bunch of flowers and was preparing to place the water and flowers in the vase when attacked. The red car Mersina had driven to the cemetery was where it was parked and police took photographs and measurements of nearby tyre marks

Police, including Senior Constable Michael Hradeck, attached to the Crime Scene Section of the Victoria Forensic Science Centre, attended the homicide scene. Senior Constable Hradeck arrived at 6.26am and noticed several tyre marks in the car park. These were photographed and, near the south entrance, the red Telstar stood locked with its automatic transmission indicator in the "park" position. Police removed a key from the right pocket of Mersina's pants and were able to open the car.

Also attending the scene was Senior Sergeant Wayne Ashley, of the Crime Scene Section of the Victoria Forensic Science Centre, who had qualifications and experience in bloodstain evidence. He said in a statement that he arrived at 11.45am and that his examination centred around the bloodstains at the murder scene, from plots 36-38, row M.

He noted: "The bloodstains on the ground in front of the monument at Plot 37 showed heavy staining that had been absorbed into the loose dirt and stones, with some stones being disturbed. Hair fibres were present within the bloodstains and samples of the bloodstains and fibres were collected."

There were many other bloodstains, even on the top and down the eastern side of the monument on plot 37 and cast-off stains from directly above Mersina's body.

Senior Sergeant Ashley stated: "The deceased's upper clothing had been pulled up over her head from the back and was bundled across the front of her chest area. The upper clothing was still covering her arms. The deceased's arms were folded at the wrists and her left arm and hand was on the ground. The upper clothing consisted of a brown patterned top, white undergarment and a partly exposed bra. The deceased was also wearing grey-coloured trousers, white patterned socks and no shoes.

"There was blood staining in the form of smears and contact marks to the deceased's face, blood staining to the exposed lower torso with blood soaking into the top of the trousers. There were wounds to the exposed torso of the deceased. There were further bloodstains on both trouser legs from the upper thighs to the cuffs.

"Several stains had soaked through the material, particularly from around the knees area. There were large and small bloodstains on the clothing of the deceased ... There were bloodstains on both hands of the deceased and each hand displayed wounds. There were also hair fibres attached to both hands. Each hand was bagged for protection with some loose hairs being removed from the right hand ... The deceased's socks were bloodstained with droplets of blood on the top of the socks as well as smears or contact marks on the left sock around the ankle area.

"A pair of optical glasses were located on the ground between the deceased's legs. They appeared to be bent and the lenses scratched. A pair of black ladies' shoes were located at the rear of pot-plants at the southern end of Plot M36. The right shoe was upright and the left shoe was lying on the left side. The location and proximity of the shoes to each other suggest that they were placed there at a later stage."

Police removed several items from the scene for examination and these included the spectacles, hair fibres and the shoes. They also examined the car Mersina drove to the cemetery and took numerous photographs.

The post-mortem was performed by Professor David Ranson, a vastly experienced pathologist employed as the Deputy Director of the Victorian Institute of Forensic Medicine and head of the Institute's Forensic Pathology Division. Professor Ranson, who also had been involved in the Margaret Maher case, started the post-mortem at 5pm on November 2, about 12 and a half hours after the discovery of Mersina's body. However, he had been at the cemetery from 9am and noted:

"Examination of the body revealed that there appeared to be a number of incised wounds of stab type to the front of the chest and abdomen and to the front of the neck. Some abrasion-type injuries appeared to be present to the back of the shoulders … Whilst there was a large quantity of blood staining over the hands, chest and abdomen, there was much less blood staining present over the face and neck."

Immediately before the post-mortem, Professor Ranson made notes on the clothing Mersina was wearing and to the damage caused by the incisions. He also noted that Mersina was wearing a white metal chain, carrying a yellow metal ring and stones, around her neck and there were yellow metal earrings in the lobes of both ears.

His notes on the clothing were important as they revealed much about the viciousness of the murderous attack. Professor Ranson noted:

"At the time of the autopsy the body was clothed in a black and cream coloured striped T-shirt which was extensively bloodstained and had been pulled over the head of the body so that the front and back of the garment lay over the front of the chest of the deceased, with the arms still being present in the sleeves of the T-shirt. Numerous defects were present in the T-shirt both in the front and the back of the T-shirt.

"However, the material of the T-shirt was scrunched up in such a way that multiple layers of the clothing lay folded adjacent to each other. Beneath the T-shirt was a white vest with a lacy neckline at the front which showed extensive blood staining and multiple defects in the material. The vest had been pulled over the head and neck of the deceased so that it lay scrunched up over the front of the chest with the arms of the deceased still present through the shoulder loops.

"Beneath the vest was a white bra which was extensively bloodstained and showed numerous defects in its fabric. The bra appeared to be correctly fastened at the back and was appropriately positioned over the breasts. The lower half of the body was covered by long grey trousers which showed blood staining and soil staining of the surface in areas together with a number of defects in the material."

There were fragments of soil, grit and hair over the body, with other small fragments of vegetable material. There also was a partly burnt match stick adherent to the skin on the back of the body.

Professor Ranson noted that the body was 155cm in length and weighed 45kg. Mersina was petite and obviously no match for her killer. Her eyes were normal and showed no sign of strangulation. However, there was bruising to the lower right leg and left thigh, with an abrasion on the right side of the forehead, about two centimetres above the right eyebrow. There were five other abrasion areas clustered over the lower part of the right cheek, near the chin.

In relation to the neck and face, the most serious injury was "an incised wound of stab type that measured five centimetres in length" to Mersina's neck. There also was a "scattered collection of irregular abrasions extended across the front of the neck", along with three "small incised superficial stab wounds".

Much more severe stab injuries were found on Mersina's chest, with one wound extremely deep. There were numerous other stab wounds to the chest and it was obvious Mersina had been the victim of a frenzied attack. There also was a stab wound to the abdomen, but the killer had concentrated on the chest, particularly in the region of the breasts.

Professor Ranson said of the chest wounds: "Situated almost in the middle of the chest and some 2cm below the horizontal nipple line was a large gaping complex incised wound of stab type comprising an almost horizontal incised wound 7cm in length from the lower border of which was a further vertical incised wound measuring 1.5cm in length.

"The wound gaped to a veracious degree and at times, depending on the position of the body, the wound gaped in excess of 3cm. In the depths of the wound, incisions could be seen in the portion of the cartilage and bony tissue comprising the inferior end of the sternum, or breast-plate. These incisions in the hard tissues of the sternum were orientated in a C-shape with a vertical lower incision measuring in excess of 3cm in length and two separate horizontally arranged incisions in the hard tissue lying beneath the horizontal component of the skin incised wounds.

"The vertical incised wound in the hard tissues of the sternum appeared to pass posteriorily and inferiorily (back and below). The incision in the sternal hard tissues to the left of the midline appeared to pass laterally to the left and the incision in the hard tissue of the sternum to the right of the midline appeared to pass laterally to the right. On turning and moving the body, a large quantity of blood flowed from this complex wound arrangement."

There were numerous other chest wounds and Professor Ranson noted that membranes around the heart had been "widely damaged with multiple wounds". He also noted that the epicardium (the outer surface of the heart) "showed evidence of trauma with an incised wound up to 2cm in length situated in the anterior wall of the left ventricle some 3-5cm from the apex".

In layman's terms, Mersina suffered terrible internal injuries and Professor Ranson indicated that "approximately one litre of liquid blood was found in both pleural cavities and the lungs were collapsed". He said:

"Examination of the chest wall revealed incised wounds of stab type passing between the ribs and the sternum as follows:

"An incised wound of stab type passed through the anterior chest of the right side between the first and third ribs.

"An incised wound of stab type passed through the anterior chest on the right side between the second and third ribs.

"Two incised wounds of stab type passed through the anterior chest on the left side between the fourth and fifth ribs.

"An incised wound of stab type passed through the anterior chest on the left side between the sixth and seventh ribs."

There were other severe injuries, including an incision to the left lobe of the liver measuring 8cm in length and a depth of 2cm. This in itself was a measure of the ferocity of the attack as the knife penetrated deep into Mersina's liver.

Professor Ranson noted other injuries, particularly the cuts to the fingers on Mersina's right hand and stab wounds to the upper left arm and lower parts of her legs.

Otherwise, Mersina had been a perfectly healthy 25-year-old. The cause of death was noted as "stab wounds to chest and abdomen".

In a supplementary report, Professor Ranson stated: "Having regard to the injuries of Mersina Halvagis, it is noteworthy that the injuries comprised a series of incised wounds of stab type to the front of the chest that were focused on the area between the breasts, as well as a few isolated injuries below the area of the breast involving the lower part of the chest on the left side anteriorly and the region of the left side of the upper abdomen.

"A series of incised wounds were present over the front of the neck and incised wounds were also present over the limbs, including the stab type wounds to the side and distal right thigh and … upper left arm. A slicing incised injury was also present to the region of the left knee.

"Many of the incised injuries of stab type to the front of the chest involve the severing of underlying bony cartilaginous structures indicating that some of these would have required a considerable degree of force for their causation. The depth of penetration of these injuries was also extensive in some cases.

"Other incised injuries were present in the body, particularly those over the palmar aspects of the hands, a feature which may be in keeping with the defensive type injuries where the palm of the hand was used to ward off an attack from a cutting object that is being wielded against the front of the upper part of the body."

Professor Ranson noted that there was a "focusing and clustering" of the injuries to the chest and, significantly in light of the eventual arrest, trial and conviction of Peter Dupas, "many of the injuries being located in the region of the breasts". Mersina had suffered terribly, even if the horrendous attack was brief, as Professor Ranson noted 85 separate injuries. Little wonder police desperately wanted to see the monster who did this pay for his cruel and terrible crime. Mersina Halvagis not only had been attacked, but viciously slaughtered when she was unable to defend herself. The number of wounds and the ferocity with which she was killed meant a monster was at large.

The location of the murder lent itself to enormous public interest, as did the callous nature of the slaying. Until November 1, 1997, Mersina was just another young woman enjoying life. From the day after her death her name became synonymous with horror and, eventually, the man who killed her became one of the most detested men in Australian criminal history. Peter Dupas had written his name in blood and it was only a matter of time before police brought him to justice. His vile crime was so vicious that police left no stone unturned to charge him and have him convicted, no matter how long it took.

Mersina's slaying was huge news in Melbourne, even though the city was caught up in the excitement of the impending running of the 1997 Melbourne Cup. The *Herald Sun* of Monday, November 3, ran news of the killing under the headline SLAIN AT GRAN'S GRAVE, with the sub-heading POLICE FEAR RANDOM ATTACK. It read:

"Police fear a woman savagely stabbed to death as she tended her grandmother's grave may have been the victim of a random attack.

"Mersina Halvagis, 25, was found dead from multiple stab wounds at Fawkner Cemetery, a few paces from where she had placed flowers at her grandmother's burial site.

"Police said the bank worker's body was found face up and her clothes were in disarray, indication there had been a struggle."

The newspaper quoted the Homicide Squad's Detective Senior Sergeant Rowland Legg as saying: "It was a particularly brutal attack and we are not discounting the fact it was random." He added that Mersina had not given any indication to friends or relatives that she felt threatened in the days leading up to her death. He told the *Herald Sun:* "Everyone describes her (Mersina) very positively and without any enemies as we know."

Although Melbourne newspapers were buzzing the next day with the latest news on the running of the Melbourne Cup, Mersina's death was still big news. The *Herald Sun* had a report on page two and even ran a side-piece titled MERSINA'S LAST HOURS, plus a plan of the Fawkner Cemetery.

The small piece on Mersina's lost hours, accompanied by a map of where she had travelled on the day she was killed, read:

"FRIDAY NIGHT: Mersina Halvagis leaves her Mentone home and drives to her fiancé's parents' home in Mill Park.

"SATURDAY, 3.30pm: Leaves the Mill Park house to visit her grandmother's grave at Fawkner Crematorium.

"3.45pm: Ms Halvagis buys flowers at cemetery gates then drives to the Greek Orthodox section.

"4.30pm: Stabbed to death.

"8pm: Cemetery gates close.

"SUNDAY, 2am: Ms Halvagis' father reports her missing to police.

"4am: Ms Halvagis' fiancé and his father drive to the cemetery after becoming increasingly concerned for her safety. They see the car she drove.

"4.30am: Police called to the cemetery where they find Ms Halvagis' body."

The page two lead item was headlined MURDER STUNS FAMILY, with members of Mersina's heartbroken family telling reporter Mark Buttler of their grief.

The report read: "They held hands and tearfully told of their love for a young woman who disliked cemeteries but always found time to light a candle or leave flowers at her grandmother's grave."

The report quoted Mersina's 28-year-old brother Nick as saying that her death had changed their lives. The report continued: "Nick Halvagis, flanked by brother Bill, 20, and sister Dimitria, 23, said Mersina's loss was a shocking blow in a tight-knit family where the siblings still lived at home with their parents in Mentone." Nick then described his sister as "a soft, caring person" and told of an incident involving Mersina.

He said that when approached by a young homeless girl for money to buy socks, Mersina walked the girl to a clothing shop and bought her a pair. Nick added: "I reckon if you got all the people who ever met her in the same room, you'd get the same story — that she's caring, soft and non-argumentative."

Sister Dimitria said: "It's not fair ... none of it makes sense. I just don't know what to do now. No one's got the right to take our sister away."

One man thought he had this right, merely to satisfy his own deviate needs — Peter Dupas. At the time, Nick Halvagis asked the public to help police catch his sister's killer. He said it was "like a jigsaw puzzle" and the police, with painstaking dedication, started putting the pieces together.

One of their first witnesses was the woman who served Mersina at the cemetery kiosk that terrible afternoon. Elva Hayden, the catering manager of the Fawkner Tea Rooms, said in her statement to police:

"On Saturday, the first of November, 1997, I commenced working at the tea rooms at about 8am. I worked until 4.40pm. I have to catch the 4.46pm, a train which stops right outside the cemetery. The tea rooms sell tea and coffee, sandwiches and drinks. We also sell flowers.

"On Sunday, the second of November, 1997, I started work at the tea rooms at 8.20am. I had heard on the radio this morning on the clock radio that the body of a girl had been found at the Fawkner Cemetery.

"The police have approached me today and have asked me if I recalled selling flowers and bottles of Sprite lemonade to anyone the day before. I have checked the cash register roll today and found I made a sale of flowers to the value of $6.50 at 3.47pm, and then a sale of $1.60 twice which has prompted my memory that I had sold two bottles of Sprite; this sale was at the same time as the flowers.

"I now recall this sale; the customer was a girl who looked to me to be about 30 years old. She had shoulder length dark brown hair, she wasn't very tall and she was on her own in the shop. She bought the flowers first and then apologised and said she wanted a couple of bottles of Sprite. I also recall she bought statis flowers. The stems are long at the moment and they require to be tied on the stems. All the flowers are tied anyway with string.

"I have taken the relevant section of the cash register and given (it) to the police today. There were some people around the cemetery at that time. I had made several more sales after this one, the last being at 4.19pm. Our security man, Steve Hume, was with me in the shop when this girl was in buying flowers and drinks. Steve stayed with me until I locked the shop up at 4.40pm. He then goes about his normal duties of locking up the toilets and gates around the park."

Hume, one of the cemetery's funeral supervisors, told police in his statement that one of his duties was to lock the gates to both the main and northern sections of the cemetery and, before locking these gates, had been in the tea rooms having a cup of tea with Elva Hayden. He said in this statement:

"Whilst there I recall hearing a voice of a girl ordering some flowers, I think a candle and some Sprite soft drink. I didn't see the girl; I had my back to her. I normally stay at the shop until Elva closed it as she is on her own. After she closed the shop I believe at about 4.30 to 4.45pm, (I) then normally walked towards the station and I continue with my duties.

"I don't recall exactly what gates I did first but from memory I then drove to the main gate in Sydney Road and closed half of the gates and then drove to Box Forest Road and turned left and went to the pedestrian gate at the rear of the Greek Orthodox section." Hume then stated that he saw an elderly man in a brownish Datsun, but no one else. He added that if anyone was left in the cemetery after the gates had been closed they could exit through an emergency gate which opened automatically. He completed his duties and left the cemetery about 6pm. He finished his statement by saying: "I am normally the last employee of the park to leave."

But, on this particular evening, there was someone still in the cemetery grounds. It was Mersina Halvagis, and she was dead. It now was a matter of tracking down her killer and, later in the investigation, proving it was Peter Dupas.

Police exhausted every possibility in a painstaking investigation. They checked and rechecked every possible clue and carried out a vast range of forensic investigations. Unfortunately, there was no DNA evidence on which to base their investigations, but police put everything under a microscope, often literally. They studied the tyre tracks, examined the cigarette butts, sought expert guidance from criminal psychologists and spoke with dozens of witnesses. Nothing was left to chance, but little turned up.

The investigation was so thorough and the net cast so wide that police were able to draw up a list of 100 possible suspects and were able to eliminate all but one from their enquiries. That one remaining suspect was, of course, Dupas. Police twice interviewed him about Mersina's murder, but he refused to make any comment whatsoever.

Some witnesses came forward soon after news of the murder had hit the deadlines, but others contacted police after appeals through Crime Stoppers. One of the witnesses contacted Crime Stoppers but did not properly identify herself and this created a problem for police as she had vital information, but was unable to be traced because of the security surrounding Crime Stoppers, an anonymous resource. Police eventually tracked the witness down and her evidence added considerably to the case against Dupas.

The witnesses gave varying accounts of events on the late afternoon of November 1, 1997, when Mersina was murdered.

Some witnesses told only of screams they heard at the time of Mersina's murder, while information from other witnesses pointed to Dupas, but without any definitive proof that he was her killer.

In relation to the screams, machine operator Arthur Joaquim told police that he was visiting the cemetery with his wife Aidia, two sons, a nephew and a niece for the funeral service of a niece. He said in a statement to police:

"Almost 4.30pm to 4.45pm, I was standing next to the grave with (my) family when I heard a woman scream. It had to be a woman because it was a woman's voice. The woman screamed twice. It was a fast scream, and sounded like someone was afraid. There was a scream for a few seconds. Not even one minute later I heard the second scream. The second scream was very short also — did not take long at all."

Joaquim said he was shown a map of the Fawkner Cemetery and, from this, was able to tell police the screams sounded as if they had come from the north, in the direction of Box Forest Road — the same direction as Mersina's grandmother's grave. Joaquim said his family also heard the screams and that he learned later than a woman had been killed at the time he heard the screams.

Ten-year-old Lisa Tinker spoke with police after her father called Crime Stoppers the day after the murder. She said she was visiting the cemetery with her mother the day before to attend her grandfather's grave. In a statement made more than six years later in the lead-up to a coroner's inquest, she said:

"I remember it was a cold and windy day. Mum and I went to the grave to place some flowers and clean it (the grave) up. I was standing on top of my grandfather's grave cleaning the top of it. My grandfather's grave is a bit taller than the other graves. I was facing towards Box Forest Road whilst I was doing this.

"Mum was bending down putting some flowers down. As I was standing on top of this grave I heard what sounded like a scream. The scream started out as a high-pitched noise which dropped away.

The scream didn't last long. The scream sounded like it came from some distance away and somewhere in front of me. I recall thinking that the scream sounded young because of the pitch and it also sounded alarming. I can still recall this scream in my mind. I can recall this scream because it sounded frightening and that's why it has stuck with me.

"When I heard the scream I said to Mum, 'Oh Mum did you hear that scream?' Mum said, 'Oh, just hurry up, it's night, we have to go.' When I heard the scream I looked in that direction but I didn't see anything that concerned me. Not long after we packed up and left a short time later. I recall that I kept on thinking about this scream on the way home. I recall thinking to myself that the scream had to be something because of the way it sounded. The next day I heard about the girl being murdered at the cemetery."

These witnesses merely heard what had occurred at the cemetery that fateful day and did not see anything at all out of the ordinary, or what might have caused the woman to scream. However, witnesses came forward to tell police they had seen a man in the cemetery that day and on other occasions.

For example, a woman contacted police on February 5, 2005, after watching television and seeing Peter Dupas on the news. As soon as Stefanie Pawluk saw his face she said out loud to her husband: "Oh my God, I think that's him."

Pawluk was referring to a man she saw at the cemetery "a long time ago" and told police:

"My mother died about 18 years ago and she is buried in the Ukraine Section of the cemetery. I used to visit my mother's grave very often until something happened that frightened me. Sometime prior to the girl (Mersina) that was killed ... I was at the cemetery visiting my mother's grave. I recall I was there on my own and that I couldn't see anyone else around. I went to my mother's grave and began tending to it.

"In this section of the cemetery which I would like to point out is the Ukraine Catholic Section, all of the memorial stones are low to the ground. Because of this I was able to see some distance around me. Whilst I was tending the grave I noticed a man walking through the cemetery. He was in another section of the cemetery on my right-hand side when I saw him.

"I saw that this man was walking very fast and he was looking around in such a manner that I thought was very strange. He kept on walking towards me and I recall thinking 'this is very strange — he is coming straight towards me'.

"I watched as he walked all the way over into the same row that I was in. When he got into my row, he was still some distance away and walking very fast and still looking all around him. I could tell that he was not looking at the graves.

"At this stage I got frightened because of the way he was acting. I immediately got up and started walking quickly towards my car that was parked not too far away … I straight away got into my car and locked the door. All of the other car doors were already locked. At this stage I looked up and saw that he had followed me to the driver's door of my car."

The woman was terrified but even years later could recall his face from what she saw on television and was able to give police a description. She said:

"He stood very close to my car and just looked at me. I was very frightened. I saw that he was wearing either glasses or sunglasses, but I'm not sure which. He had blond hair and looked as though he was between 30 and 40 years old. I don't know how tall he was except I believe he was taller than my husband, who is about five foot six inches tall. I think he was wearing jeans and a cream coloured denim type top. I think this top had buttons on the front. His hair wasn't long."

Of course, it could have been a description of one of hundreds, if not thousands of men, but the significance of Pawluck's statement to police was that the man she saw bore a striking resemblance to the one she saw on the television news — Dupas. She said she could recall thinking as she watched the television: "It looks like this man but I can't be sure. My husband was with me when I saw this and I recall that we discussed it."

Pawluk's husband, Valentine, also made a statement and said at the outset that he had been married to his wife for 46 years and "Stefanie is always truthful and reliable". His statement continued:

"A long time ago Stefanie came home from the Fawkner Cemetery and told me something that happened to her whilst she was there … Stefanie told me that on this day she was very scared by what she saw. Stefanie said she was at her mother's grave crying and praying and she saw this man walking along the road looking to his left and right. Stefanie said that he then turned into the same line that Stefanie was standing in and crying (Pawluk later changed this to "praying"). Stefanie said that his head was turning left and right, and that's when Stefanie decided she should leave …

"Some time after this happened, Stefanie and I were at home watching television when we saw a picture of a man that police had already arrested. When Stefanie saw this man on television she said to me 'he looks like the man I saw coming towards me at the cemetery'."

Another woman, Janet Morton, also had a terrifying experience at the Fawkner Cemetery in either July or August, 1997, and contacted Crime Stoppers in September, 2004, after seeing Dupas' photograph in the *Herald Sun*. She said: "As soon as I saw the photo I think I said something like 'that's the bastard that day in Fawkner'. I then read that this man was Peter Dupas and that he was in trouble for doing something to another girl (Nicole Patterson)."

Mrs Morton was at the cemetery to research her family tree and, after being dropped off by her husband, she stood in a rose garden and started reading plaques. She then saw a man standing opposite her on the other side of the garden bed. Mrs Morton gave a quick smile as if to say "hello", but the man ignored her and then bent down to do something in the garden.

Mrs Morton said in a statement: "I recall that this made me feel foolish because he didn't respond to my smile. He was a soft sort of looking fella and was a bit pudgy. He was just an ordinary looking man. I recall that he was wearing blue clothes, the sort that truck drivers might wear. I think he was wearing a long-sleeve shirt and I believe he may have been wearing a T-shirt underneath."

The description of the man as being "pudgy' was significant, as was the reference to him being "an ordinary looking man". Dupas was the sort of man who would never stand out in a crowd. Ordinary looking, yes, but also a cold-blooded killer.

Mrs Morton said she went to another area and, after writing down a name from one of the plaques, saw the same man again. She continued:

"I noticed this same man walking into the same area I was in. I didn't think anything of it at this stage. From there I walked to another area that had walls with more niches in them. This area was about 50 yards away from the first lots of walls and quite some distance from the rose garden where I first saw him.

"I was searching the walls for another particular name and as I did this I saw that this same man had followed me there. This time I got concerned and I left immediately. I saw that he had been looking at me when I glanced over.

"From there I walked over to the older section of the cemetery. I was searching for two particular graves and I had my head down trying to read all of the names. I was there for maybe 20 minutes when I suddenly heard something and looked over towards my left. Straight away I saw this same man coming straight at me with a look in his eyes that really frightened me. He was so close and coming so fast at me that I put my left hand up and began walking backwards. I'm not sure but I think that I may have either screamed or yelled something at him."

Mrs Morton, more than likely, was being stalked and, from her description, the stalker was Dupas. Little wonder she screamed. Mrs Morton said that the man had a startled look on his face as she screamed. He briefly stopped in his tracks and then walked away. Mrs Morton continued in her statement: "The look on his face when I turned to face him was almost like a rabbit in a spotlight type of look, just very startled.

"He walked off to some nearby trees and went and stood behind them. I could see his feet behind them. I could see his feet below the two bushes that he was standing behind. I turned and ran as fast as I could and I recall that I even jumped over one of the gravestones as I ran. I ran over to the road and then ran down the middle of the road as far as I could. I recall that I began to feel puffed and I could see some people in the distance. So I began to slow down."

Mrs Morton then saw her husband driving towards her and, when she got into the car, told him what she had experienced. She took her husband back to where the pudgy man had walked towards her so frighteningly, but there was no sign of him.

It was such a traumatic experience that Mrs Morton said: "I don't get scared this easily and there is only one other time in my whole life that I have been this frightened and that is when I nearly got hit by a train one night. This man frightened me so much that it took me about six years to return to that spot to continue my research."

It appears Mrs Morton had a lucky escape, but the description of the man who had scared her was invaluable. It was another link, albeit a circumstantial one, in the chain police were building to prove that Dupas had killed Mersina Halvagis.

Besides, there was more, much more. Other women reported being stalked by a man who bore a remarkable resemblance to Dupas. Coincidence? Certainly not, police believed. One of the other women who reported an unnerving experience at the Fawkner Cemetery was young schoolteacher Seval Latif, who visited her mother's grave about noon on October 5, 1997 — less than a month before Mersina was stabbed to death.

Ms Latif arranged to meet sister Ayshe at the cemetery and, after opening her car boot to take out some water containers to place flowers at her mother's grave, had "a terrible sensation of danger".

She told police: "I looked up and saw a man approaching me from the roundabout of Seventh Avenue. I was facing north and turned to my left to see him. At this stage he was only about four metres away from me.

"He did not look to be normal; he looked very focused striding purposely towards me. When I looked up I appeared to startle him. Prior to seeing him I would have been filling containers for about three minutes during which I would not have seen him …

"When I saw him he sort of jumped in his spot and turned left and followed the path of some trees running along the eastern side of the creek. He was standing in a northerly direction. He did not appear to have a purpose there and was not looking at any tombstones."

Ms Latif said she was concerned by his appearance and kept watching him until she had finished filling the containers with water. She then drove her car to another section (Islamic) of the cemetery to visit her father's grave and was sitting, crying by the memorial when she again "had a horrible sensation of danger".

She continued in her statement: "Again he was striding along the road towards me purposely, and I felt he was trying to get me with my head down. I stood up and was taller than him. He appeared to be intimidated by the fact I caught him out and he seemed confused as to what he was going to do. He then turned right and began to walk down a row of graves about three rows from the grave I was at. I stopped, turned and was watching him. His shoulders appeared to slump as if he was contemplating what to do."

Yet this wasn't the end of Ms Latif's ordeal as the mysterious man bobbed up in front of her again, this time in the Protestant section of the cemetery. Again, Ms Latif said, the man seemed "focused" on her and started to walk towards her. Terrified, she turned her back on him and started walking to the driver's side of her car. Fortunately, her sister then turned up and the man walked straight past the car.

Ms Latif gave police this description of the man: "This male was about 45 to 50 years old. He looked Anglo, as in Australian. He was about five feet eight. He was stocky with a bulging pot. His hair was very short, grey and receding and was bald at the top. He did not have any facial hair. He never said anything. The look in his eye was the scary part."

In some ways this description did not fit Dupas, but police could not disregard the fact that another woman reported that she had been stalked at the Fawkner Cemetery in the lead-up to Mersina's death.

Ms Latif made this statement on November 19, 1997, just 18 days after Mersina's death. Almost three years later she contacted police again after seeing a photograph of Dupas in the *Herald Sun*. She rang the Homicide Squad and asked to speak with anyone dealing with the murder at the Fawkner Cemetery.

In June, 2001, she made another statement in which she told police: "On the day I saw this man's photo (two days before she made this statement), I can remember vividly what happened. I was at work and I went and collected the newspaper on that day ... When I got to the classroom, I placed it down on my desk and the paper unfolded.

"On the front page of the paper was the photo of the man. I can remember saying to myself, 'Oh God, that's him'. I immediately began to relive what happened on that day at the cemetery. I was glued to the article and read it. I knew prior to reading the article that he was the man who came at me. The photo in the paper showed that he had more hair. On the day I saw him at the cemetery, he didn't appear to have as much hair; in fact he appeared to be balding at the front. I don't know whether or not his hair was brushed back and off his forehead on the day I saw him.

"I continued to read the article and this confirmed that it was him. I am not sure what was in the article that confirmed this in my mind, but I am totally sure that when I first saw that photo of the man, I knew he was the man at the cemetery."

Ms Latif was upset all that day after seeing the photograph and said in her statement that she had nightmares "reliving the fear back that I felt on that day at the cemetery". Ms Latif went with her fiancé and three police officers to the cemetery the Saturday after she contacted the Homicide Squad in August, 2000. She showed them where she was when confronted by the stalker and what he did in his approach to her. She later said in her statement: "I told them on that day again that I have no doubt the person I saw in the photo was the same person who came at me."

Married by the time she made her 2001 statement and now Mrs Dillon, she added her dreadful experience had altered her pattern of visiting her father's grave. She had visited the cemetery weekly for nine years before being stalked, but then went far less often, and never alone.

Importantly, she said in her statement: "I have absolutely no doubt that the person who came at me was going to hurt me and I believe the only reason he didn't was that I stood up and my height threw him."

It appeared the coward who preyed on women had been spotted before he could swing into action and backed off, intimidated by being seen, especially by a potential victim who was bigger than him and therefore a prey not as easily overcome as someone as small and light as Mersina proved to be when she was murdered almost a month later.

She added in her statement: "The first time I saw him, as I said in my first statement, I had my head down and I felt something was wrong and I felt the hairs on the back of my neck stand. I looked up and he was striding at me. I startled him and it was his reaction and the fact that when he walked off he paid no attention to any of the graves that alerted me that something was not right.

"I got the impression that he was trying to get at me when my head was down. When I went to my dad's grave. I was so consumed by grief, I didn't think of this man. I again got the same feeling of danger and I looked up. It was then he came at me again and this time I stood up and towered over him and startled him. It was this point after he had come at me twice when my head was down, I knew he was out to get me."

It was obvious that Dupas was stalking a potential victim and another woman, middle-aged Enza Romanella, also told police of a horrible experience at the Fawkner Cemetery in 1997. Mrs Romanella could not remember the date, but knew it was the Saturday before Mersina was murdered. This meant it was October 25 and, as usual on a Saturday afternoon, she was visiting her late husband's grave in a special lawn area near the cemetery's front gate.

Mrs Romanella was kneeling and placing flowers on the grave when she realised someone was standing near her. When a male said to her "excuse me", she looked around and saw a man wearing a zipped khaki jacket. He was holding a piece of paper in his left hand but, perhaps more sinister, he had his right hand in a jacket pocket. The man then told Mrs Romanella: "I can't find the grave of my mother (or brother)." She asked him if he was looking for a grave on the lawn, but the man pointed to a commemorative wall. He then asked her: "Can you come and help me look?"

It all seemed so innocent and Mrs Romanella had no concerns at this stage. However, she said in a statement to police:

"We walked over towards the walls and we looked along walls one and two. He did say a name or number, although I can't remember what it was. He told me without me asking. At this point this man asked me to come over and look with him at the others (graves behind a wall). As soon as he asked this, something came over me and I became scared. I felt as if someone was saying don't go with him. I walked back to a park bench, which was close by and sat down. I said to him: 'You go and look for the grave.'"

Mrs Romanella said the man appeared to be agitated when she said she wouldn't help him further and he walked away. She said she became scared when the man asked her to go behind the wall with him and noted that he kept his right hand in his jacket pocket the whole time he was with her. Did this man have a knife in his hand?

Three years later Mrs Romanella was standing in her kitchen watching the television news when she saw an image of a man who had been arrested on a charge of murder. It was Dupas. She said in her statement: "As soon as I saw him I was shocked. I recognised this man on TV as the man that I spoke to at the Fawkner Cemetery in 1997 …

"I remember his eyes and his face and I am sure that the person I saw on TV on that time is the same person. The first time I saw him, it was about this man being charged about a girl (Nicole Patterson) in Northcote. I can't remember anything else said and I am sure that on the first occasion when I saw him, there was nothing said about the girl (Mersina Halvagis) at the Fawkner Cemetery. It was later on, when he was on TV, maybe a week or two later that there was mention about the girl at Fawkner."

A niece of Mrs Romanella, Lina Fichera, told police that her aunt told her a week or two after Mersina's murder of the man approaching her at the cemetery. Mrs Romanella told her the man "never took his hand out of his pocket". The niece asked her: "What do you think he did that for?" However, Mrs Romanella could not give any obvious explanation, but added: "I got scared all of a sudden."

Another woman to experience an unnerving ordeal at the cemetery told police she was "terrified to go back". Mrs Patricia Nemeth, in her 60s at the time of the cemetery murder, was with a four-year-old grandson when she visited her parents' graves one

Saturday afternoon when she walked across a road to get some water for flowers while her grandson sat on grass near her parents' graves. It was then that she spotted a man acting suspiciously and, importantly, she had seen him at the cemetery twice before.

She said in a statement to police: "When I first saw this man, I thought 'where did he come from?' as he just seemed to appear from nowhere. I could see that he kept looking at us and this made me nervous. As I walked towards the tap, the man walked towards me. I thought at first he might have been coming for water, but I couldn't see any cup or container.

"As he came closer, I noticed this man had his right hand in his jacket pocket. I immediately felt he was going to hurt me. I just felt terrible and knew I had to get out of there. He got within about three or four feet of me. If I had reached out or moved a bit, I think I could have touched him.

"This man didn't say anything to me. The fact that he came at me and didn't speak or say something troubled me. I am sure that, thinking back on it, he was definitely not going to the tap. I was the only one there as my grandson was across the road about 20 or 30 feet away. I looked this man straight in the face and I could see he had pasty skin on his face. It was his eyes; they were blank. There was something peculiar about him."

Mrs Nemeth was able to describe this pasty-faced man. She said: "This man had thin gold rimmed glasses on. He was wearing a jacket which was fawny colour and similar to that of a duffle coat. It was down below his waist but it didn't go below his knees. It had two big pockets on it. It was a colour somewhere in between cream and green. He was very agitated. He would have been in his late 30s or 40s, I would say. His hair was brownie or mousy colour."

Mrs Nemeth, sensing danger, rushed back to her grandson and put him in the car and locked the doors. She turned to the little boy and said: "We won't be coming back here again." Later, at home, she told her husband that the mysterious man "scared the daylights out of me".

She thought of contacting police as soon as she heard of the cemetery murder because: "I immediately thought of this man and felt sick. I went hot and felt shocking at the thought." Mrs Nemeth told her husband: "That could be the man I saw." But, for some reason she could not explain, she did not contact police until after she saw a newspaper photograph of Dupas being led into court over the murder of Nicole Patterson.

Mrs Nemeth told police: "I only saw the side of his face, but immediately I knew that he was the same man that came at me at the Fawkner Cemetery, the week before the murder of the young girl there. As soon as I saw his photo I knew it was him. I felt sick and I told my family, 'I know this man. I've seen him. He was the one at the cemetery.' I didn't read the article as I felt sick.

"I later saw another article with a photo of this man's full face. Again I felt sick when I saw this photo, as I know that he was the man that came at me in the cemetery." Mrs Nemeth told police she told her son-in-law: "I looked the murderer in the face. This is the man I stared in the face. He frightened us to death and we left the cemetery." Before making her statement, she went with police to the cemetery to show them where she saw this man. Mrs Nemeth closed her statement with the chilling comment: "I am 100 per cent sure that the man that came at me at the cemetery is the man I saw in the paper regarding the murder of the other girl (Nicole Patterson)." She was sure it was Peter Norris Dupas!

The problem for police was that this was merely circumstantial evidence, despite the fact that Mrs Nemeth was certain the man at the cemetery was Dupas. There also was her recollection that the man had his right hand in his jacket pocket. Again, was this for concealing the knife in his hunt for an intended victim?

And there were other witnesses who told similar accounts of being stalked at the cemetery. One woman, Laima Burman, told police of how a man approached her at the cemetery early on the morning of November 1, 1997 — just hours before Mersina Halvagis was murdered.

Mrs Burman was doing maintenance work in the Latvian section of the cemetery when a man came up to her and asked if she worked at the cemetery. She told him she did (standing in for her son with voluntary work because he was overseas) and the man told her that he had just found his adoptive mother's grave and that he was completing his family tree. When Mrs Burman offered to help him, he gave his name as John Roberts and gave her an incomplete telephone number. She then gave him a rake so he could do some tidying around the grave he claimed was his adoptive mother's. Yet when she returned to the grave, there had been no tidying up.

Mrs Burman told police: "I found this man to be most unusual. When this man told me that he hadn't seen his adopted mother, I wondered how this could be as I believe the normal circumstances are that a person is adopted because the biological mother has either died or disappeared for whatever reason. She also was puzzled by the fact that the headstone on the grave the man claimed was that of his adoptive mother had a Latvian name, yet the man gave an Anglo-Saxon name.

The woman also told police the man smelt of alcohol and, most sinister of all, twice asked her what was behind a nearby hedge. Mrs Burman later kept an eye on the gravesite the man pointed out, but it never appeared to have any maintenance or care.

She gave police this description of the man: "He would be aged in his late 30s, he had fair to light brown straight collar-length neat hair. He was wearing prescription glasses, he was of medium build and about five feet seven inches tall. He was on his own and I recall that he was wearing what looked like white runners. He was also wearing what looked to be black tracksuit pants which were gathered at the bottom. He had a waist-length jacket on. It was light coloured and was done up halfway."

Most significant of all, Mrs Burman said the man kept his hands in his jacket pockets the entire time she was speaking with him. She added: "I also noticed a tear in the area of the right pocket. The pockets were positioned in the lower section of the jacket. The jacket had either a zipper or buttons that were hidden under the fold."

When Mrs Burman heard there had been a murder at the cemetery she provided police with a computer drawing "depicting a likeness" of the man she had seen there on the morning Mersina Halvagis was stabbed to death. She also indicated to police that she believed the drawing was "a 65 per cent likeness". In fact, it was a truly remarkable likeness by graphic artist Timothy Hardiman.

Mrs Burman made this statement in April, 1999, but made a second one after being shown photographs of a possible suspect and then a third one 16 months later, on August 19, 2000. She was holidaying in Echuca with her husband three days earlier when she took a telephone call from Detective Acting Inspector Greg Hough, of the Homicide Squad, who asked if she could try and identify something for him. He gave her no further information, but he contacted her again soon after she returned to Melbourne from her holiday.

On August 16 the Burmans had driven to Kyabram and bought a newspaper. Mrs Burman told police in this third statement that the papers were stacked on a counter and the front page item immediately caught her attention. There was a photograph of a man wearing glasses and she realised it was the same one she had spoken to at the cemetery.

Mrs Burman said: "I kept looking at the photo and I put my little finger over the photo on the right side of his head. I did this so I could get a better view of him straight on, as I saw him for most of the time at the cemetery. I repeated this several times while we were in the shop. I immediately kept saying to myself 'that's him, that's him'. She said that after her husband had bought the newspaper, they went outside the newsagency and sat on a bench.

Mrs Burman added: "I was shaking inside and I am not sure whether my emotions were showing outwardly. I was upset and I had lots of thoughts going through my head. I saw the front page and I saw his photo. I was drawn by the big headline and when I had a good look at the photo, he was familiar. I know that person in the photo is the one I was with."

The Burmans returned to Melbourne two days later and, on the morning of August 19, Det. Acting Inspector Hough contacted her again. He asked her what she did on her holiday and Mrs Burman told him she had read the papers. The police officer replied: "I hoped you weren't going to say that". He then asked: "Was that the man you saw at the cemetery?"

"Yes, it was," Mrs Burman replied. Det. Acting Inspector Hough then asked her not to read any more newspapers or watch television until she made another statement, which she arranged to do the following day.

In this statement she said: "I have often thought about that day at the cemetery and the time I was with that man. I have thought of what he was saying to me. I thought at the time I saw the photo of the man, that he looked a little bit older than what he looked like on the day he spoke to me, but it definitely was him."

It was another witness able to place Dupas at the Fawkner Cemetery on the day of the murder, and there were others. For example, Horst Weller and partner Patricia Rodrigues told police they saw a man they believed was Dupas on November 1, 1997. Weller knew this with certainty as his father had died just 11 days earlier and was visiting his grave. Ms Rodrigues went with him to visit her late husband's grave.

Weller did not contact police until early in 2005 after seeing Dupas on television in relation to the murder of Margaret Maher. When police asked him why it had taken him so long to report what he had seen and experienced on the day of Mersina's murder, he told them he was "scared to get involved especially with my family tells me that Dupas could arrange for me to be harmed or even killed". Weller even apologised to Mersina's father George for taking so long to come forward and said "I just want forgiveness".

In the statement he made to police on March 22, 2005, he told of the visit he and his partner made to the cemetery between 3pm and 4.30pm on the day of Mersina's murder. He said that after he and Ms Rodrigues walked through the gates he saw two feet behind a tree. He said to his partner: "Look, there is someone standing there."

Then, as he kept walking, Weller had a quick look at the man who had been standing behind a tree. The man stared at him for several seconds and Weller noted his metal-framed glasses. Weller said: "I remember that they were prescription type glasses because I could see the glare of light shining off them and I could clearly see his eyes. I remember thinking that he had a look in his eyes as if he was startled by something as they were opened wide and I could clearly see the whites of his eyes."

Just like other witnesses, Weller also noted that the man had his right hand in his jacket pocket. He was not too concerned at the time, but thought to himself: "What's his problem?"

Weller gave police this description: "This man looked as though he was younger than me but I can't pick what age, maybe 45 or 55 years old, but that's a guess. I remember he had ginger coloured hair and I could see what looked like silver strands on his left side. I couldn't really see his left side. I don't recall how long his hair was at the back but he had a fringe that was brushed forward and the side of his hair was straight down.

"I think he was maybe about my height, but it's hard to say as he was slightly hunched forward. I am five feet seven inches tall and I wouldn't think he was much taller than me. He was wearing a dark blue jacket with a zipper up the front. The jacket had a collar on it that was a different material and was a dark colour as well. The jacket was like a nylon-type material. I recall he had dark trousers on but I can't recall if they were blue or black. He had dark shoes on but I can't recall what type. I don't think he was wearing joggers or anything like that. This man looked a bit plumpish but I wouldn't describe him as fat."

Weller and his partner did not see the man again but after seeing Dupas on television said: "I can't recall how long after the murder I saw this picture of Dupas on the television. At the time of seeing this picture of Dupas, I straight away thought to myself that I know this man's face. I thought about it for a while and I recalled that this was the same man that I saw this day at the Fawkner Cemetery."

There appeared to be discrepancies in these witness statements with, for example, descriptions of the jacket worn by the man in the cemetery ranging from being light-coloured to dark blue. Also, the colour of the hair varied from ginger to brown. One constant, however, was that the man had his right hand in his jacket pocket and had a strange, frightening appearance. Police therefore wanted more evidence, even though there were other witnesses who gave similar accounts of seeing a strange man at the cemetery. These other witness described similarly eerie experiences, with two of them hypnotised to refresh their memories after they had contacted police.

One of these witnesses, receptionist Angela Rowe (later Baran), made an initial statement on January 3, 1998, just two months after Mersina's murder. She arrived at the Fawkner Cemetery just before 4pm on November 1, 1997, and, after walking towards the grave she was visiting, "felt as if someone was watching me". Ms Rowe then saw a man walking towards the graves where she was sitting.

She said in her statement: "When I saw him he was looking in my direction and he did not appear to be looking at the graves or anything like that. I don't think he was carrying anything. I looked away and then looked back a couple of seconds later and couldn't see him. I thought I had better leave because I thought, 'where did he go?' and I felt something was not right."

The description of the man Ms Rowe gave police also varied from other witness statements, but had some similarities. She could not remember what the man was wearing, but stated that he had "very blond short hair, messed as if it had gel in it". She added: "It looked too blond to be natural, like it was dyed and you could see some dark bits on the side and at the roots." This part of her evidence was significant as police later tracked down Dupas' hairdresser, who gave them some extremely interesting information.

Police believed Ms Rowe could provide them with further details and therefore arranged for her to undergo hypnosis. It was explained to her that in hypnosis the memory "tends to work better the more relaxed you are". In preparation for hypnosis, Ms Rowe totally relaxed and made herself "feel like a rag-doll".

Then, under hypnosis, she explained that she was at the cemetery to visit an aunt's grave. Ms Rowe also told of how the man stood looking at her and then disappeared. She said: "The main thing that stood out, (was) that he had very, very blond hair" before adding that the man had "pinkish skin". Ms Rowe also recalled that the man was wearing a blue jacket and was "looking at me in a strange way".

Ms Rowe's evidence under hypnosis did not provide police with a great deal more evidence, but it added to their conviction that the man responsible for stalking woman at the cemetery and then killing Mersina was the same man. And they were convinced that man was Dupas.

Police recontacted Ms Rowe in May, 2005, and asked her if she had any further thoughts about what had happened the day she saw this strange man and Mersina was killed at the cemetery. She told a detective, Paul Scarlett, that she was home with a friend, Sarah Roe, when she flicked through a copy of the *Herald Sun* and noticed a photograph of Dupas.

She said in a further statement: "As soon as I saw the picture I said to Sarah: 'Oh my God, that looks like him; he's got the same skin.' I definitely said something along the lines of 'but I'm not sure because this man has brown hair and the man in the cemetery I saw had blond hair'."

Ms Roe also told police of her friend Angela seeing Dupas' photograph in the newspaper and of how Angela had told her a few years earlier of her unnerving experience at the cemetery. She said she could remember having a conversation with her friend about how someone could change their hair colour.

She said: "I can recall telling Angela that you can change your hair colour but not your skin. When Angela was telling me about this, I got the impression that she was frightened. I recall that the picture of Dupas was very big and it took up about half the front page … A couple of months ago I saw (on the news) the parents of the girl (Mersina) who was killed. I rang Angela and told her that it was on the news and that the police were offering a reward. Angela told me that she didn't care about the reward …"

Finally in this litany of witnesses who saw a mysterious man at the cemetery, 72-year-old Katica Melnik contacted police late in 2004 after she had seen police on television asking for witnesses to come forward. Mrs Melnik also had seen the grieving Halvagis parents on television and wanted to get what she had experienced off her chest.

Mrs Melnik often went to the Fawkner Cemetery to tend her parents' graves and, on November 1, 1997, asked friends Anna Wisnovska and Cveta Gurgevsak to join her because they too had relatives interred in the Ukraine Section. The trio reached the cemetery soon after 3pm and, after visiting the graves of Mrs Melnik's parents, they walked over to what they believed to be the Greek Macedonian Section.

One of the trio, Cveta Gurgevsak, walked ahead and when her friends caught up with her they noticed she was speaking with a male stranger. She said in her statement to police that the man turned his head away from her after he had spotted her. She added: "The way this man did this made me think he was a bit shy or something. I remember he was wearing glasses, but they weren't sunglasses. He had both hands in his pockets."

The trio left the cemetery around 4pm and, next day, Mrs Melnik heard there had been a murder at the cemetery. She said: "I remember feeling sick when I found this out." Some time later, Mrs Melnik was watching the television news when she saw a photo of a man accused of another murder. It was Dupas. She told police: "As soon as I saw this man's face, I straight away knew that I had seen him before somewhere. I recall thinking for the next hour or so, where I had seen this man before and it was then that I remembered that he was the man I saw at the Fawkner Cemetery on the day that the girl was killed … I remember that I couldn't sleep that night thinking of this man."

In a later statement, Mrs Melnik said: "When I first saw this man that I think is Dupas, he turned his head away from me and I recall thinking that he appeared a little confused or something."

The evidence from all these witnesses might have been comprehensive, but it was all circumstantial and police knew they had a lot more work ahead of them before they could charge Dupas with the murder of Mersina Halvagis. They knew with a fair degree of certainty that Dupas was the killer, but they knew they would find it difficult to prove this in a court of law. A man so many witnesses said was Dupas or looked remarkably like him had either stalked them or had been at the cemetery, but there was no forensic evidence. Regardless, police kept plugging away, even though Dupas later was locked away, never to be released. Police wanted finality and, more importantly, closure for the Halvagis family.

They therefore left no stone unturned in their investigation and, for example, questioned Dupas' hairdresser and optician, hoping for a vital breakthrough or, at least, further links in the chain of circumstantial evidence. They would never close their files on Mersina's murder.

Because of witness statements referring to the hair colour and style of the man seen at the cemetery, police contacted hairdresser Domenica d'Alberto, who told them he had been cutting and styling Dupas' hair on a regular basis. In a statement made to police in April, 1999, d'Alberto said he had operated his business "Mim's Hair on the Move" for five years and advertised his visiting hairdressing services in Leader newspapers servicing the northern suburbs.

After checking his appointment book, d'Alberto was able to tell police he first called on Dupas at Coane Street, Pascoe Vale, on February 18, 1997 — almost nine months before Mersina was murdered. Importantly, he told police he changed Dupas' hairstyle from an undercut to a blended one. The appointments then were about six weeks apart and d'Alberto bleached Dupas' hair every third visit. He said: "I would bleach it enough so that it had a streaked effect, which meant there would be very light blond tips. They at times would be almost white blond ... his hair style was very fine or limp and I just used to cut it like a bowl cut."

After further checking his records, d'Alberto was able to tell police that Dupas had his normal haircut, with the bleaching, on October 21, 1997 — just 10 days before Mersina was murdered. Dupas then made an appointment for December 10 and although this booking later was cancelled, d'Alberto noted in his appointment book that Dupas had asked for a change in colouring, "possibly because I was putting too much bleach in or possibly for another reason".

Could that reason have been because Dupas knew he had to change his hairstyle and colour so that no one could recognise him?

The appointment was re-booked for five days later and d'Alberto last cut Dupas' hair on March 25, 1999. Exactly a month later, d'Alberto went to the St Kilda Road Police Headquarters and was asked to describe how Dupas looked in 1997. There were three pictures drawn on a computer and the first showed Dupas at the time the hairdresser first met him. The second was how he looked when he changed his hairstyle and the third was of Dupas wearing glasses. The third photo was important as Dupas did not always wear glasses when he saw d'Alberto.

The hairdresser made another statement six years later, on May 20, 2005, after police had received further information on Dupas and his possible involvement in the cemetery murder. After again telling police of when he first styled Dupas' hair, d'Alberto said in a statement: "Since having made that first statement to police I have had plenty of time to think about my dealings with Peter Dupas. I recall that I used to think that Peter was always a bit odd."

One of d'Alberto's concerns arose after he told Dupas he had a friend in the Victoria Police. Dupas then kept asking his hairdresser questions about this police officer and whether he was still seeing him. He also asked for the officer's name, but d'Alberto told Dupas it was none of his business.

In relation to Dupas wanting to change his hairstyle, d'Alberto said: "According to my diary I cut Peter's hair on October 21, 1997, and it was at around this time that Peter one day asked me to change his hairstyle. I recall the conversation with Peter because he became quite irate that I couldn't do anything with his hair. I recall thinking that I was feeling uncomfortable with his aggressive attitude and I had to say something to him to calm him down."

Dupas told the hairdresser that he wanted his hair style changed because he was planning a holiday to Queensland and that he didn't need a bleach as the hot sun would do this up north. The hairdresser told police: "Peter was just so determined to change his hairstyle."

Dupas also was determined to change the style of spectacles he wore. He claimed he had damaged a pair while at work, but police believed he had damaged them when he attacked Mersina so viciously. Police therefore asked Dupas' optician, Jack Sgourakis, to tell them about Dupas changing spectacles. Sgourakis, who ran the "World of Specs" business in Mahoneys Road, Cambellfield, told police that Dupas had his eyes tested on November 7, 1997 — six days after the cemetery murder.

Mr Sgourakis said Dupas previously had separate reading and distance glasses but now wanted bi-focals. He also told police that Dupas had not changed his distance glasses for five years and his reading glasses for 12 years. Yet, incredibly, he was having his eyes tested for new glasses less than a week after Mersina's murder.

Police also interviewed the optician who tested Dupas' eyesight at Mr Sgourakis' practice. Isabella La Rocca, after telling police of minimal changes in Dupas' optical prescriptions, said in her statement: "I also recall the patient presenting with a small fresh cut on the left cheekbone which I would also have queried. The reason for this query is that if you receive a blow to the cheekbone, it could potentially cause a blow-out fracture to the eye. That would be serious if that happened to any patient. To my knowledge he dismissed it and said it happened at work. As such, it wasn't noted on the patient file. I can remember the cut in that there was no skin over it and looked as if it had been there a day or two and not just happened that day."

Police checked whether Dupas had injured himself or damaged his glasses at work and spoke with the production manager, John Kazakis, at Blue Diamond Furniture. He said the firm where Dupas had worked had 16 factory employees and it was company policy for employees to report injuries, even "the smallest injuries" from a bump to a splinter. He said he explained this policy to Dupas, who therefore must have known the correct procedure. Yet when Mr Kazakis checked the injury book, there was no report of any Dupas injury around the time of him ordering new spectacles.

Mr Kazakis said in a statement: "There is no record of Peter Dupas damaging or breaking his glasses at work. I believe that if Peter had have damaged or broken his glasses at work he would have told me or reported it. It is a practice of the management to replace or assist anyone that breaks or damages personal property at our factory. If Peter had have broken or damaged his glasses at work we would have replaced them or we would have helped him out with payment. I cannot remember any discussion with Peter about him damaging or breaking his glasses."

Police, through the circumstantial evidence they had uncovered, suspected early that Dupas had killed Mersina. They therefore spoke with him at the Coburg Police Station on February 12, 1998, just three months after the murder. The meeting, as police noted at the time "was held in an attempt to ascertain Dupas' knowledge, if any, in the murder of Mersina Halvagis".

Police had tried several times to contact Dupas, but failed to find him at his home in Pascoe Vale. They finally left a calling card at his home and he contacted them and accompanied them to the Coburg station later that day. It was not a formal interview but, rather, a "meeting", with Detective Senior Constable Stuart Bateson, of the Homicide Squad, taking handwritten notes.

These notes read:

*He (Dupas) was released from prison in October, 1996.*

*He was currently living with his girlfriend (whose name he refused to divulge) at Coane Street, Pascoe Vale.*

*He rented these premises.*

*He was employed by Blue Diamond Furnishings, Temple Drive, as a factory hand.*

*He had been so employed for six months.*

*His employment hours were from 7am to 4.30pm weekdays; however he regularly worked one or two hours' overtime.*

*His only knowledge of Mersina Halvagis' murder consisted of what he had read in the newspaper (he was unable to give details of what he had read).*

*He had never been to the cemetery.*

*He did not know of anyone who was buried there.*

*He knew that the cemetery was located on Sydney Road, Fawkner.*

*He stated the closest he had been to the cemetery was an occasional visit to the nearby K-Mart store.*

*He did not know what he was doing on the day of the murder.*

*He currently owned a white Nissan Bluebird station wagon, which he purchased in December, 1997.*

*That at the time of the murder he owned a chocolate brown Ford Cortina which he sold in December, 1997 (to a workmate).*

*He was still occasionally seeing a psychologist by the name of Dr Askar Stirrup of the Brunswick Clinic, Brunswick Road, Brunswick.*

*That his girlfriend was overseas from October, 1997, and did not return until January, 1998.*

*That his hair was regularly coloured by a hairdresser which he believed was known as "Mim's Hair on the Move".*

Bateson noted that Dupas looked much younger when wearing sunglasses and that the suspect had blond tips in his hair, which was parted to the side. He also noticed that Dupas kept brushing his hair to one side to keep it off his forehead. With Dupas' permission, the detective took a photograph of him from the shoulder up.

Dupas rang Det. Senior Constable Bateson the following day to confirm the name of the hairdresser and that, after checking his work records, now could say he was not working on the day of the murder. However, Dupas still could not recount his movements that day. Dupas told police nothing they did not know and insisted he knew absolutely nothing about the murder.

Meanwhile, police were gathering further information in the hope they could charge Dupas with the murder of Mersina Halvagis and, as part of their investigation, had the clothes the dead woman was wearing examined by forensic scientist Jane Taupin, who drew comparisons between this and the Nicole Patterson murder.

On February 28, 2001, Ms Taupin received several items for investigation. These included the trousers Mersina was wearing when she was killed, her long-sleeved T-shirt type top, singlet and bra. Ms Taupin also received a copy of the autopsy report on Mersina's death and relevant photographs in relation to the crime scene and autopsy. She then set about examining the clothing and noted that all four items had been damaged.

Ms Taupin stated that there were six areas of stab-type cuts to the front of the heavily bloodstained top, indicative of six thrusts with a weapon. There also were five stab-type cuts to the back, although some of these might have been caused by the "bunching" of the velour-type material. There also was a slash-type cut to the top of the left sleeve.

The white camisole type singlet with lace trim also was heavily bloodstained and had four areas of irregular damage, with a maximum dimension of 4.5cm. The white bra, which had a lace centrepiece, had five stab-type cuts to the front and two to the band to below the left cup.

Mersina's trousers, which also were heavily bloodstained, had a stab-type cut to the front of the waistband of about 3cm in length. There also was a series of cuts to the lower left front leg and an irregular stab-type cut to the back of the right knee. Finally, there was some damage to the middle back and right back belt loops.

In relation to a comparison of the clothing worn by Mersina and Nicole, Ms Taupin stated under the heading of "stab-type cuts":

"There were numerous stab-type cuts to the clothing of both of the deceased. The multiplicity of the cuts was a distinctive feature in both cases. Some of the cuts in both of the deceased's clothing penetrated many layers or were through thick material such as elasticised straps.

"Although allowances were made for different garment compositions, the profiles of the cuts indicated they may all have been produced by a sharp, smooth single blade (that is, a single cutting-edge) knife. The maximum width of this blade was estimated to be in the order of 2.5cm or 3cm. There were no outstanding features in any of the cuts that may have indicated a particular style of blade.

"It should be noted that knives are mass-produced. Thus even though it was considered that the one knife may have produced all of the stab-type cuts, it was not possible to make a statistical estimate of the quantity of knives capable of producing such damage."

Ms Taupin also reported that although Nicole's clothing also had been cut by scissors, there were no scissor cuts detected to Mersina's clothing. She said in conclusion:

"There were multiple stab-type cuts detected to the clothing of Mersina Halvagis. These cuts were similar in profile to the multiple stab-type cuts detected to the clothing of Nicole Patterson. No scissor cuts were detected to the clothing of Halvagis."

This statement futher convinced police that Dupas also had murdered Mersina, but they also knew it was only one piece in the jigsaw of evidence they were preparing to take Dupas to court and they needed more evidence. They were determined not to allow the worm wriggle from this particular hook.

Police officially interviewed Dupas on August 6, 2002, in relation to Mersina's murder. They knew from the evidence they had collected that their case against him was reasonably strong, if not conclusive, and felt they might get some answers, even though they knew the cold-blooded killer had a propensity for stone-walling and ignoring their questions. They took him from the Port Phillip Prison to the Homicide Squad offices at police headquarters in St Kilda Road and although Dupas was willing to answer questions about his age and whether he was a permanent Australian resident, he then clammed up completely! He even refused to answer the question of whether he once had lived at Coane Street, Pascoe Vale. Again, he was quietly spoken and asked to speak up.

The interview was conducted by Detective Inspector Greg Hough in the presence of Detective Senior Sergeant Phil Shepherd.

Hough, after the usual preliminaries of informing Dupas of his legal rights, asked him: "Are you aware of the murder of Mersina Halvagis?" Dupas would have had to be living on Mars not to know of this murder, but set the tone for interview by saying "no comment".

The interview continued:

Q: Mersina Halvagis was a young lady who had attended the grave of her grandmother at the Fawkner Cemetery. Now, she was attending to the grave, and paying respects to her grandmother when she was murdered. She was repeatedly stabbed by someone, who I believe to be you, with a knife. Do you have any comment about that?

*No comment.*

Q: Were you the person that repeatedly stabbed this young girl?

*No comment.*

Q: OK. The focus of injuries to this girl was to her breasts. She was repeatedly stabbed. Now, do you have a fetish with breasts?

*No comment.*

Q: And you're currently in — serving sentence in regards to the murder of Nicky Patterson. Is that correct?

*No comment.*

Q: During that murder, of which you are convicted, you severed the breasts of that young lady. Is that correct?

*No comment.*

Q: Which would indicate to me that you have some fetish for the female breast. What do you say to that?

*No comment.*

Q: Another injury that occurred to — to Miss Patterson — was an injury to the region of the right eye. That same injury, which was around about the right eye, the right temple region, a similar injury is located on the temple, right temple area of Mersina Halvagis. What do you say to that?

*No comment.*

Q: And, due to your involvement in Miss Patterson, I've gleaned a bit of information to that which makes me believe that you're involved in this murder of Mersina Halvagis. Now I believe that the injury to the right eye, or the region of the right eye, is by you either punching or striking them to catch them off guard.

*No comment.*

When Dupas refused to comment whether he had been to the Fawkner Cemetery, Hough produced a photo image produced with the help of one of the witnesses who claimed to have seen a man looking like Dupas at the cemetery.

Q: Who's that?
*No comment.*

Q: Who does it look like to you?
*No comment.*

Q: Mr Dupas, I put it to you that that is you in the face image. What do you say to that?
*No comment.*

It was obvious Dupas was not going to answer any question whatsoever in case he incriminated himself, but Hough continued the questioning, even trying to get some form, any form, of realisation that the police knew he had killed Mersina.

Q: OK. That face image was compiled by a witness who was at the Fawkner Cemetery on the day of the murder of Mersina Halvagis, at a location approximately 75 metres away from the murder scene. Now, I say to you that that person who's made that face image there was describing you on that day. What do you say to that?

*No comment.*

Q: And I say that — or I would suggest that on that day you tried — tried to coax the witness into a secluded little area, not far from where Miss Mersina Halvagis was murdered. What do you say to that?

*No comment.*

Q: The person who spoke to the witness who compiled that face image gave the name of John Roberts. Do you know John Roberts?

*No comment.*

Q: And did you give the name John Roberts?

*No comment.*

Q: There are three other witnesses who have been approached by a male fitting your description, behaving in the same or similar manner to this person here, who was seen there on the day of the murder, and who I say is you. What would you say about that, the fact that three women have come forward and said there's a male at the cemetery, fitting your description, behaving in the same manner as that person?

*No comment.*

Dupas must have know by this stage of the interview that there was considerable circumstantial evidence pointing to him being Mersina's killer, but he refused to budge on his stance of refusing to comment on any question, even when Hough asked:

Q: I suggest to you that it's you, and on these occasions, you were seeking out a suitable victim to murder. What do you say to that?

*No comment.*

Hough then switched tack and asked Dupas questions about the jacket seized from the house in Pascoe Vale and identified as the one Dupas was wearing when he killed Nicole Patterson.

Q: The description given by this person who made the photo image, relating to the day of the murder, gave a description of the jacket. Now, the description was of a jacket with a tear to the right pocket area of the jacket. Does that description sound familiar to you?

*No comment.*

Q: The jacket was described by this person was a khaki or light coloured jacket, and the person who approached her on this day, who I believe is you, had his hand in the right pocket at all time. What do you say to that?

*No comment.*

Q: I'll just show you a photo of the jacket (shows Dupas the photo after taking it from a paper wrapping), and that's the front of the jacket. Now, as you can see in that light, there's a difference in colour, merely because of the shade of lighting. Can you see that?

*No comment.*

Q: OK, this jacket that I just showed you the photo of the jacket, there's a tear to the right pocket region. Can you see that?

*No comment.*

Q: OK, this jacket that I just showed you the photo of was seized from your house in Coane Street in Pascoe Vale as a result of the murder of Nicky Patterson. Now, do you agree that that occurred?

*No comment.*

Q: That jacket was the jacket you wore on the day you murdered Nicky Patterson. And I believe that jacket is the same jacket as described by the lady who made this face image and described you. What do you say to that?

*No comment.*

Hough, still getting no response from Dupas, then switched his attention to the stalking of other women and his appearance, both before and after the murder.

Q: Was it your intention, when you approached the other women in the weeks leading up to the murder of Mersina Halvagis, to kill them?

*No comment.*

Q: Can you tell me why you picked a defenceless female in an isolated cemetery to murder?

*No comment.*

Q: There was another witness on the day of the murder who came forward and informed us of a male who had dyed hair. That male was in the vicinity of the murder of Mersina Halvagis on that day, and that male had glasses that looked like sunglasses on. What I'll do shortly is show you a video. No, I won't. What I'll do is show you a photo. Who is that?

Hough showed Dupas a photo and asked him "is it you?" Again Dupas replied "no comment" and the detective pointed out that the glasses were photo-chromatic and therefore would appear to be normal glasses in certain light, yet sunglasses in different, brighter light. Dupas wore photo-chromatic glasses and, as his optician told police, had them changed after Mersina's murder.

The detective also asked Dupas about trying to obtain a false alibi after being worried that someone had seen him at the cemetery and then asked the pudgy man in glasses opposite him questions in relation to the similarities between the Patterson and Halvagis murders.

Q: There are certain similarities and I'm not sure whether I've actually stated these to you, but in Miss Patterson, in her murder, that you've been convicted of and currently undergoing sentence, she was killed by an extremely sharp — what's classified as an edged-weapon. She also had an injury to the right eye or temple region, a bruising. So did Miss Halvagis. She had an injury, bruising to the right eye. What do you say to that?

*No comment.*

Q: Is it coincidental that these have occurred in (a) the murder that you have been convicted of and (b) the murder that I say you've committed?

*No comment.*

Q: Another similarity in the murder of Miss Patterson, that took place in her house, an event or occurrence that you orchestrated. And I say to you that you orchestrated that so you could have control. What do you say to that?

*No comment.*

Q: And when you look at the comparison between Miss Patterson's murder and Mersina Halvagis' murder, it's similar. And that is that you orchestrated an environment where you had complete control of your victim. Now, those three similarities alone that I've said — the injury, the sharpness of the weapon, the orchestration of the environment — suggest that you're the killer; the killer of Mersina Halvagis. What do you say to that?

*No comment.*

Q: One other similarity in both of these cases is that there's no indication of sexual assault. Now, that is strange because a young woman normally doesn't get murdered just for the sake of it. But in both of these cases, Nicky Patterson, that you're convicted of killing, and Mersina Halvagis, it occurs. There's no motive in either of them, apart from a person who has got a drive that makes them do these things. What do you say to that?

*No comment.*

Hough then moved on to the question of Dupas' telephone records and how there had been calls to escort agencies while girlfriend Iolanda Cruz was on holiday in South Africa. The detective even suggested that Dupas was a "psycho-sexual offender", but there still was no reply but "no comment". After suggesting Dupas' sexual drive had caused him to commit such horrific crimes, Hough turned to trying to shame Dupas and make him feel guilty.

Q: It's a tragedy she (Mersina) has been murdered. An innocent kid who did nothing. She was tending her grandmother's grave, and living life. And what I suggest is that you come along and decided to take that life away. What do you say to that?

*No comment.*

Q: And that occurred because you couldn't control sex — psycho-sexual drive. What do you say to that?

*No comment.*

Q: It's pretty hard, I would suggest, to actually sit back and realise what's occurred to that young girl, and accept the fact that you were the one that did it. What do you say to that?

*No comment.*

Hough also asked Dupas questions about Mersina's actual death, including what the monster might have said to her as he was killing her and whether or not she pleaded for her life. Again, the replies were "no comment". Hough continued:

Q: 'Cos she certainly fought. Now, Mr Dupas, the evidence that I've shown you there from witnesses, your criminal history, your drive, your sexual drive that you couldn't control, I think is enough evidence to make you realise that you did kill Mersina Halvagis. Am I wrong?

*No comment.*

Q: A young girl who was going to get married, had everything to live for, was the daughter of a loving, devoted family, minding her own business and tending to her grandmother's grave was preyed upon, I suggest, by you through your psycho-sexual drive. Now, if there's anything that you can tell us about this I would be greatly appreciative, and I think you would too. Do you agree?

*No comment.*

At this stage of the interview, however, Hough could tell that Dupas was reacting to these highly emotional questions, not in remorse, but probably in realisation that the police knew with certainty he had killed this innocent young woman.

Q: You seem to be fairly emotionally swollen, choked up. Is that because realisation has hit home, or is it because you cannot bring yourself to admit what you've done.

This time, there was no reply whatsoever, not until Hough asked Dupas "what is it?" and got the usual reply of "no comment". Hough then asked Detective Senior Sergeant Shepherd if he wanted to say anything, but he replied "not at this point, no". Hough therefore continued the interview with Dupas and at one stage suggested it was Dupas' habit to take victims by surprise and, in one early case, approached his victim by walking along a nature strip so that she couldn't hear him. He also questioned Dupas about changing his hairstyle and spectacles to alter his appearance, all questions receiving the same monotone reply of "no comment". Hough, before eventually handing over to Shepherd, told Dupas he had a wonderful opportunity to open up and at least say he did not kill Mersina.

Q: This in an opportunity for you to say "it wasn't me". But you haven't done that … if I was in your shoes, and I was being interviewed over a murder, it would be the first thing I would say — "it wasn't me, I never murdered Mersina Halvagis". But you haven't said that. You've chosen not to say that, and you've chosen to exercise your rights (of not saying anything). Now, in the exercising of your rights, I can deduce from that that you're exercising those rights 'cos you don't have to say anything or you can't bring yourself to say "it wasn't me", because you know you did murder Mersina Halvagis. What do you say to that?

*No comment.*

Shepherd took over and repeated that Dupas had been seen at the cemetery before asking the already convicted killer whether he had a breasts fetish. Dupas was shown a video featuring a suggestive T-shirt worn by his partner Iolanda. It featured different sized breasts on different women and Shepherd asked Dupas whether he had given this T-shirt to Iolanda. Again, the reply was "no comment".

Shepherd also asked Dupas questions about the change of spectacles before ending the interview by telling Dupas: "You may be charged with the murder of Mersina Halvagis. You are not obliged to say or do anything unless you wish to do so, but whatever you do say or do may be recorded in evidence. Do you understand that?" There was no audible reply and the interview ended at 7.40pm; it had lasted 50 minutes.

Dupas was not immediately charged with Mersina's murder and at that stage it virtually was a stalemate and police, despite their most strenuous efforts, could do nothing about it. They had no other suspect, but needed more evidence to charge Dupas with the murder of Mersina and, more importantly, have him convicted on that charge.

Then came the breakthrough police had been so desperately wanted for so long. And it came from a completely unexpected source — from within a prison.

## CHAPTER TEN

# The Breakthrough

Police and, in particular, Detective Senior Constable Paul Scarlett, refused to concede that Dupas would get away with murdering Mersina Halvagis. They worked countless hours on the case, checked and re-checked every lead and pored over countless pages of statements and tiny fragments of evidence. Apart from anything else, they wanted to give the Halvagis family closure. Mersina's father, George, rang them every working day to know if there had been any developments. Sadly, they always had to tell him nothing had turned up. Their tremendously hard and painstaking work always seemed to hit a deadend — until they got the breakthrough they so desperately needed.

Scarlett had contacted several prisoners where Dupas had been incarcerated in the hope that one of them might have heard the already convicted killer mention his involvement in Mersina's death. To this stage police were always falling just short of having enough evidence for the Office of Public Prosecutions (OPP) to give them the go-ahead to bring Dupas to trial for Mersina's murder.

Scarlett eventually contacted convicted drug dealer and former high-profile solicitor Andrew Fraser by telephone. Fraser was incarcerated in the Fulham prison in the Gippsland city of Sale and Scarlett knew he had had regular contact with Dupas. It was common knowledge that Fraser and Dupas had developed some sort of friendship and Scarlett hoped that Dupas might have opened up to Fraser. However, the detective also feared that if Dupas had sought Fraser's counsel, the former solicitor might have advised him to keep quiet.

Fraser had practised as a criminal lawyer for more than 30 years, but was arrested on September 13, 1999, on a charge of knowingly being involved in the importation of a commercial quantity of cocaine. The then 50-year-old pleaded guilty and, despite hoping for leniency, was sentenced to seven years' jail, with a minimum of five years before being eligible for parole. He knew criminal law inside out and Scarlett hoped his contact with Dupas in prison would glean at least some information.

Scarlett explained: "We knew Dupas had been hanging around with Fraser in the prison and when I rang Fraser I expected him to tell me to go to hell. I therefore made the phone call fearing the worst and that this would be another deadend. When Fraser came to the phone I asked him if Dupas had said anything to him about Mersina. I was shocked, but delighted when Fraser told me, 'you had better come and see me'.

"I rushed to Sale and saw him the very next morning, but not before we made elaborate precautions. Fraser was very much in fear of his safety as he had seen what could happen to those who had been seen as dobbers and violence in jail can be frightening. Fraser knew he would be taking a risk and, apart from anything else, he regarded Dupas himself as extremely dangerous.

"I met Fraser in the prison officers' mess and security was tight. He appeared nervous and I thought to myself 'is this the breakthrough we need? Is he trying it on with us?' I need not have worried as Fraser provided us with the evidence we so desperately needed.

"There later were suggestions that Fraser gave us this information because there was a $1 million reward for information leading to the conviction of Mersina's murderer, but this reward was offered six months before I spoke with him. If he was only interested in the reward, he would have contacted us. As it was, we contacted him on the off-chance that Dupas had let something slip.

"It was a very delicate operation and, despite all our efforts to impose maximum security, one prison officer made a comment about what we were up to and I had to pull him into line. He had not been malicious or intentionally trying to upset our plans, but merely had been a bit silly with loose lips. When I explained to him that we were interviewing Fraser as part of our plan to charge someone with Mersina's murder he was very, very apologetic. He indicated that he also would like to see closure on this case and told me, 'I'll keep my mouth shut'. And he was as good as his word."

Fraser's statement was so pivotal to the eventual case against Dupas in the murder of Mersina Halvagis that it is reproduced here in full. He stated from the Fulham prison in the Gippsland city of Sale on June 28, 2005:

"My name is Andrew Roderick Fraser, date of birth April 5, 1951. I am currently a prisoner at Fulham Correctional Centre, Sale, serving a term of imprisonment for being knowingly concerned with the importation of a commercial quantity of cocaine and trafficking cocaine.

"I was imprisoned on November 13, 2001, and was moved to Port Phillip Prison ('PPP') in February, 2002. I was placed against my wishes into the protection until, Sirius East at PPP. There I remained until being finally moved to mainstream at PPP on June 12, 2003, and thereafter, on January 5, 2005, moved to Fulham Correctional Centre.

"While at Sirius East, I met Peter Norris Dupas and became close to him. We were the two gardeners for the protection units and spent a large proportion of each day together working in the garden. We also undertook education together studying horticulture and used to watch gardening and associated programs together on TV.

"I have been approached by Detective Senior Constable Paul Scarlett, of the Homicide Squad, who enquired as to whether as a result of my association with Dupas I knew anything of the murder of Mersina Halvagis and further would I be prepared to give evidence against Dupas. I am able to say that Dupas discussed Halvagis with me and made certain admissions, voluntarily and against his interests and, subject to certain preconditions being met, I am prepared to execute a formal statement and give evidence if required.

"By way of background, I say that in jail the etiquette is that you never ask another person what they are 'in' for, or the circumstances surrounding their incarceration; to be honest, to be nosey is to invite violence and I have witnessed such attacks.

"As a result of the foregoing, I did not ask Dupas any questions and was early in the piece concerned not to upset him, or appear overly inquisitive as I consider him to be probably the most dangerous person I have met and I did not want to be attacked. It was only over a period of time Dupas and I started to talk and it was only after the (Margaret) Maher investigation got into top gear that he was clearly rattled and opened up to me more.

"At this point, I should say a little about Dupas; he is very quiet, suspicious, introverted or introspective, socially inept and reticent to talk. Even when discussing matters of interest, he tends not to speak in flowing phrases, rather grabs of sentences, short, followed by long breaks. I did observe when agitated or anxious he would start to shake and on occasions became teary and often when that happened, he could clam up and the conversation would be over. He was very difficult to communicate with, but over the period from when I went to PPP and Dupas was moved to Barwon, approximately one to two months before I went mainstream, he opened up to me as much as I think he is capable of.

"I also think based on years of dealing with these types of offenders, that he had blocked a lot of his offending out of his mind and when the memory returns, this is when he becomes distressed.

"The first indication of Dupas' involvement with the Halvagis murder came before the Maher investigation. At Port Phillip the protection unit is divided into three — Sirius East and West, with West divided into two, A and B side. This is done because of the different types of protection required. East's for the worst of the worst, that is considered everyone wants to get. This is where I was placed.

"West's roughly divided into sexual offenders on one side and those too violent or unreliable to be in the general population. The garden area therefore had different access times for the three units. At the back of Sirius East is a small 'chook pen' exercise yard and this looks on to the garden and the other units can see into this yard when they are in the garden. It is separated by a mesh fence.

"Dupas and I were alone walking in the 'chook pen' when one of the other units had use of the garden. It was early in the morning and before the Maher investigation caused Dupas to be interviewed. He had not mentioned Halvagis to me at all. A younger Greek prisoner — I don't know his name — came right up to the fence and said 'you are Peter Dupas'. 'Yes'. He then commenced to berate Dupas saying Halvagis was a cousin of his. Dupas was an animal; he knew Dupas had killed Mersina and that if he got the chance he would kill Dupas.

"This verbal attack was out of the blue and Dupas was clearly shaken by the barrage. He turned to me and said, his exact words were: 'How does that cunt know I did it?' I was surprised at his admission because he was saying he had done it. I remembered this because it was significant.

"About a week later we were in the veggie garden when I noticed Dupas was looking at one of the upper windows of Sirius West; he was starting to shake, a sure sign to me he was agitated. I asked what he was looking at and he told me he now knew which cell the abusive one was in and he was going to try and 'knock' him because he would not be allowed to go around saying such things. I took this utterance seriously.

"A short number of days later we were again in the garden when Dupas said that he knew when that person would be going to the doctor and he was going to jump him then and kill him. He told me in no uncertain terms not to be in his way and it would be better if I was elsewhere as he did not want me involved. He took the garden fork and put it where it could not be seen near the pathway. Luckily that person did not go to the doctor that day and was shortly thereafter moved. Nothing further came of that incident.

"When the police let the media know that Dupas was again being investigated for the Maher murder, Dupas' demeanour changed markedly; it was at this time he started to ask me questions. It was never a discussion, always short questions or series of questions that seemed to have no starting or finishing point, but to me it was clear that he was asking me about Maher and seeking my opinion.

"As s464 (of the Crimes Act) was served and he was obviously and deeply distressed, he asked me about the procedure and I told him he could decline to consent and he did not have to answer questions. I referred him to a private practitioner for advice as he was dissatisfied with Legal Aid.

"At this stage I am unsure of exact chronology, but with further thought and checking of dates I will be sure. You must remember this approach came out of the blue and I had not prepared a draft prior to this.

"When Dupas was interviewed pursuant to s464 he came back to jail and he immediately sought me out in my cell; he was upset and said he thought he would not only be charged with Maher, but also maybe with Halvagis. I thought it was time to try and gently coax the story from him. I asked what the new or extra evidence they had for Maher. Dupas said there was mention of forensic evidence, a glove. He then made a surprising admission to me that he left no forensic evidence at Fawkner. This clearly meant Halvagis.

"He also referred to the other 'old sheila' down the road. He lived in Pascoe Vale and I took this to mean the old lady in Brunswick whose murder remains unsolved *(Dupas is a suspect in the murder of 95-year-old Kathleen Downes, who was stabbed to death in a Brunswick nursing home on December 31, 1997)*. After this admission and due to his stressed state, we did not have any other relevant conversations until after he was charged and he received his brief for Maher.

"Needless to say, as soon as he received the Maher brief, he asked me to read it, which I did. The first thing I noticed was a similar fact to the psychologist — I forget her name (psychotherapist Nicole Patterson) — that he was convicted of killing and explained the allegations were similar, ie, a frenzied knife attack and subsequent mutilation. I also indicated the same modus operandi applied to Halvagis. Dupas repeated he left no forensics at the scene and no one, not even the deceased, would have seen him as he attacked from behind as she was either kneeling at or bending over her grandmother's grave — a frank and surprising admission.

"I emphasised the potential problem with the glove containing DNA traces at the Maher scene and he again stressed he left no DNA or forensics at the Halvagis scene.

"I cannot recall at what stage of proceedings he was moved to Barwon but he was subsequently convicted and sentenced in the Maher matter.

"About mid to late 2004, I became a prison listener at PPP. This is a peer support job and prisoners discuss their problems with you. I was in mainstream by this time but was one of the designated listeners for protection. I was called to see a prisoner at Sirius East and I was surprised to see it was Dupas; he was back at PPP for some court reason which I do not recall.

"There had been more publicity and media speculation regarding Halvagis and again he was upset. The crux of this conversation was again that he could not be charged because of lack of evidence, ie, no forensics left at the scene by him and no one could have witnessed the attack because no one was around. This is the first time he actually stated as a positive that he knew there were no witnesses; it was clear to me that there was only one way he would have known that fact and that is, he is the killer.

"He did not seem in the least bit perturbed by this conviction regarding Maher; he effectively said 'oh well'.

"I did not have any further discussion with Dupas after that. PPP would have a record on the running sheets of when I went to see Dupas for the last time."

Fraser indicated at the end of this statement that he was prepared to give evidence if required and admitted that some events might be out of order as he would have to check dates.

In further comments to his draft statement, Fraser told Scarlett: "When you first arrived and spoke to me unannounced, I was caught somewhat by surprise regarding the matters and accordingly the previous 'can say' statement I provided was missing some important details. You must appreciate that it is only since your representations that I have given this matter detailed thought.

"Hereunder are now further aspects of this case that have come to mind since my previous statement. If further detail comes to me I will advise ...

"The additional matters are: In the discussion I had with Dupas in the cell about Halvagis and him not leaving any forensics at the scene, I add that his body language is easy to read; he sits upright when anxious or stressed, stares ahead, starts to shake (and can even be a bit teary) and he folds his hands and clamps them between his knees. He rocks back and forth a little, but it is noticeable.

"This is how Dupas was sitting when talking about Halvagis but then he jumped up and did a little pantomime of a person leaning over, which I took to be Halvagis, followed by his demonstrating a stabbing motion of the other person. He lifted his hand up about shoulder high and executed a swift, sharp downward motion. He did not speak while he did this, but the meaning was obvious and not at all ambiguous; he was demonstrating the killing of Halvagis.

"He then sat back on the bed, hands between his knees and the conversation was over.

"I should say here that all his admissions are short and not detailed. Dupas is very introverted and I would say almost sociopathic. He does not relate well to others and has great difficulty talking to others. His conversations with me were always short and sometimes finished abruptly as above described.

"The first occasions Dupas made any mention of any killing was well before he was charged with the Maher matter."

Fraser then named two prisoners, Ray Edmunds (known as "Mr Stinky" because of his distinctive body odour) and Paul Gorman. Edmunds had been found guilty of murdering teenagers Abina Madill and Garry Heywood near Shepparton in 1966 and sentenced to life imprisonment without the possibility of parole, while Gorman had been sentenced to 13 years' jail for rape.

"Ray Edmunds, Paul Gorman, Dupas and I were in the workshop doing 'nuts and bolts', ie, putting sleeves and nuts on locks in bolts. No one else was there and we went there occasionally to have a quiet chat. It was on this day (I don't know the date) that I was talking to Edmunds about his sentence. At this stage, he had served about 20 years and I asked him how he handled it. His response was he had done what he had done, a bad offence, regretted it and had paid and was continuing to pay a heavy price. Gorman then admitted his offences (rape) and said he was near the end of his sentence and upon release he would probably re-offend as he could not help himself. Dupas was next to Edmunds and Edmunds said, 'what about you, Pete'? Dupas hesitated and all was quiet; he then haltingly admitted the killing of Nicole Patterson.

"I was surprised because he pleaded not guilty. He was not remorseful, rather off-hand in fact. 'What's done is done and I have to wear it.' I then admitted my offence as I did not want to be the odd man out.

"Finally, as evidence of propensity to violence and in addition to the comments made about the planned attack on another prisoner in the garden I previously mentioned, there was another incident between Dupas and another prisoner. Dupas is quite spooky, very quiet and you have no idea what he is thinking. We were sitting at a table having dinner and he indicated another prisoner who he perceived had slighted him in some way. Dupas was mumbling about getting him. I thought nothing more of it until before lockdown when he kept saying he was going to get him in the morning. To 'get' in jail means to attack with a view to inflicting serious harm or death. Dupas mentioned this a few more times that evening. He was shaking and I took this threat so seriously I mentioned it to the officers. On lock-up Dupas told me he was going to get him first thing next morning because the staff are usually outside having a coffee and a smoke and the unit is quiet.

"On let-out Dupas came flying up the stairs; this was unusual because he has a bad knee and avoids the stairs, even to come to my cell. I saw he had an implement which looked sharp in his hand. He said, 'where is he?' and I told him the person in question had been moved last night. He appeared deflated and went back downstairs. My opinion is that he stewed on this all night and had worked himself into a state by the next morning. He was ready for and capable of anything in my opinion."

Fraser made several alterations to his statement but no significant change in relation to what Dupas told him about the Halvagis murder, except to say that after saying there were no forensics at the murder scene, Dupas pointed to a speaker on the cell wall as if to indicate "no more talk". Fraser added: "With that he jumped to his feet, turned and faced the bed and used a downward opening motion of his arms and indicated a person bending forward. He stood back and, with an arm movement, then indicated himself and further he indicated a raised right arm and then a downward stabbing motion. This indicated to me how he had killed Halvagis and why she would not have seen him."

Fraser, who said he was contacted by the Homicide Squad and "did not approach the prosecution", also said in his statement after reading the first two drafts:

"It has been annoying me that I have not been able to adequately describe the way Dupas communicates. I have previously described it as speaking in grabs or snatches; the word I have been searching for is 'disjointed', in other words his conversations do not flow. In addition he appears to keep himself under a tight rein and occasionally things get the better of him and he will utter something that he almost instantaneously regrets and he clams up again.

"You can almost watch the pressure build; he becomes obviously anxious, commences to shake, with a little sweat around the temples. He then utters whatever it is he says and almost immediately you can see him check himself and the conversation is over.

"I have had many years dealing with criminals and I have dealt with many murder trials. It is my opinion based on that experience that Dupas is probably the most dangerous and unpredictable person I have ever met.

"I have now recalled when on my run on Wednesday, June 22, 2005, that in the garden at PPP, Dupas and I regularly found contraband hidden in the garden — drugs, knives and, on one occasion, part of what I would describe as an incendiary device. Dupas always threw these items into the rubbish bin and instructed me to do likewise, otherwise the bringing of these items to the attention of the officers usually resulted in a lock-down and search and you could be locked down for days as has happened on more than one occasion following items being located in the jail.

"On one day I recall clearly I was weeding a garden bed outside Sirius West Unit and uncovered a substantial home-made knife. The knife appeared to me to be made from a table tennis brace and was very professional. One side had been ground down (usually done on one of the concrete pathways) and had a taped handle. I called Dupas over and showed him the item, as was usual when we found something. He looked at the knife — he was on my left — and took it from me. He started to move the knife up and down as if feeling the balance of the item. He started to sweat and looked at me with a very strange look on his face. I was apprehensive at this time and he uttered one word — 'Mersina' — (I am unsure of the spelling) and handed the knife back. I put it in the bin but was shaken by the incident. I had no doubt that he was referring to the deceased Halvagis and had no doubt he was telling me he had stabbed and killed her with a similar instrument.

"I was so concerned by this that the next day I checked the bin had been emptied and that the knife was gone."

Fraser signed this statement at the Sale Police Station at 12.36pm on June 28, 2005. It was the missing piece in the Mersina Halvagis jigsaw and police now knew they had moved close to charging Dupas with her murder.

With Fraser giving police the breakthrough they needed with these secretly recorded statements, along with his agreement to provide evidence for the prosecution of Dupas, they drove Dupas from the Barwon Prison to Homicide Headquarters on September 2, 2005, for another interview, this time conducted by Detective Senior Constable Scarlett.

Dupas knew why police were taking him for questioning and Scarlett recalled: "He initially was very nervous, although he knew we were going to question him about Mersina's murder. He was dressed in prison clothes of white T-shirt and green tracksuit, with sneakers.

"He chatted about various matters on the drive to police headquarters and referred to his camping trips before he was imprisoned and about his woodworking. Immediately after we arrived, however, he asked one of the police officers to examine his body. He told him: 'These coppers are going to bash me'.

"We had nothing of the sort in mind and the interview was merely procedural. We knew he would tell us nothing about the murder and, sure enough, as soon as we started questioning him his demeanour changed completely. From being quite talkative in the car, he became the opposite. It was like he had put a steel shutter down and went into prison mode in replying 'no comment' to our questions.

"Earlier, he had his head up, even though he wouldn't look us in the eye. But, as soon as the interview got under way, he had his head down. He tried to keep a dead-pan expression on his face, but having dealt with him previously, I looked for certain little tell-tale signs. For example, he sometimes would move his eyes as if the questions had hit a mark. Interviewing Dupas was a very unusual experience as it was like trying to open a locked door without a key."

The interview opened at 11.30am and, again, Dupas was willing only to give his name and date of birth, etc. When Scarlett told him he would be asking questions about the murder of Mersina Halvagis,

Dupas clammed up with his usual "no comment". He even used this reply to whether he knew of the murder or whether he had ever been to the Fawkner Cemetery. Scarlett even asked him directly: "Did you attack and stab Mersina Halvagis at the Fawkner Cemetery on November 1, 1997?" Following the usual "no reply", Scarlett suggested to Dupas that "this might be an opportunity to put forward any explanation, any circumstances that you would like to talk about." Again, the reply was "no comment".

The interview was adjourned briefly and, on resumption, Scarlett told Dupas: "Since you were interviewed in 2002, a number of new facts and circumstances have come to light. And from these facts, numerous people have identified you being at the Fawkner Cemetery in the weeks leading up to Halvagis' death." He then asked: "Are you able to give any explanation as to why these people would say this?"

Following a barely audible "no comment", Scarlett dealt Dupas a savage blow when he said: "We've taken a witness statement from a person (Andrew Fraser) who has stated that you have made admissions to Halvagis' death. Are you able to give us any comment about that?"

Scarlett recalled that this question definitely shook Dupas, even though the already convicted killer tried desperately to disguise his emotions. He said: "Dupas had been around the block many times in regard to police interviews and knew how to clam up, but this question seemed to rattle him temporarily. I believe it was a real shock for him to discover that we had a statement from a key witness."

Although Dupas mumbled his customary "no comment" he must have known he was about to be charged with a murder committed almost eight years earlier.

Before he closed the interview with the obligatory legal warning, Scarlett told Dupas: "OK Peter, this matter will be reported and you may or may not be charged with the offence of murder in relation to Mersina Halvagis."

Although the investigation had dragged on for almost eight wearying years, the end was in sight for Dupas in relation to Mersina's murder and, following this interview, there was a rapid chain of events.

On September 11, 2006, the now 55-year-old Andrew Fraser was released from the Fulham correctional facility at Sale. He was freed two months before his listed earliest release date (November 11) following an agreement between the Office of Public Prosecutions and the state and federal governments in exchange for his co-operation in the Halvagis case. The state government was willing to give Fraser an early release but, because he had offended under Commonwealth law, the federal government had to approve his release. The red-tape frustrated police, but Fraser walked a free man at 11am on September 11 and, within hours, Homicide Squad officers travelled to the Port Phillip Prison to charge Dupas with the murder of Mersina Halvagis.

An inquest into Mersina's death opened at the Coroner's Court on November 19, 2005, with the Director of Public Prosecutions, Mr Paul Coghlan QC, acting as counsel assisting the Coroner, Mr Graeme Johnstone. Newspaper reports that morning suggested the Coroner would hear:

- Nine witnesses say they saw Dupas in the Fawkner Cemetery before the murder.
- Witnesses stating they saw Dupas was within 20 metres of the murder scene at around the time of the vicious attack on Mersina.
- Evidence from a woman who was believed to have been Dupas' original target.
- A crime profiler suggesting the attack had all the hallmarks of previous crimes committed by Dupas.

- Testimony that Dupas lied about how he received a facial injury around the time of the attack.
- Testimony that he tried to change his appearance after the murder.
- Testimony that he described one of his killings to a sex worker.

Holding this inquest was a minor triumph for the Halvagis family, which had fought long and hard to see Mersina's killer brought to justice. George Halvagis told reporters: "We don't want to be told about suspicions; we want to see the evidence on who killed Mersina. I have a great deal of faith in Paul Coghlan. I met him two years ago and he promised us then he would do everything he could to help us. Now all we want is the truth, but nothing will bring Mersina back."

Newspaper reports also indicated that Dupas would be expected to give evidence, but noted that he previously had refused to answer police questions on the cemetery murder and also that he had the right of refusal to answer questions on the grounds of self-incrimination. The net was closing in on Dupas on another murder investigation but, interestingly, he also was named in the lead-up to the inquest as the possible killer of three other women — Helen McMahon, who was bashed to death on a Rye beach on February 13, 1985; Renita Brunton, who was stabbed to death in her used clothing shop in Sunbury on November 11, 1993; and Kathleen Downes, the 95-year-old woman who was stabbed to death in a Brunswick nursing home on December 31, 1997.

The inquest was never completed because of police inquiries but it mattered little in the long term as Dupas already had been charged and was to go on trial for the murder of Mersina Halvagis.

Although the inquest was truncated, it took a terrible toll, not only on the long-suffering Halvagis, but also on Paul Scarlett, whose 67-year-old father was diagnosed during the inquest with a malignant brain tumour. "It was a very harrowing and emotional time," Scarlett said. "I took many calls about my father's health during the inquest and the coroner even was kind enough to give me his personal support.

"George Halvagis also was tremendous to me at this time and I shall never forget the kindness and sympathy the Halvagis family gave me at such a terrible time, especially as they also were going through a difficult and highly emotional period. My father died six months later and George attended the funeral; he simply was amazing and I have nothing but the highest respect for him and his wonderful family."

Scarlett also had nothing but praise for his partner Rania, also a police officer, who gave him unstinting assistance during his years of trying to bring Dupas to justice for Mersina's murder. She had joined Victoria Police after serving as a police officer in Tasmania and was at Port Arthur on April 28, 1996, when gunman Martin Bryant shot 35 people dead. Rania heard the shots and rushed to assist and was so proficient in her duty that she was selected by the Tasmanian police force to meet Prime Minister John Howard on the tenth anniversary of the shootings.

Scarlett said: "Rania's assistance was invaluable as she did a lot of the spade work, typed up all sorts of documents, gave advice and even travelled to Sale with me when I spoke to Fraser. Rania might not have been an official part in the investigation, but she played a massive role in helping us in charging Dupas with Mersina's murder. I cannot thank her enough."

The Supreme Court of Victoria on December 12, 2006, ordered Dupas to be presented directly to trial for the murder of Mersina Halvagis, bypassing the usual committal hearing process. The jury was selected on July 9, 2007, and the trial, in front of Justice Phillip Cummins, lasted 22 days. The Crown was represented by Mr Colin Hillman SC, while Dupas' defence counsel was Mr David Drake, a Victorian Legal Aid-funded barrister.

In a pre-trial hearing, Mr Drake told Justice Cummins that Dupas had reached the international status of "some famous icon of evil" and that when he typed Dupas' name into his internet search engine it showed 78,000 hits. Mr Drake's junior counsel, Mr Mark Regan, said an American website described Dupas as "a predatory sex monster of the worst kind, a cruel and calculating fiend who meticulously went about his depravity and could then melt into a crowd in a heartbeat".

Dupas' two lawyers argued that Dupas was so infamous he could not get a fair trial. However, Justice Cummins disagreed and the trial went ahead.

The prosecution presented its case with meticulous care, with witnesses telling the court of being stalked at the Fawkner Cemetery, of Dupas' change of hairstyle and spectacles. There was evidence from forensic experts and a crime-scene video recorded at Fawkner Cemetery the morning after the murder was shown to the jury.

Fraser, in his evidence, performed a repeat of the macabre pantomime Dupas had used to show him in prison how he had killed Mersina — this evidence presented in front of the Halvagis family sitting in court.

The jury was asked to study the ripped right pocket of a Dupas jacket and also was told that while Dupas' de facto wife was overseas from September, 1997, to the following January, Dupas rang 29 numbers for escort agencies, massage parlours and personal contact services. The evidence seemed overwhelming.

However, Mr Drake told the jury that Fraser did not come forward until a reward had been announced and that Fraser was a "disgraced, imprisoned bankrupt and struck-off solicitor".

The defence also suggested that Mersina's fiance, Angelo Gorgievski had been untruthful in his evidence. Mr Drake put to him: "You hadn't rung her throughout the night on her mobile phone, I suggest, because you knew she wouldn't answer it. And you ran up that aisle precisely to the body because you knew where it was."

"No, I did not," Gorgievski replied.

Mr Drake continued: "Mr Gorgievski, did you have anything to do with the death of your fiancée, Mersina Halvagis?"

"No, I did not, I loved her. I still love her."

The jury of eight men and four women took just over a day to find Dupas guilty. Mersina's mother Christina clutched rosary beads as the verdict was announced, while Dupas remained motionless.

Outside the court, Mrs Halvagis broke down in tears and was enraged that Dupas laughed at one stage of the trial. She said through her tears: "He laughed, he laughed."

She added: **"He will rot in hell; he will rot in hell."**

Mersina's brother Nick told of how difficult it was to sit in the same room with the man who had killed his sister. He said to reporters: "We sat opposite a guy who has now been convicted of three murders of innocent women. I don't know how any person could sit in that room with the lowest form of human existence and not get angry."

He said he and his family felt her absence every day. He said: "You might be going to work and you hear a song that has no relevance to your sister, but you think of her. Her death was a very small part of her existence, but we are going to do our best to remember those 25 years."

Mersina's father George told the assembled reporters: "I just want to say this message. I want that animal to have nightmares … I want him never to go to sleep and think that he is OK; he will never be OK."

Mersina's brother Bill said he did not believe Dupas got what he fully deserved and added: "My sister is no longer living and he gets to live his life. My sister is never going to speak again, never going to talk with us again. We cannot imagine, and I don't think anyone here can actually imagine, what she really went through or any of his other victims what they went through. We will be there to the end for her and, you know, we will live on for her. The whole family will."

Gorgievski said the trauma of being forced to relive the events of finding Mersina's body and of having to defend himself had left him unable to eat for a week. "I was absolutely taken apart," he said. "I was beside myself. I was sick the whole week. I didn't think it would have affected me in that way, but it hit me as hard or even harder than in 1997 (when Mersina was murdered)."

He told the *Herald Sun* he could not understand why the legal system allowed lawyers to probe the personal history of witnesses, yet would not allow a jury to know the details of what someone such as Dupas had done in the past.

Of Dupas, he said: "He's a monster. I can't put it any other way. It's sad because he should be underground and these innocent women should be alive and prospering and creating their own families and enjoying life."

He said he thought at one stage: "Give me a few minutes with him. I'm not a big person, but I'm sure God would help."

Gorgievski also told the *Herald Sun:* "I have a very strong support base. I have had a lot of support and I have been able to move on, but it's taken a while for me to get back involved in life. My parents are my pillars. They've always been there for me, no matter what, and they loved Mersina like a daughter."

Justice Cummins sentenced Dupas on August 16, 2007, in unusual circumstances, with some controversy. It was the first televised sentencing since Justice Bernard Teague sent axe murderer Nathan John Avent to jail for 21 years in 1995. The Avent sentencing was even more controversial as it later was claimed that Justice Teague, with the TV cameras whirring, might have been too harsh. The Court of Appeal later cut three years from Avent's sentence.

This is what Justice Phillip Cummins said in sentencing Dupas, running through the events that fateful day and the evidence presented in court:

"Peter Norris Dupas, you have been found guilty by a jury of the murder at Fawkner Cemetery on Saturday, November 1, 1997, of Mersina Halvagis. The Fawkner Cemetery should have been a place of peace and of reflection; instead, in your hands, it was a place of murder.

"Believing the cemetery to be a place of peace and of reflection, Ms Halvagis went there that Saturday afternoon to do honour to her grandmother. At 3.47pm in the Fawkner Cemetery tea rooms she purchased flowers and two bottles of Sprite. She drove her fiancé's car, which she had for the day, to the northern section of the cemetery close to Box Forest Road and parked at the Greek Orthodox section. She took her flowers and one bottle of Sprite and walked along Row M to her grandmother's grave, No. M33. There she intended to tend her grandmother's grave and to spend time in peace and reflection, doing honour to her grandmother.

"Her last actions were typical of her: a fine young woman, in a place of peace and beauty, thinking not of herself but of others, devoted, considerate and good. Then you struck.

"Just as Ms Halvagis' presence at the cemetery was typical of her goodness, your presence at the cemetery was typical of your evil: cunning, predatory and homicidal. You were a strong man, with strong arms and hands. Ms Halvagis was but 45 kilograms in weight and 155 centimetres in height. You were armed with a lethal knife, until at the moment of the attack was hidden in the jacket you were wearing.

"You had approached another woman and were seen by others in the area during the day. Your grandfather's grave was only 128 metres to the west of that of Ms Halvagis' grandmother. When Ms Halvagis walked alone along Row M, stopped at her grandmother's grave and commenced to tend it, you attacked. From behind.

"Your attack was swift, savage and brutal; but directional. Ms Halvagis sought to turn and escape. Her slashed left fingers and hand show that she tried to defend herself from your knife. But she had no chance against your strength, your knife and your hate. You inflicted 33 stab wounds to Ms Halvagis. There were a further 20 incised wounds caused by your knife. Of the hundreds of photographs in this case, there are three which are especially haunting: photograph 55 showing Ms Halvagis' flowers and bottle of Sprite beside her grandmother's grave, M33; photograph number 68, showing Ms Halvagis' body slumped between the graves M35 and M36; and photograph 175, of the autopsy of Ms Halvagis, showing the concentration of your knife attack on her upper body.

"So savage was the stabbing that it broke through Ms Halvagis' bones — the lower sternum and the ninth thoracic vertebra. The knife passed through her lungs. It penetrated her neck and it cut through her heart. You left the body of Ms Halvagis slumped dead on the grave site M36, three sites from that of her grandmother. Then, with your bloody knife, you vanished from the scene. But it was your cunning that was to bring you undone. For you left no forensics at Fawkner — words which would come back to haunt you.

"Throughout that Saturday Mr Halvagis' fiancé, Mr Angelo Gorgievski, was working ... at Epping. He finished there at 6pm. When that evening and into the night nothing was heard from Ms Halvagis, he commenced extensive searches for her. Ultimately he and his father found the vehicle he had provided for Ms Halvagis, in the dark and locked cemetery. He immediately called police who arrived. The police and Mr Gorgievski entered the cemetery and shortly after 4.45am — 12 hours after you had murdered Ms Halvagis — in the darkened cemetery, Mr Angelo Gorgievski found her body. He reacted exactly as an innocent and loving person would.

"Despite extensive investigation, for years you were not positively identified as the murderer. The month before you murdered Ms Halvagis you had murdered, by knife attack, Ms Margaret Maher at Somerton. You were not identified as the murderer. Eighteen months after you murdered Ms Halvagis you murdered, by knife attack, Ms Nicole Patterson at Northcote. You were arrested for that murder three days later. You were convicted of the murder of Ms Patterson in August, 2000, and sentenced to life imprisonment with no minimum term. You were convicted of the murder of Ms Maher in August, 2004, and again sentenced to life imprisonment with no minimum term.

"One of the persons who saw you in the Fawkner Cemetery on November 1, 1997, was Mrs Laima Burman. On April 15, 1998, at the St Kilda Road police complex she created a computer image, exhibit J at the trial, which bore a striking likeness to you. Your conviction in August, 2000, for the murder of Ms Patterson received extensive publicity. At the time Mrs Burman was on holiday in northern Victoria, on August 16, 2002, in a newsagency in Kyabram, she saw the front page of the Melbourne *Herald Sun* which carried your photograph in relation to the murder of Ms Patterson. Mrs Burman recognised you as the man in the Fawkner Cemetery. The net was starting to close.

"Mr Andrew Fraser, formerly a solicitor, in November, 2001, pleaded guilty in the County Court to serious drug offences deriving from his cocaine addiction. He was sentenced to seven years' imprisonment with a minimum term of imprisonment before being eligible for parole of five years.

"In January, 2002, he was placed in a protection unit, Sirius East, of the Port Phillip Prison at Laverton. He was given the task of gardener. There was one other gardener in the same unit — you. At that time you had been sentenced for the murder of Ms Patterson at Northcote and you were being investigated for the murder of Ms Maher at Somerton.

"You had legal issues in the Maher matter, including procedural requirements before you were charged with her murder. You sought to gain advantage of the former solicitor, Mr Fraser, being in your unit, in relation to the Maher matter. One of the problems in the Maher matter was DNA — from a glove left at the scene. You discussed this with Mr Fraser, and then you added: 'I left no forensics at Fawkner.'

"When you were charged with the Maher murder, you asked Mr Fraser to examine the brief served upon you. He did so and discussed it with you and, in particular, the forensic evidence of the glove. Again you said 'I left no forensics at Fawkner'. You said that Ms Halvagis would not have seen you because you attacked her from behind. You then, in your cell, performed a macabre silent demonstration of the attack. Some time later you again said to Mr Fraser that you had left no forensics at Fawkner. The remorseless verbal recitation three times in prison of your cunning at Fawkner helped bring you undone.

"By good police work, Detective Senior Constable Paul Scarlett, then of the Homicide Squad, noted that you and Mr Fraser were together in the Sirius East Unit from January, 2002, to March, 2003. He approached Mr Fraser later in Mr Fraser's sentence when he was in Fulham Correction Centre, Sale. Mr Fraser made a statement of the events and conversations between him and you in Sirius East. Ultimately you were charged with the murder of Ms Halvagis and, after a month-long trial, in which you remained silent as was your right, you were found guilty by the jury of her murder."

Justice Cummins then turned to the Halvagis family and said:

"The Court has been deeply impressed by your dignity throughout these painful and emotional proceedings. You are a fine family. Through these 10 years you have shown courage, and love and loyalty to Mersina. You have never wavered. The jury's verdict will not bring Mersina back, but I hope it brings to you some sense of juctice and of resolution. To you, Mr and Mrs Halvagis Senior, and especially to the younger generation — you, Nick, Dimitria and Bill — I encourage you to look to your own creative futures and to embrace those futures. I am sure that is what Mersina would wish."

Justice Cummins then turned to Mersina's fiancé, Angelo Gorgievski, and told him: "Your conduct was exactly that of an innocent and loving person. You have suffered the added pain of Mr Dupas' counsel in public court asking did you have any involvement in the death of Ms Halvagis. When you were asked that question the person, other than you, who best knew the answer sat silently in court — the true killer, Mr Dupas. You, Mr Gorgievski, had no involvement in Mersina's death whatsoever. You lovingly cared for her and had the horror of finding her body. I hope that in your life you can now move forward with your family."

To the police and, in particular, Inspector Greg Hough, Detective Senior Sergeant Jeff Maher and Detective Senior Constable Paul Scarlett, Justice Cummins said: "This has been an extensive investigation. You have demonstrated excellent police qualities: intelligent application to the task, initiative, persistence and integrity; I commend you."

Justice Cummins continued: "At the commencement of this trial an application was made on behalf of the accused for a permanent stay of proceedings. The application was premised on two grounds: a suggested incapacity to receive a fair trial because of the accused's notoriety, and a suggested lack of utility because the accused was already serving two life sentences with no minimum terms. I refused the application.

"The jury, by its care and conscientious application to its task, and its intelligent address as demonstrated by its questions during deliberations, undoubtedly gave the accused a fair trial. The fairness is a commendable Australian characteristic and the jury demonstrated it.

"As to the second ground, utility, the answer is that victims matter. Ms Halvagis matters. Every victim matters. I would like to say something further about Ms Halvagis and other victims of crime. The law has always given, and rightly so, scrupulous attention to proper process to ensure accused persons receive fair trials. That process should never be deflected or diluted or diminished. Further, the criminal law is founded upon the protection of society as a whole. It is a public, not a private matter. Thus proceedings are brought by the State, not by the victim.

"Even so, I do not think the law has given sufficient attention to the rights of victims. Because Mr Dupas could not be sentenced to any further term of actual imprisonment beyond that which he already was serving, the trial was a vindication of the rights of Ms Halvagis — the bringing of justice to her killer — and of all victims of crime."

Finally, Justice Cummins returned to Dupas and told him: "You took from Ms Halvagis the most basic right of all — her right to life. She was a fine young woman aged 25 and you cut her life from her. You left her family and loved ones bereaved. You are now 54 years of age. Before November 1, 1997, you had been convicted three times of violent rapes of women — in 1974, 1980 and 1985 — and sentenced to imprisonment. You have no remorse for the terrible crime of the murder of Ms Halvagis: none. You have no propects of rehabilitation: none. You do not suffer from any mental illness. Rather, you are a psychopath driven by a hatred of women. For the murder of Mersina Halvagis, I sentence you to life imprisonment. I refuse to set any minimum term. Life means life."

Justice Cummins had just three more words to say, but they spoke volumes. "Remove the prisoner," he said and, indeed, Dupas was removed fromn society for a third life sentence, never to be released.

The *Herald Sun* the next day reported the sentencing under the headline JUDGE PUSHES VICTIM RIGHTS. The report centred on Justice Cummins' call for a change in the weight given to victims' rights by the justice system.

Mersina's father George told the newspaper that the sentence would not bring his daughter back and added: "In my heart I know if he (Justice Cummins) could have given him any more he would have." Mr Halvagis said he was relieved for his other children that the trial and sentencing was over.

Mersina's brother Bill said: "We will be there to the end for her. We will live on for her and be strong for her — the whole family will."

The *Herald Sun* again saw fit to run an editorial on Dupas. Under the headline IN DEFENCE OF VICTIMS it read:

"Supreme Court Justice Phillip Cummins thinks the law has not given sufficient attention to the rights of victims.

"Thus the judge has acknowledged a view widely held by the public in recent years.

"He was sentencing serial murderer Peter Dupas to life in jail for the brutal killing of 25-year-old Mersina Halvagis. Dupas killed Mersina with a frenzy of stabbing as she tended her grandmother's grave in Fawkner Cemetery on November 1, 1997. The monster is already serving two non-parole life terms for the murders of two other women and is suspected of killing others. Justice Cummins described the killer as a psychopath who had no remorse and no prospect of rehabilitation.

"But the obviously moved judge's words to Mersina's devastated family injected a refreshing touch of humanity into the judicial process.

"He said that 'victims matter ... Ms Halvagis matters ... this trial was a vindication of the rights of Ms Halvagis ... and of all the victims of crime'.

"Calling for a fairer balance between the rights of offenders and those of the victims, the judge said the Sentencing Act should be amended to state specifically that one of the purposes for which a sentence may be imposed is 'the vindication of the rights of victims'.

"He told the family they were fine people who had shown dignity, courage, love and loyalty to Mersina, adding, 'I hope it brings you some sense of justice and resolution'.

"His words of comfort to the family also give the wider community cause for renewed confidence in the justice system."

Also, *Herald Sun* columnist Andrew Bolt commented on Justice Cummins' decision to have the sentencing televised. Under the headline JUSTICE SEEN TO BE DONE, he wrote:

"Judge Phillip Cummins on Monday ended the argument. More trials should be televised.

"I doubt many Victorians would have felt more satisfied by a court verdict than they were by Cummins' sentencing of Peter Dupas.

"For me, the satisfaction didn't really come from the sentencing itself — life with no set minimum for the murder of Mersina Halvagis in 1997.

"After all, that meant little really, given Dupas was already serving two life sentences for two other murders.

"The power of the moment came instead from the way Cummins said what he did — and on camera.

"Rarely will Victorians have seen justice being so emphatically yet sensitively done — and in a case that has emotionally affected so many ...

"As Cummins has shown, the handing down on camera of such a powerful verdict gives reason to think a watching public is left feeling justice has indeed been done. It also gives reason to hope a few might even hear it."

## CHAPTER ELEVEN

# Rotting in Hell

Barring unforeseen circumstances, Peter Norris Dupas will never be released. He will spend the rest of his days — and many hope these will be few — behind bars and walls capped with coils of razor-wire. Dupas currently is in Port Phillip Prison, leading a life of regimented futility. Almost every step, every movement is monitored and the outside world be but a dream.

Dupas spends much of his time at woodwork, sometimes making ornamental bridges for the prison's garden. The rest of his time would be spent in such utterly boring circumstances that he is, indeed, rotting in a hell on earth.

However, the multiple killer has plenty of time to think and, hopefully to reflect on his hideous crimes. After he was convicted of murdering Nicole Patterson, the *Herald Sun* of August 23, 2000, in a special feature titled "Caged for Life", ran the headline: "Killer urged to confess any secrets".

Through the *Herald Sun*, Nicole's parents, Pam O'Donnell and Bill Patterson, urged Dupas "to bring peace of mind to George and Christina Halvagis, the parents of Mersina (Halvagis)", who had closely followed the trial for Nicole's murder.

More, however, they urged Dupas to confess to other heinous crimes he has been alleged to have committed. Mr Patterson said: "It's not just our daughter, it's others ... I hope there's a part of him that he can find in himself the capability of letting go some of those dark secrets he has in his mind. He's going to go to the grave with a lot of secrets."

Nicole's parents since have seen Dupas convicted of the Margaret Maher and Mersina Halvagis murders and Mrs O'Donnell still lives in hope Dupas eventually will confess, beg forgiveness and offer light on other unsolved murders he might have committed.

She said late in 2008: "I would like to think that Dupas some day will repent and tell everyone he is sorry for what he has done. I do not expect this, but this is what I hope. Nothing can extinguish the pain, but a confession would help in some very small way."

After Dupas lost his appeal for the conviction of killing Nicole Patterson, the *Herald Sun* reported that police could question him on other murders and specifically referred to the Margaret Maher case, as well as two still unsolved murders, of an elderly woman in Brunswick in 1997 and of the woman killed at Rye in February, 1985.

Since that report Dupas was convicted of the Margaret Maher and Mersina Halvagis murders, but remains a suspect in the murder of three other women, Helen McMahon, Renita Brunton and Kathleen Downes.

Helen McMahon was killed on February 13 (the day before St Valentine's Day), 1985, at the Rye back beach on Victoria's Mornington Peninsula. She was murdered just days before Dupas raped the young woman at Blairgowrie (see Chapter 2) while he was on day release with his parents at nearby Frankston.

Police have never disclosed certain details involving McMahon's murder, but it is known that her head was bludgeoned so severely that she died of a brain haemorrhage. She had fought for her life as her hands were bruised, but the killer had overcome her in a vicious attack.

McMahon had left a caravan park at the seaside village of Rosebud on that fateful day and walked to sand dunes to catch the sun. In seeking a lonely and sheltered position, she attracted more than the sun and her killer struck with savage intent.

One of the most significant features of the murder was that the woman's breasts were covered by a blood-stained towel. Was this part of some breasts fetish? Only the killer knows. Although Dupas was not a suspect at the time, this changed because of subsequent events and the files on this particularly savage murder are still open.

While Dupas was living in Woodend with his wife Grace, middle-aged shopkeeper Renita Brunton was stabbed to death — in the chest — at her Exclusive Pre-Loved Clothing store in nearby Sunbury on November 5, 1993.

The shop was open for business that morning, with several potential shoppers calling in to inspect goods. Then, early in the afternoon, strange noises came from the back of the shop, but no one went to investigate. With the shop still open after the usual closing time of 5.30pm, a shopper went to the back of the shop and discovered Brunton's blood-soaked body. The chest wounds and the fact that Peter and Grace Dupas shopped in Sunbury that day still interest police.

Frail 95-year-old Kathleen Downes, who lived at the Brunswick Lodge Nursing Home, went to bed early on the night of December 31, 1997, and staff soon after locked and secured the home for the night. Early the next morning, a staff member noted that the door to Mrs Downes' room was open. She stepped inside to investigate and was horrified to discover the old woman's bloodstained body on the floor. Incredibly, a monster had stabbed the old woman in the neck — and until just before the murder Dupas had lived close to the nursing home. Police traced a seemingly inexplicable call from where Dupas lived to the nursing home, but there was no direct evidence of any involvement in the silver-haired grandmother's murder.

Dupas should have at least three murders on his conscience — if he has a conscience. One American commentator suggested that if killers like Peter Norris Dupas were bugs he would like to step on them and squash them. Like a bug, or perhaps a maggot, Dupas instead will crawl and wriggle through the rest of his life in a confined area, never to be released. For that, at least, we can be grateful.

Hollywood movie star Clint Eastwood said early in 2009: "I never sympathise with the accused unless there is a chance the accused is not guilty. I don't sit around saying 'Gee, the person had a strange childhood and that's why he's doing this horrible thing. Poor Jeffrey Dahmer (American killer/cannibal). He's just had a bad childhood and that's why he's eating people.' Wait a second! This person should be removed from the planet."

# About the Author

JIM MAIN is one of Australia's most respected journalists. He studied law at the University of Melbourne, but preferred to pursue a career as a writer. He worked on the Melbourne *Herald* before spending almost two years on Fleet Street with the *Daily Express*. On return to Australia he combined journalism with studies for his Bachelor of Arts degree (majoring in History) at La Trobe University. The author of more than 50 books, he is a winner of the Sir William Walkley Award (Australian journalism's most prestigious award) and, while in London, a Lord Beaverbrook Award. He has written six other books on Australian murder cases.